Manhood and Politics

NEW FEMINIST PERSPECTIVES SERIES
Rosemarie Tong, *General Editor*

CLAIMING REALITY:
Phenomenology and Women's Experience
Louise Levesque-Lopman

UNEASY ACCESS:
Privacy for Women in a Free Society
Anita Allen

MANHOOD and POLITICS

A Feminist Reading in Political Theory

Wendy Brown

Rowman & Littlefield
PUBLISHER

ROWMAN & LITTLEFIELD

Published in the United States of America in 1988
by Rowman & Littlefield, Publishers
(a division of Littlefield, Adams & Company)
81 Adams Drive, Totowa, New Jersey 07512

Library of Congress Cataloging-in-Publication Data

Brown, Wendy
Manhood and Politics
Bibliography p. 215

Includes index.
1. Political science—History.
2. Sex role—History.   I. Title.
JA81.B66   1987   320'.088042   87–12850
ISBN 0–8476–7576–9
ISBN 0–8476–7577–7 (pbk.)

5 4 3 2 1

Printed in the United States of America

To the memory of my mother

Contents

vii

Preface

THIS IS A FEMINIST BOOK about political theory, but it is not a book about women. In the introduction to *Reflections on Gender and Science*, Evelyn Fox Keller remarks, "the widespread assumption that a study of gender and science could only be a study of women still amazes me: if women are made rather than born, then surely the same is true of men. It is also true of science."[1] It is also true of politics and political theory. Everything in the human world is a construct—upon this, most students of the humanities would agree today. Everything in the human world is a gendered construction—upon this, feminist scholars have been insisting for the last decade and this book is another strand of that insistence. Political theory, a genre of theory concerned with Western history's most exclusively masculine purview, is fairly saturated with various modalities of masculinity. The classic works in political theory do not simply narrate the historical exclusion of women from politics and the relegation of women to subordinate spheres and statuses, they also comprise a rich articulation of masculinist public power, order, freedom, and justice.

For those who have followed closely the extension of feminist criticism into every crevice of every discipline over the last decade, the idea of a feminist inquiry that is not primarily concerned with women is easy enough to grasp. But for those relatively unversed in contemporary feminist thought, the idea may seem incoherent. Colleagues who learned that I was working on a feminist study of manhood and politics often heard *only* the word "feminist" and assumed that I was working on "the woman question"—women in politics, women in political theory, or women as political thinkers. One referee for the book cited Susan Okin's *Women in Western Political Thought* as its "nearest competitor," a work for which I have the highest esteem but as its title makes clear, is about women, not men

1. Evelyn Fox Keller, *Reflections on Gender and Science* (New Haven: Yale University Press, 1985), p. 3.

ix

or manhood in Western political thought. A feminist book concerned with politics and political theory that did not have women as its primary focus could not be fathomed—no receptors existed for it inside a worldview in which feminism is about women while everything else is human, that is, male, that is, human.

This kind of deafness has a vitally political edge, indeed precisely the edge with which this book is concerned. Consider again Evelyn Fox Keller's amazement at those who are uncomprehending about the reach of gender analysis into the construction of science itself—is this incomprehension really so amazing? Like antiracist campaigns that are kept within the bounds of minority civil rights, feminism limited to women's issues, whether women's literature or women's rights, can be accepted by those outside these bounds without seeming to challenge or indict their existence. Feminism construed as solely concerned with women can be variously endorsed, coopted, tolerated, or marginalized by nonfeminist men without much trouble or trauma to themselves precisely because it is not their issue. Such feminism can be "added in" to curriculum, nodded to in lectures, given its own panels at academic conferences, permitted to caucus in professional organizations, requested in job candidates, and converted into Title IX statistics. Such feminism is not seen as having anything to do with men save for the occasional affirmative action conflict over scarce positions or the odd dishwashing squabble when everyone in the family is tired.

The importance of bringing feminist angles of vision to domains other than those explicitly occupied by women goes beyond the ways it renders more difficult the practice of marginalizing or coopting feminism. "Second wave" feminist scholarship has travelled an enormous distance since its beginnings two decades ago and the course of these travels has been marked by two major shifts of emphasis. The first entailed a move from documenting the omission or outrageous depictions of women in traditional scholarship to the trenchwork of redressing these omissions and depictions. Legions of feminist scholars undertook the task of recovering our history and literature as well as painstakingly ferreting out the misogyny and myths in the accepted histories. In the course of this work, "woman" also became women—specifically constructed creatures of particular races, classes, epochs, and cultures rather than figments of the "eternal feminine" or its modern, white, middle-class variant. The second shift entailed a move from recovering ourselves to critically examining the world from the perspective of this recovery—developing critiques of the gendered quality of our inherited discourses, disciplines, institutions, and practices. Together these changes represent a move from margin to center (and one that could have only happened in this order), from a focus upon women's experience in the margins to an analysis of the world that produced that experience. Through this move, feminist scholarship is throwing off a designation as interest group advocate and is becoming citizen, in the deepest, fullest sense of the term. Increasingly, we have something to say about the methodologies and epistemologies informing every disciplinary niche—from primatology to bureaucracy, biology to representation, sexology to moral theory. Naturally, there are many who would like to return us to the ghetto. Some, like Allan Bloom in his new bestseller, *The Closing of the American Mind*, are explicit about this wish; others are the people Keller is amazed by, those who simply "cannot imagine" gender as an issue for any but women.[2]

In addition to being a move from margin to center, the contemporary feminist focus upon the socially male constructions of various disciplines, discourses, and institutions helps to make good on a fine old injunction to theory "not simply to interpret the world but to change it." For as we attack these constructions and map ways to transform these disciplines, discourses, and institutions, we are striking at the jugular of male dominance. We are also joining feminism to the difficult task of imagining and sketching alternatives to the existing orders of knowledge and power, a sign that we now feel ourselves to be enough a part of history to take responsibility for the future.

This book is written in several different voices, a phenomenon shaped in part by the texts under consideration and in part by my own multiple political and scholarly commitments. With regard to the texts, I am easily influenced by others' moods and styles; hence, the chapters on Machiavelli are allusive and playful while the chapters on Weber are sober, straightforward, and depressing. This was not intentional and such "merging" with a text is certainly a questionable virtue; indeed, there is something distinctly gendered about it, but a raised consciousness is not the same thing as a revolutionized psyche. With regard to the multiple commitments, I say here only what every scholar with fierce political cares has probably experienced. At times I am transfixed by the artful genius of the classical political theorists. This was the intellectual aesthetic that attracted me to political philosophy in the first place; not the politics but the magnificance of Plato drew me in. At other times I am moved by the urgent demands of a world rife with troubles and injustices, including but not only those perpetrated by masculine dominance, and at such moments, attention to textual nuance and interpretative subtlety may

2. Allan Bloom, *The Closing of the American Mind* (New York: Simon and Schuster, 1987).

give way to anger and impatience at the practices dignified and justified by the canonical texts in political theory. Of course, there is a self turning against a self here; strands of a life strung in high tension with each other are warring in a manner Plato called symptomatic of a "disordered soul" but which he also used to characterize the anarchist stage of democracy, a stage I always thought he judged a bit harshly.

The devotee of political philosophy and the impatient citizen are not the only factions making an appearance on these pages. There are times when men—their airs, antics and institutions—appear nothing short of ridiculous to me, times when I am inclined mainly to parody their lofty theoretical utterances and self-descriptions. At other times, I am thoroughly fascinated by the tensions and contradictions contained in the constructions and imperatives of manhood, and I am perfectly content to poke about in these complexities. But there are other times when the devastating consequences of masculine dominance, rather than its absurdity or internal tensions, are before my eyes and at these moments, when the sanity and survival of women and the world appears to be at stake, a fierce, even angry voice emerges. This particular multiplicity of voices, of course, is one that appears in feminism itself as an opposition between characterizations of women as powerful, albeit undervalued, social actors, and women as subjected and victimized. The truth is that we are both, just as masculine dominance has both its utterly laughable and utterly horrifying moments. A feminism which abjures either dimension will fail to capture the range of women's experience in its analysis and the range of women in its ranks.

The different voices in this book, then, appear not as a literary device but because they are all inescapably present in a political, feminist student of political theory and the world. Happily, at least a portion of the women's movement is learning to let such multiple voices emerge without hushing, hierarchalizing, or even typologizing them and at the same time, without surrendering to ethical relativism. We are learning, sometimes with great awkwardness, to be not simply tolerant but genuinely democratic *and* discriminating about difference and about identities that are fractured, fluid, and plural. Perhaps political theory will someday follow suit.

I have many people to thank for their companionship to this project. When it was a dissertation, I was privileged to work with Sheldon Wolin, whose rigorous intellect, subtle readings of texts, and complex political values taught me what to reach for. For their encouragement, teaching, and critical readings of parts or all of the thesis, thanks are also due to Michael Brint, Linda Fitzgerald, Amy

Gutmann, Cindy Halpern, Manfred Halpern, Timothy Kaufman-Osborn, Marion Smiley, and Bernard Yack. The American Association of University Women and the Woodrow Wilson Foundation Women's Studies grant program provided financial support and affirmation at the right moment.

During the years when teaching and other obligations rendered the dissertation-to-book transition an erratic affair, I was sustained by many others. For tending my spirit, engaging my work, or inciting me with their own, I am especially indebted to Lila Abu-Lughod, Tim Cook, Peter Euben, Gail Hershatter, Michael MacDonald, Polly Marshall, Joshua Miller, Carol Ockman, Wendy Strimling, Rosemarie Tong, and Elisabeth Vogel. Francine Davis, my research assistant at Williams College, worked cheerfully on tedious details; the College itself was generous with both time and money for completion of the manuscript. And unfailing in their good humor and support has been my family: Elizabeth and Donald Fennelley, Francis Kalnay, and the Browns—Cecil, Dick, Greg and Roger.

Finally, there are three people who made all the difference. Kirstie McClure poured encouragement into my work, warmth and wisdom into the rest of my existence. Valerie Hartouni combed the manuscript when I no longer could, offered many and excellent suggestions for revision, and cared for me exquisitely. Arnie Fischman provided everything from workspace and printers to laughter and solace whenever I needed them, gave marvelous readings to early incarnations of this work and was an extraordinary teacher of political thinking. For these riches of mind, body and spirit, I am deeply thankful.

1

Introduction: Politics, Manhood, and Political Theory

For most of Western history, the expectations, sensibilities, and life activities of human beings have been divided into two, generally contraposed orders: male and female. While associated with the natural phenomenon of human physiological difference, this division has been a conventional, humanly-constructed one. Simply in view of the variety of its historical and cultural permutations, it cannot be called natural, inevitable, or biologically determined. Gender is a human affair, a protean arrangement of meanings, values, and activities born of human mind and endeavor, yet so thoroughly "naturalized" over time that the constructed character of the arrangement has been lost upon most of Western history's inhabitants.

With a few notable exceptions, the situation of women and the ideological antimony between female and male have been uninterrogated and unchallenged by even the most radical thinkers of any previous epoch. Yet, in a span of less than two decades, these matters have been the subject of one of the most remarkable revolutions in the history of human consciousness. At the level of ideas and attitudes as well as location and action in the world, "what a woman is" has been thrown into question. No longer are women everywhere assumed to harbor specific virtues, vices, mental or physical limitations. No longer are we universally regarded as the necessary and sole bearers of a particular kind of work—child-raising and family making.[1] Women are more in the public world, the heretofore male world, than at any previous moment in history. We are engaged in

1

vocations and activities never before conceived as appropriate to us or within our capacities.

For conservative or reactionary students of history and society, these developments appear as the inevitable outcome of the unravelling of Western civilization, symptomatic of a general disintegration of morals, social boundaries, family, and authority. For the moderate or resigned, they may be explained by a Tocquevillian perspective on liberalism: the dynamic of liberal egalitarianism steadily dilutes and diminishes all significant distinctions between members of society. And for liberals of the optimistic stripe, these developments epitomize the best in liberalism: ever-increasing opportunity for each individual to realize her or his potential and aspirations.

In fact, the recent, dramatic transformation in the status of women is far more "materialist" in origin than any of these popular accounts would suggest. By far, the most important factor eroding women's time-honored place in the Western world has been the transformation of the household realm accomplished by capitalist development. The rise of industrial manufacturing revolutionized the formal and material basis of the family and familial economy. The household as a primary productive unit began to diminish, especially in the nonagrarian sectors; commodification of labor on a mass scale gave rise to an increasingly atomized work structure in which the individual, rather than family or household, became paramount; landed property declined in importance relative to other forms of property ownership and use; and the roles of property and inheritance as the underpinnings of marriage for the middle and upper strata began to diminish. In short, capitalism in its adolescent years powerfully subverted the material basis of familial households and the confinement of women within them. This phenomenon has vastly accelerated since its origins in the 18th century as more and more household functions are commercialized and as capital (hence labor) continues to become more mobile. This is the material side of developments rendering women's traditional roles, activities, and identities increasingly superfluous and, concomitantly, more socially and psychologically hollow or suffocating.

A second and related development over the last three centuries has had enormous impact upon the ideological and structural situation of women. This is the emergence and dissemination of the liberal doctrines of universal equality, liberty, suffrage, and opportunity. In the formulations of the early liberals, "universal" excluded not only women but the nonpropertied masses. However, due to the abstract nature of these doctrines—their grounding in the *concept* of the individual rather than in the concrete content of an individual's life circumstances and endeavors, the exclusion of women and others from basic civil and political rights had a blatantly illogical and untenable quality about it. Early feminists such as Mary Wollstone-craft, Harriet Taylor Mill, and John Stuart Mill seized upon just this "contradiction" in liberal thought and practice: if citizenship and its attendant rights and opportunities are no longer conferred upon certain social strata or rooted in certain characteristics but redound to individuals irrespective of their socio-economic station, then women must be counted among these individuals. In short, 18th and 19th century struggles to extend the "rights of man" to the nonpropertied masses implicitly raised the question of the rights of women.[2] Within this discourse of enfranchisement, rights, and privileges lies the origins and perspective of what we know today as "liberal feminism." The limitations of this kind of "emancipation" should be immediately obvious: as rights, liberties, and opportunities within civil society are pursued and defended, the structural barriers to genuine freedom imposed by the organization of the economy, the family, and political power are ignored if not effectively buttressed and legitimated by the struggle to extend citizenship and opportunities to a previously disenfranchised group.[3]

In the United States in the 1960s, these very institutions and structures of power became the focus of popular political attack. Institutions and ideologies incompatible with genuine freedom, lurking beneath and within the doctrines of liberalism, were assailed by the civil rights movement, the antiwar movement, and a host of political and theoretical spin-offs from these movements. Yet, as the barriers to freedom and dignity for racial minorities, the poor, and the colonized in the Third World were challenged, the situation of women was at first ignored. This time, however, because so many women were involved in these struggles and because there was such a sharp irony in fighting for the freedom and dignity of those particularly marginalized by Western society while eschewing those things in the largest marginal group of all, the scattered cries of feminists through the centuries converged into a deafening roar. This, combined with the general liberalization of mores engendered by the "sexual revolution"; the repudiation of valueless careers and soulless families by middle class youth; and the recent experience of women cast *en masse* into the labor force during World War II only to be thrust back into the home a decade later, gave birth to a women's movement of proportions that took even those involved by surprise.

The scope and pace of the changes resulting from the "second wave" of the women's movement are almost impossible to grasp. This movement has dislodged social and ontological assumptions and transformed the lives of women and men to an extent probably unparallelled by any other social or political movement in history. Yet contemporary political, social, cultural, and economic life is utterly infused with the history of an uninterrogated division between the spheres, activities, characteristics, and values associated with each gender. The historical division between men and women as well as the subjugation of women is inscribed in the history of political and social thought, arrangements, and institutions. We are the inheritors of a world literally divided into institutionalized conceptions and practices of "masculine" and "feminine." Thus, despite the fact that many have now come to reject or at least to question traditional notions and practices associated with women and men, we live in a world in which political, economic, and private realms are rooted in and shaped by these traditional arrangements and practices.[4] As Marx reminds us, "the tradition of all dead generations weighs like a nightmare on the brain of the living." Or in Freud's more succinct turn of phrase, "the dead are mighty rulers." The power of dead generations, of history, is even more forcibly present in the traditions and institutions of "masculine" and "feminine" spheres than in any single woman or man. Individual change, however difficult, is relatively accessible compared to what is involved in interrupting a social or political tradition, a form of activity, discourse, or intercourse. Traditions and institutions, humanly constructed yet by definition now separated from the hands and minds that gave them life, not only lack the capacity for self-transformation, they elude our attempts to alter them until we fully apprehend them, and the latter is tremendously difficult while living within them.

More than any other kind of human activity, *politics* has historically borne an explicitly masculine identity.[5] It has been more exclusively limited to men than any other realm of endeavor and has been more intensely, self-consciously masculine than most other social practices. The extent to which both the theory and practice of politics has been bound up with protean yet persistent notions and practices of manhood is not limited to the origins of politics in "warrior leagues," nor to ancient beliefs about the realization of manhood through political life, nor to modern declarations about the "manliness" of political heros and leaders. The historical relationship between constructions of manhood and constructions of politics emerges through and is traced upon formulations of political foundations, political order, citizenship, action, rationality, freedom and justice. What counts as political and what is excluded from politics, what is considered pernicious, threatening, or inappropriate to politics is also affected by this relationship. It is this relationship between manliness and politics, as it has been inscribed in traditional political theory, that this study seeks to lay bare, analyze critically, and ultimately press toward transformation.

II

The writings of Aristotle, Machiavelli and Weber are the specific focus of this work and an account of this selection is in order. To begin with, a study of these thinkers makes it possible to situate the inquiry within ancient, early modern, and contemporary periods of Western Civilization such that elements of longevity, continuity, and change in the manhood-politics relation can be explored. In fact, I argue that a thin, uneven line of development in the manhood-politics relation can be perceived in the course of Western history. This line begins with Plato's overthrow of his more "mystical" predecessors and his concommitant establishment of a specifically Western tradition of politics and thought. But it is Aristotle who most succinctly and unapologetically establishes politics as a distinctly male sphere and masculine activity. In Aristotle's political and ethical theory, we greet man's pursuit of a kind of freedom *against* natural necessity and the body, his concern with dominating these things, and his development of a political rationality to facilitate such domination.

By Machiavelli's time, these ideas and practices have been largely cut loose from their formally ethical foundations and give rise to a world in which power is quite starkly pursued for its own sake. Political rationality has grown more forthrightly instrumental, and the ends of politics pertain to a relatively narrow conception of political glory by comparison with the rich conception of the "good life" cherished by the ancient Greeks. For Machiavelli, woman, nature, and the "uncontrollable" are bound together in the guise of *fortuna* and are cast as the explicit antagonist of political men in search of political glory, freedom, and power.

By Weber's epoch in the late nineteenth century, with capitalism and the bureaucratic organization of political and social life firmly under way, the manhood-politics relation has reached an impasse, indeed a crisis that is part and parcel of a cultural and political crisis. This crisis has a double character. On the one hand, the quest for manhood as freedom from constraint, as domination of men and the environment, and as thought and action liberated from sensual and emotional aspects of being, results in a bureaucratic and capitalist machinery in which man is utterly ensnared, unfree, and by Weber's own account, inhuman. In the process of his quest for a particular (masculine) kind of freedom, man has built an "iron cage" that dominates and reduces him to a soulless automaton incapable of shaping his world, performing as a political or intellectual "hero," or exercising the liberty to which he has aspired. On the other hand, the crisis manifests itself politically: the manhood-politics dialectic has produced a political-economic order that appears out of control even to those who supposedly control it and thoroughly dominates the human beings it was designed to liberate. It is commonplace and almost tedious to rehearse the ways in which we are today on the brink of economic, geopolitical, or ecological disasters and the helplessness with which these dangers are confronted even by those in power.

I am not suggesting that there are iron laws of development in the manhood-politics relation akin to either Marx's laws of economic development or Hegel's reason in history. Sustaining the argument at either the Marxian or the Hegelian levels would fly in the face of post-modern critiques of such views of history, critiques to which I am largely sympathetic. What I am arguing is that there is a definite if nonlinear and unspecifically determined process of historical development—a traceable genealogy—in the manhood-politics relation. And it is precisely because this development has reached or produced a point of crisis that the present work is possible and of immediate political relevance. A political crisis signals the crumbling or exhaustion of existing modes and practices and the need for alternative approaches to collective existence. That alternatives to prevalent ways of thinking about, organizing, and acting within our polities are in order is a matter upon which many Western intellectuals would easily agree. The argument that a specifically feminist approach to these fundamentals of human society is in order is grounded in the critical, interpretative chapters of this book.

The span of history covered by Aristotle, Machiavelli, and Weber is only one aspect of their place in this work of interpretation; there are other reasons for the choice of these particular thinkers. First, each is importantly "mainstream" within the tradition of political theory. That is, while each challenged certain prevailing ideas and practices of their times, none bears the radically critical posture toward their specific political and intellectual milieu that is the hallmark, for example, of Socrates, Rousseau, or Marx. All three theorists were committed "realists"; they sought to give theoretical coherence to the existing order of things and devoted themselves to working within its range of possibilities. Consequently, a focus upon Aristotle, Machiavelli, and Weber makes possible the qualified claim that something of an historical reality—an actual practice of politics and not just the turns of mind of particular thinkers—is represented in their thought.[6]

Second, in a study seeking to discern something new about the nature of politics in Western thought and practice, it is important to look to theorists who have a strong and full conception of politics—where it comes from, what its purpose and meaning is, how and why it should be cultivated or valued. (Ironically, this rules out a fair number of "great" political theorists.) The politicalness of their times as well as of their thought made Aristotle, Machiavelli, and Weber appropriate choices in this regard. For it was not simply personal values that led these thinkers to place politics at the center of their worldly concerns, but the fact that they were inhabitants of particular epochs where political life enjoyed a centrality unknown, for example, in our own culture and times. This is especially so with Aristotle and Machiavelli. In Nietzsche's words:

> Consider the Greeks. . . . Certainly history knows of no second instance of such an awful unchaining of the political passion, such an unconditional immolation of all other interests in the service of this political instinct; at best one might distinguish the men of the Renaissance in Italy with a similar title for like reasons and by way of comparison.[7]

Even within these intensely political times, there is an unusually strong concern with political life harbored by each of the theorists considered in this study. In diverse ways, each sought to assert the value and autonomy of politics as a unique and ennobling dimension of human existence. Aristotle pursued this aim in the intellectual context of antipolitical Platonist philosophy. Machiavelli championed power-politics and an invigorated, politicized citizenry amidst Italian cultural crisis as well as against the prevalence of Christian doctrines and Papal hegemony. Weber sought to redeem and reassert the value of political life in the face of modern forces of bureaucratic rationalization and against what he considered to be the antipolitical doctrines of pacifists, Marxists, and romantic idealists.

Thus, the nature, character, and meaning of politics is accentuated by these theorists by virtue of both their historical context and their particular passions and aims. Besides its usefulness for this work, this also means that each puts forth understandings of politics that are not to be lightly dismissed, even as they are subjected to critical scrutiny. For each comes to terms with their political milieu and formulates the project, purpose, and possibilities of politics in ways that are profoundly important, especially given the status and condition of politics in our own age. Thus, from each we can learn not only what is wrong with politics rooted in a masculine tradition but what is compelling about it such that it calls for transformation rather than thoroughgoing condemnation or abolition. That each of these thinkers subverted the inspiring or even liberating aspects of their political formulations is partly related to the fact that these formulations were bound to an ethos of manhood.

A brief preview of the self-subverting aspects of the work of these theorists will illuminate part of the strategy of this study. Aristotle is distinguished by his doctrine that a life lived in freedom and collective deliberation with others is the ultimate good for human beings. For him, political life was the expression of a noble, complete human existence. Another aspect of Aristotle's perspicuity lies in his recognition of the variety of activities and relationships constitutive of human existence. Aristotle grasped our multifaceted character as reproducers, producers, thinkers, actors, friends, citizens, and lovers and recognized that each of these are ineluctable elements of being human. Moreover, he knew that all of these elements of our being, as they manifest themselves in various relationships and associations, must be articulated and explored in any comprehensive political theory. But Aristotle subverts his own rich understanding of what it means to be human in his effort to structure individual and collective existence according to a hierarchy of values in which manhood, defined in a narrow and alienated fashion, is at the top. He thwarts his own insight into our multiplicitous nature with his project of devaluing and diminishing all those elements of life that are not, by his definition, manly. Aristotle, renowned as the political theorist who recognized that the human being is a natural being and is but one small part of an intricate cosmological order, savaged this important perception as he cast humanity in the terms of an elite group of males estranged from and seeking to dominate nature, bodies, and the majority of the human population. Similarly, his establishment of politics as the consociation of free and equal citizens who deliberate together about who they are and what should be undertaken by and for them is distorted by a formulation of freedom defined by male domination of women, necessity, and the body. Moreover, this formulation of freedom is one that ultimately makes incoherent the value Aristotle seeks to ascribe to politics and political activity themselves.

Machiavelli presents a similar picture. On two very crucial issues, he stands as a powerful critic of much of the political theory that comes both before and after him. First, he pulled the human body back into politics and, in the same sweep, revealed the hollowness of political philosophizing that forgets, denies, or repudiates the body. Second, Machiavelli approaches political theory with a willingness to bear, even celebrate, the enormously complex web of agents, actions, and perceptions that make up the world of human and political life. If he had a single message for those who engage in politics, it is that everything alive or moving is a part of the political world and that one must at all times act according to this knowledge. The political actor must not only cast his eyes widely but must recognize how much of the political realm is a matter of perception and the organization of "appearances." Machiavelli also perceived the futility of fixed methods, purposes, and rules for politics. He viewed human life as historically conditioned and changing, and located the value of politics within this history and flux, not in some external, metaphysical, or spiritual source. The effective political actor attends closely to context in order to draw forth new possibilities; his concerns, techniques and visions cannot issue from an external book of ideals or strategies.

But if Aristotle subverts his extraordinary insights through the masculine content he gives them, how much more extreme is this tendency in Machiavelli's thought. For the body that gains *entrée* in Machiavellian politics is without qualification a male, extremely "macho" one. This body ceaselessly seeks power over others, beats, rapes, displays, unfeelingly seduces and plunders. This body also reveals only its dominating and driven aspect and keeps in the shadows all that sustains it, all that it wants, needs, and offers aside from its passion for domination. Moreover, even as Machiavelli witnesses the complex web of forces and perceptions constituting the political world, he entreats political actors to overcome and deny this multiplicity, to proceed singly and boldly, to impose their own purposes and forms upon what is alive and ever in motion. He advises striving for maximum control over context, while his attunement to the extent to which context is uncontrollable suggests both the danger and the inappropriateness of such an approach. His scepticism about the possibility that human beings could work within context in such a way as to simultaneously respect and develop this context pertains to the limitations of character in the politically virile men he studied and admired. Manhood is Machiavelli's beacon and his downfall.

If Machiavelli's work is the most extreme version of the self-subversion in masculinist political theory, certainly the case of Max Weber offers the greatest pathos. One need not perform elaborate hermeneutical feats to see that Weber decried and dreaded in one gesture what he bore to life and power with another. He abhorred the massive system of domination and rationalization capsulating man's quest for power as domination, freedom as control, sensient being as rational mind. But Weber also stood by these things, encoded and empowered them, embodied and strove for them, demanded our allegiance to them. Weber even spies the contradictory nature of man's quest for domination on its own rocky shoal: in his studies of economy and society, bureaucracy and power, he recognizes that the particular nature of Western man's reach for freedom and power has bred man's own enslavement and powerlessness, in addition to the inordinate oppression of others. The tragedy lies not only in Weber's controversion of his own understandings through his ultimate attachment to manly quests, deeds, and monuments, but in the way it was borne inwardly by Max Weber, the man. The contradictory dimensions of his work and cares literally crushed and paralyzed him and he could not heal himself. He—his fidelity to manhood—was his own poison.

III

In addition to an understanding of why particular theorists have been chosen for this work, the reader may want to know how this project differs from other "feminist critiques" of political theory. To begin with, I am less engaged in a critique than in a rereading of past political theories for the light they shed upon a newly discovered problem. Moreover, while the problem I am addressing issues from a feminist angle of vision, it does not deal solely nor even centrally with women. Most definitions of feminism, and most feminist theory and practice, tend to focus upon the denigration of women, the heretofore hidden or devalued sphere of women's work, or the exclusion of women from male arenas of achievement, remuneration, and recognition. This is as much the case with feminist treatments of political theory as with feminism in other disciplines and feminist practice in the everyday world.

Feminist approaches to political theory can be loosely grouped into two general categories. The first involves examining the ways in which past political theorists have justified their (usually low) regard for women and their exclusion of women from political life.[8] This approach tends to be somewhat limited since women *were* historically barred from the public realm, as were the concerns and activities relegated to women, namely, production and reproduction in the household. A study of this by itself shows how this exclusion was justified, or how misogyny and sexism manifest themselves in various thinkers and epochs. The result is often little more than a chronicle of "sexist attitudes." This approach is also beset by its dependence upon what past political theorists actually said about women, and since most theorists devoted their attention to a realm where women had no visible part, few of them said very much. Indeed, what they did say tends to be rather foolish, in the nature of unreflective afterthought or reiteration of the platitudes and attitudes of their epoch.

Most political theorists of the past simply did not bring the insight and creativity for which they are renowned to their reflections on the nature and proper place of women. Aristotle: a thinker esteemed by posterity for his perception of the human condition as one that moves subtly and complexly between nature and convention, left all this genius behind when he sought to fit women into his schema.[9] Kant and Hegel: thinkers whose hallmark in the tradition of Western thought is the near impeccability of their logic, collapsed into mumbo-jumbo when they strove to offer a rational account of women.[10] Rousseau: a thinker who mourned the loss and dreamed of the recovery of the "natural man," celebrated and developed the "unnatural woman" and identified man's vice as woman's virtue.[11] Marx and Engels: thinkers who sought for the radical root of man himself reached only as far as man made himself (production), neglecting altogether the activity, consciousness, and social relations entailed in the reality that man does not make himself but is the product of woman's assigned life-long tasks (reproduction).[12]

So what does one learn by discovering that for Hegel, women are subrational plants; for Rousseau, passive citadels of virtue; for Aristotle, deformed males; for Marx (that remarkable theorist of work!), unproductive elements of the labor force; and for Jean-Paul Sartre, holes and slime that men are always wont to plug up or run from for fear of getting caught in a bog of unfreedom?[13] One learns just that, how women were thought about or the permutations of women's oppression on an ideological level. Unless what these thinkers ascribed to women and decried in public life is considered in light of what is valued in men and the male world, this approach tends to leave one trapped in the blatantly anachronistic or flatly misogynist elements of a given theorist's work and to reduce feminist criticism to criticism of theorists' attitudes and statements about women.

A second feminist approach to the tradition of political theory involves combining analytic philosophical techniques with a neo–Marxist critical method. The question this approach brings to political theory is some variation upon the following: when women are added to the supposedly generic term, "man," can any given political theory still "work" or is the theory "inherently sexist?"[14] C. B. Macpherson asked precisely this kind of question of the classical liberals with regard to those they excluded from citizenship on the basis of property ownership, and he found classical liberal theory to be "inherently bourgeois."[15] The theories of Hobbes, Locke, and others he claims, are coherent and workable only if the proletariat is excluded from full citizenship and participation in social and political life. Their propertyless status inherently excludes them from the justice, freedom, and participation in civil society propounded by liberal theory and this, in turn, shows the extent to which liberal conceptions of justice, freedom, and participation are inherently bound up with serving and entrenching the capitalist mode of production. Feminists such as Susan Okin, Lorenne Clark, Lynda Lange, and Carole Pateman have sought to conduct a similar kind of analysis of political theory with regard to women and modes of reproduction.[16] Their concern has been to "prove" that women and reproductive work cannot be added to a theorist's conception of man without rendering other parts of the theory incoherent. This would then "prove" that past political theories are not merely incidentally sexist, i.e., sexist at the level of attitude, but inherently and fundamentally so.

This approach is fruitful insofar as it highlights a realm of work and activities that are excluded from political life, upon which politics rests while denying validity and value to them. But it is limited in both its conception of political theory and its conception of feminism. It tends to reduce texts in political theory to systems of definitions and arguments that either add up to a coherent and persuasive case or fail to do so. The offerings of political theory are generally richer than this: there are important elements of perspective, equivocation, tone, narrative, irony, and ambiguity that are lost if one simply distills these texts into a series of propositions. With regard to feminism, this approach brings to light a realm and its inhabitants who have been denied political status, but it does not substantively challenge the characteristics of political life itself. (If one could prove, for example, that nothing in John Rawls's formulations of politics inherently excluded women from political life and women's work from political consideration, then according to this method, Rawls would count as a feminist political theorist.)[17] Barriers to female political citizenship and leadership are of primary consideration in this approach, while the nature and quality of political life itself remain largely uninterrogated.[18]

This uninterrogated terrain is precisely the one occupied by this study. That most political theorists of the past refused women a place in the political order is beyond doubt, as is the fact that this exclusion is not incidental nor easily rectified. But the challenge feminism can make to the history of political theory goes beyond identifying ways in which women have been denied political or even human status and ways in which this denial is locked into various theoretical constructions. Most importantly, the political aim of engaging past political theories for feminist purposes can go beyond seeking a place for women in the existing political order or attempting theoretical reconstructions in which the "invisible" work traditionally performed by women is incorporated into political thinking and practice. The challenge that strikes at the heart of all past political constructions is that the politics men have made by and for themselves is saturated with highly problematic, often dangerous, ideals and practices of manhood. The radical critical possibility of a feminist perspective on the tradition of political theory thus lies in grasping the ways in which what we know as politics is a politics constructed according to specific notions, practices, and institutions of masculinity. The radical practical possibility emerging from this understanding lies in constructing a politics that is divorced from its historical identification with manhood.

IV

How does one discern something as subtle and often elusive as the relationship between manhood and politics in political theory, especially if literal readings of theorists' accounts of gender are more limiting than helpful in such a project? To begin with, there is simply no "method" to be called upon for this work. Rather, texts must be opened with the question of this relationship in mind and with a readiness to consider every aspect of these texts potentially relevant to the question: metaphysical, ontological, and polemical constructions; implicit as well as explicit utterances about what women and men are and are not; discussions of the origins and purposes of politics, of constituent elements of politics, of threats to political life and political men, of the relationship politics bears to other realms and activities. With each theorist studied, this material determines how the question I bring to the texts is addressed.

I do not approach the texts interpreted in this study nor the problem of manhood and politics in general with an "ideal type" of manhood and a prefigured understanding of its relation to politics. I do not, for example, bring a preordained conception of masculinity to Aristotle's writings and peruse his thought for evidence that his view of man corresponds to it and his politics reflect it. Rather, I have sought to discern the understanding of manhood, politics, and their relationship contained within the writings of each thinker. This does not imply an exclusive focus upon the theorists' literal statements about men and politics nor an analytical effort to correlate them. To the contrary, one must often reach far beyond and beneath such statements, even where they are proffered. This is especially so because these thinkers mostly *assumed* the appropriateness of the relation between politics and manhood and therefore did not treat this relation as a matter for careful articulation or interrogation.

How does one search "beyond and beneath" theorists' utterances? That which Aristotle designates as political or which Machiavelli calls *virtù* are partly revealed by exploring what is not political or not *virtù* in their understandings. This exploration entails more than simple reflection upon literal contrasts and oppositions: Aristotle's conception of the political is not grasped merely through comparison with his conception of the "private," "economic," or "ethical" although these comparisons, where available, constitute useful touchstones. More important, however, is the almost archeological activity involved in grasping what lies under or to the side of explicit declarations by a theorist, grasping what makes the declaration important to the theorist as well as what makes it possible. What must be repressed or pushed aside for a theoretical thread to stand bare and utterable? What cauldron of tensions bubbles beneath a claim to truth in an uneasy mind driven to theorize in its struggle toward insight? Attunement to the theoretical repression inherent in the act of theoretical expression is especially important in a study whose concern is the denied, suppressed, ignored, or assumed elements in politics and the order of man.

A second matter making a prefigured conception of masculinity an inappropriate heuristic device for this work is that biological maleness and specific ideals of manhood are not synonymous and are not even considered so by the theorists under consideration. For none of them is manhood equivalent to being male—all biological men are not manly, all men are not real men. Moreover, manhood is not always counterposed to womanhood. For the Greeks, only free men even stood the possibility of realizing their nature as men and among those who were free, *aretē* symbolized the fulfillment of manly ideals. For Machiavelli, *virtù* was the supreme expression of manliness—in cities or individual men—and very few men or cities actually evinced this quality.

Yet to say that there is no method and that "everything counts" opens rather than settles questions of interpretation raised by this kind of project. For clearly I am susceptible to historical and hermeneutic criminality in summoning the relics of the intellectual past for purposes of a highly contemporary inquiry. What is involved in reopening a dialogue with Aristotle on issues he dealt with in subterranean fashion at best, and certainly from a much different set of concerns than those I am posing? How does one appropriately and fruitfully engage in this kind of dialogue? Finally, why turn to these thinkers and their works for illumination of this subject?

I want to insist upon the difficult claim that one can read political theory as a means to historical understanding, the very kind of historical understanding so crucial to formulating contemporary feminist perspectives and projects. One of the problems with this claim lies in the status of the classic texts of political theory as works that have survived precisely because they do more and other than merely represent the dominant ideas and practices of particular polities or cultures. In this regard, the "great works" in the tradition of political theory obtain their stature, in part, from their departure from common parlance, perceptions, even assumptions of their day. This is as much the case for thinkers usually regarded as politically "conservative"—Aristotle, Hobbes, or Hegel—as for known "radicals"—Socrates, Rousseau, Nietzsche, or Marx. A noteworthy political theorist adds a new and challenging dimension, sometimes even a new location or circumference, to political understanding and self-conception. The theorist accomplishes this with the special movements and ingredients of the theoretical enterprise: abstraction from event and phenomenon to a larger and longer view of the nature, order, and relation of elements of political life. In Norman Jacobson's words:

> The great works of political theory have persisted because they are all intimations, each in its own partial way, of what persists within the consciousness of Western humanity. . . . The great works have endured because they continue to represent us in our endless complexity and contradiction. A new political theory comes into the world when its creator discovers still another way to capture a part of the richness of existence.[19]

If political theorists stand in a relationship of slight distance to their times and milieu, how and why is the case to be made for reading political theories as history? First, there is the theorist's concern with achieving a level of understanding wherein contradictory, seemingly ideosyncratic or conflicting elements of the phenomenal world can be rendered coherent or at least, understandably incoherent. Secondly, there is the significance of the Minervan owl as harbinger of what we inherit from a given historical epoch. Each of these is elaborated below.

The political theorist is distinguished by her or his attunement to the problem of *coherence* in human affairs. A search for coherence differs from a concern with harmony, stability or with resolution of tension and contradiction. And while the search for coherence involves discerning ordering principles, it does not imply order. Rather, coherence pertains to the configuration of institutions modes, mores, principles of action and process that constitute human affairs in a given time and place. Within this configuration, there may be conflicting strains and remnants from a variety of other epochs and cultures. But the theorist seeks for a level of meaning that makes sense of this *mélange* in a way that also sets forth possibility. For at its best, political theory is an endeavor that pieces together phenomenal existence such that it can be grasped sufficiently for us to know what and where we are as well as what we might become, such that we may acquire the power inherent in knowledge.

There is no guarantee, of course, as to the "accuracy" of the principles of coherence any given political theorist depicts. Indeed, political theorists have diverged upon every important proposition since the inception of the discipline and rival claims to truth may even be said to constitute the activity of the discipline. But contemporary studies of the history of political theory ought to be less concerned with truths or Truth than with meanings. Certainly it is easy enough to declare every well known political theorist "wrong" on the nature of man, manhood, woman and womanhood. Such a declaration is also uninteresting. Far more interesting and important are the sources, permutations, power, tenacity, and implications of such formulations.

To put the matter another way, even if a political theorist is quintessentially bourgeois, aristocratic, sexist, or conservative, insofar as bourgeois, aristocratic, sexist, or conservative forces and mentalities prevail in the theorist's object of study, the underlying coherence discerned and presented by such a theorist represents an aspect of the power that maintains this prevalence. Here, Marx is one of our best teachers—"Ruling ideas do rule!" and what is more, they are as likely to emerge from philosophers of the state as from ministers of state. Thus, for Marx, Hegel was not merely a brilliant, albeit misguided thinker who saw the world "upside down," but a theorist who portrayed power structures as they had to portray themselves in order to maintain their power and legitimacy, to continue perpetrating injustice in the name of justice, inequality in the name of universality, exploitation in the name of freedom.[20] Marx recognized that Hegel depicted the real power of his age in his philosophy. Similarly, while Aristotle was inarguably an aristocratic apologist, if we want to know what kind of metaphysical machinations could justify the hegemony of the Athenian aristocracy, and what kind of *Weltanschauung* such hegemony involves, and how much of Aristotelian Athens we live with today, we will do better to unpack the coherence Aristotle discerned in Athenian political life than to criticize from an external standard his politics, ethics or logic. For purposes of this work, within this coherence also lies the identity, and the power of the identity, between manhood and politics.

The coherence a theorist discerns in social and political life is often drawn from the light shed on the present by the past. This is not to say that all theorists think in explicitly historical terms, but that the project of understanding where we are and what we might do is invariably informed by a view of where we have come from. This is as much the case with Socrates' call for a radically new order as with Edmund Burke's exhortation to return to values and practices of a prerevolutionary epoch. Rousseau grasped modern alienation and decadence through conjectures about premodern existence. Similarly Nietzsche. Machiavelli diagnosed Italian political decay in terms of prior epochs of glory.

Prior orders, however, are not grasped as they were lived by their inhabitants but, rather, through their meanings for their successors. An analogy with Freud may be useful here: the analysand has potentially infinite capacities for recalling childhood experiences, but they are recalled as a component of the adult who lived through (and attached certain meanings to) those experiences, not precisely as they were experienced by the child while they transpired, and certainly not "objectively." The study of past political theories may be regarded not only as a general means of exploring the past but also of grasping the particular elements of the past we have incorporated into the present. We are, for example, Aristotelian not merely in the sense that Aristotle profoundly influenced developments in our civilization—indeed, that is far too large a claim about the role of theory as an historical force—but because Aristotle captured so many of the strands of the Greek experience that have threaded their way forward into our own. Similarly, and more controversially, I think Hannah Arendt has managed to pinpoint some of the most important elements of our inheritance from the ancient Greeks. Even her distortions and perversions of the Greek world may constitute an aspect of what we have retained or absorbed from that world. Arendt sometimes elucidates what the Greeks are to us at the very expense of establishing what they were to themselves. Here, we confront another troubling aspect of the theorist's struggle with coherence: such coherence may be inseparable from the distortion inherent in the Owl of Minerva's flight hour. The theorist bears this tension, perhaps, that meanings are obtained from a prior epoch in a manner that indisputably recasts, even violates, the "truth" of that epoch.

As with political theorists and theories of the past, so with my own attempts in the present work. For I am concerned not merely with interpreting Aristotle, Machiavelli, and Weber but with constructing a theoretical account of where we have been and where we are *vis à vis* the relationship of politics and manhood. It is possible to engage in this exploration with some acuity precisely because that relationship is now beginning to fracture. Manhood, and all that it conjures in its traditional formulations, has been under fire for nearly two decades. Its hegemony is not broken, but it has been partially undressed. The consequence for the present work is that, for the first time in history, we have a vantage point from which to examine the historical identity or partnership between manhood and politics. We can, as it were, stand in the cracks and survey the interiors of a phenomenon that, until now, has been the whole, the very medium of our existence.

This is not to suggest that we are finished with the problem nor that political theory in general only looks backward. For to say that the manhood-politics relation is cracking is neither to proclaim the relationship dead nor to suggest that this rupture will necessarily produce social and political changes worthy of celebration. Indeed, a reactionary response to such a rupture is every bit as likely and currently in evidence in the United States. Thoughtful and deliberate action is essential for a progressive transformation of this relationship and such action requires knowledge of where we have come from, what we now live with, and what these things teach us about what we want to create.

Notes

1. Women other than those of the privileged classes have always engaged in productive labor, both within the household and outside of it. This does not mean, however, that their work was ever acknowledged in the dominant ideologies about the nature, aptitudes, and appropriate activities of women.

2. The rise of the women's suffrage movement in the context of the American abolitionist movement can be understood in the same way. Like Mary Wollstonecraft's circle, which consisted of men who sought rights for propertyless men while ignoring the plight of women, many white male abolitionists were content to obtain citizenship status for male slaves while distancing themselves from the issue of female suffrage.

3. For a fuller discussion of this development of Marx's argument in "On the Jewish Question" as it applies to women, see my "Reproductive Freedom and the 'Right to Privacy': A Paradox for Feminists," *Families, Politics and Public Policy: A Feminist Dialogue on Women and the State*, ed. Irene Diamond (New York: Longman, 1983).

4. Actually, the market may be least imprinted by gender relations, i.e., despite the fact that women are everywhere economically ghettoized and disadvantaged, it may be one of the most gender-neutral spheres of activity. Of course, the ethos of the economic realm is competitive, and its ownership and control is dominated by men. But as the recent enormous female incursion into this realm has made so evident, its highly alienated aspect combined with its highly concrete nature renders it less "gendered" than, for example, politics or personal life. The economic realm is less about sensibility and involves less of human interiors than these other realms, precisely because it is alienated and concrete. Understanding sexism as most contingent and least permeating in the economic realm illuminates why a)liberal feminism, by its nature preoccupied with economic discrimination, has such a thin conception of sexism and b) Marxist-feminism, by its nature searching for economic accounts of sexism, founders in this endeavor.

5. War could be said to constitute a caveat to this claim. The relationship between war and politics is one which will be addressed frequently in the following chapters.

6. See pages 14–17 for further discussion of the problems associated with treating these thinkers as representing "real" history.

7. "The Greek State," *The Complete Works of Frederich Nietzsche*, ed. O. Levy (Edinburg: Darien Press, 1914), Volume II, p. 11.

8. For example: Eva Figes *Patriarchal Attitudes* (Greenwich, Conn., Fawcett, 1970); Mary Mahowald, *Philosophy of Women: Classical to Current Concepts* (Indianapolis: Hacket, 1978); Dorothea Wender, "Plato: Misogynist, Paedophile and Feminist," *Arethusa*, Volume 6, no. 1 (1973); Kate Millett,

Sexual Politics (Garden City, N.Y.: Doubleday, 1970); Julia Annas, "Mill and the Subjection of Women," *Philosophy* 52 (1977); Carole Pateman and Teresa Brennan, "Mere Auxilliaries to the Commonwealth: Women and the Origins of Liberalism" *Political Studies* Volume 27, no. 2 (1979); Victor Wexler, "Made for Man's Delight: Rousseau as Antifeminst," *American Historical Review* 81 (1976); Louise Marcil-Lacoste, "The consistency of Hume's Position Concerning Women," *Dialogue* 15 (1976).

9. See chapter 3, pp. 33–34.

10. R. Agonito, *History of Ideas on Women* (New York: Putnam, 1972), pp. 130–137; G. W. F. Hegel, *Philosophy of Right*, trans. T. M. Knox (Oxford: Clarendon, 1952), Paragraphs 161–165, additions 105, 107.

11. Jean-Jacques Rousseau, "Discourse on Inequality," *The First and Second Discourses*, trans. R. and J. Masters (New York: St. Martins, 1964); and *Emile*, trans. A. Bloom (New York: Basic Books, 1979).

12. Karl Marx, "The German Ideology" in the *Marx-Engels Reader*, Second Edition, ed. R. C. Tucker (New York: Norton, 1978), esp. p. 150. Feminist commentary on this feature of Marx is voluminous, in part, of course, because it is so central to the question of whether Marxism and feminism are reconcilable. A small sample of this literature includes: Lydia Sargent, ed., *Women and Revolution: A Discussion of the Unhappy Marriage of Marxism and Feminism* (Boston: South End, 1981); Michele Barrett, *Women's Oppression Today: Problems in Marxist Feminist Analysis* (London: NLB, 1980); Zillah Eisenstein, ed., *Capitalist Patriarchy and the Case for Socialist Feminism* (New York: Monthly Review, 1979); Sheila Rowbatham et al., *Beyond the Fragments: Feminism and the Making of Socialism* (Boston: Alyson, 1979); Mary O'Brien, "Reproducing Marxist Man" in L. Lange and L. Clark, eds. *The Sexism of Social and Political Theory: Women and Reproduction from Plato to Nietzsche* (Toronto: University of Toronto Press, 1979); and the lengthy (largely British) debate on the relation of housework to capital spurred by Mariaosa Dalla Costa and Selma James, *The Power of Women and the Subversion of the Community* (Bristol: Falling Wall Press, 1973) and for which a bibliography can be found in *Women and Revolution*, pp. 34–35.

13. See notes 10–12 above and Jean-Paul Sartre, *Being and Nothingness*, trans. H. E. Barnes (New York: Washington Square Press, 1966), pp. 776–82.

14. See "Introduction," Clark and Lange, *The Sexism of Social and Political Theory*, pp. vii–xvii.

15. C. B. MacPherson, *The Political Theory of Possessive Individualism* (Oxford: Oxford University Press, 1962).

16. Clark and Lange, eds., *The Sexism of Social and Political Theory*, Lynda Lange, "Reproduction in Democratic Theory," *Contemporary Issues in Political Philosophy*, eds. Shea and King-Farlowe (New York: Science History Publications, 1976); Susan Okin, *Women in Western Political Thought* (Princeton: Princeton University Press, 1979); Carole Pateman, "Women and Consent," *Political Theory*, Volume 8, No. 2 (May 1980).

17. In recent years, several feminist political theorists, including Susan Okin, have inquired into the relation between feminist concerns and Rawls' theory of justice.

18. Clearly, there are feminist studies of political theory that defy these two categories, and this defiance, happily, is on the rise. Works that survey a number of political theorists while sustaining an original argument about

gender include Jean-Bethke Elshtain, *Public Man, Private Woman* (Princeton: Princeton University Press, 1981); Arlene Saxonhouse, *Women in the History of Political Thought* (New York: Praeger, 1985); and Mary O'Brien, *The Politics of Reproduction* (Boston: Routledge and Kegan Paul, 1981). On Marx and Locke, see Linda Nicholson, *Gender and History* (New York: Columbia University Press, 1986). On the Greeks, see Nancy Hartsock, *Money, Sex, and Power: Toward a Feminist Historical Materialism* (Boston: Northeastern University Press, 1985). And on Marx, see Catherine MacKinnon, "Marxism, Feminism, Method and the State," Parts I and II, *Signs* 7, no. 3 and *Signs* 8, no. 4.

19. *Pride and Solace* (Berkeley: University of California, 1978), p. xiii.

20. *Contribution to the Critique of Hegel's Philosphy of Right*, in R. Tucker, ed., *Marx-Engels Reader*, pp. 59–60.

Ancient Greece

Arendt and Aristotle

2

Arendt: The Fragility of Politics

HANNAH ARENDT WAS FIERCELY DEVOTED to many features of ancient Greek political thought and practice that will be treated critically in this study. Arendt's rendering of Ancient Greece is also the model and inspiration guiding her argument for a resuscitated political life in the modern age, a vision that involves reviving pieces of the masculinist Athenian politics she so revered. Thus, despite her notorious license with the historical and theoretical material she analyzes, brief consideration of Arendt's adulation of ancient Greece may serve as a useful *entrée* to an interpretation of Aristotle, Arendt's favorite Greek political philosopher.

Politics is a uniquely human activity and is rooted in a peculiarly human characteristic. Although we are innately social and interdependent creatures, we construct an existence together rather than engaging in it on a purely natural or instinctual basis. Language and the ability to build institutions generate power beyond that of physical force as well as the capacity to negotiate the arrangements of this power. We also ascribe purpose or meaning to our collective arrangements and derive at least part of our individual identity from these collective meanings. From these features of the human condition, politics is born.

In perfect contrast to the notion that politics is about the arrangements, needs, and purposes of collective life, Hannah Arendt, claiming to speak with and for the ancient Greeks, insists that politics is the human activity that has nothing whatsoever to do with life or need. In *The Human Condition*, where Arendt eulogizes the Greek polis at length, she writes:

> Whoever entered the political realm had first to be ready to risk his life, and too great a love for life obstructed freedom, was a sure sign of

slavishness . . . The "good life" as Aristotle called the life of the citizen, therefore was not merely better, more carefree or nobler than ordinary life, but of an altogether different quality. It was "good" to the extent that by having mastered the necessities of sheer life, by being freed from labor and work, and by overcoming the innate urge of all living creatures for their own survival, it was no longer bound to the biological life process . . . Without mastering the necessities of life in the household, neither life nor the "good life" is possible but *politics is never for the sake of life.*[1]

Familiar to most students of political theory is Arendt's hostility toward the realm of necessity where life is created, reproduced, and maintained, and her anguish over this realm's "invasion" of the public world in the modern age.[2] For Arendt, the *raison d'être* of a polity worthy of the name is not the well-being of society, nor political, social, or economic justice, nor the articulation and realization of common values. Rather, Arendt argues, politics is centrally about immortality, a "guarantee against the futility of individual life."[3] She depicts human beings as inherently frustrated with the biological fact of their mortality and determined to overcome this fact in some way.[4] Of the two paths toward immortality taken by the ancient Greeks, philosophical thought and political action, only the latter could fulfill its aim, since philosophers merely contemplated "the eternal" and could not actually depart their earthly ground to *exist* in an eternal realm. For the Greeks as for us, she insists, the sole means to immortality is striving toward excellence of speech and deed in a genuinely public realm where this excellence can be seen and heard by others and recorded for posterity.[5]

> Only the best (*aristoi*) who constantly prove themselves to be the best . . . and who prefer "immortal fame to mortal things" are really human; the rest, content with whatever pleasures nature will yield them, live and die like animals.[6]

In Arendt's view, only those whose aims and actions embody defiance of the incorrigible fact of their mortality are fully human. Those who, by choice or by circumstance, are stuck in the muddy truths of human life—that it has a beginning, an end, and is beset with no small number of tedious endeavors in between—are not human at all but mere creatures of life. Such people Arendt calls variously "animal laborans,"[7] "idiotic" (from the Greek *idion*),[8] or simply "deprived."[9] Privacy for the Greeks, she reminds us, literally meant a state of deprivation. Hence "a man who lived only a private life, who like the slave was not permitted to enter the public realm or like the barbarian who had not chosen to establish such a realm, was not fully human."[10] Arendt's refusal of the status of humanity to slaves and barbarians (non–Greeks) is related neither to their absence of community nor to a simple lack of freedom.[11] Slaves and "barbarians" are stripped of their claim to humanity because, by force or by choice, neither participates in the quest for immortality through performances of excellence amidst a company of equals.[12]

Arendt's designation of politics as the arena for expressing individual and collective greatness does not merely lessen the extent to which politics can be relevant to human needs but utterly precludes the possibility. Politics cannot be for heroism, glory, immortality, and at the same time be concerned with mere life. Concern for life and the pursuit of freedom Arendt regards not merely as separate but mutually exclusive endeavors and Aristotle's "careless" reconciliation of the two projects bothers Arendt enormously. Overly influenced by the Platonic school, she suggests, Aristotle betrayed the true nature of politics when he "tentatively assumed that at least the historical origins of the polis must be concerned with the necessities of life and that only the polis content or inherent aim (telos) transcends life in the good life."[13]

Arendt's anxiety about the infestation of politics with material concerns has several sources. The common thread among them, however, is the identity she asserts between material life and animality.[14] Since we share with other animals the necessity of providing for our physical wants and needs—indeed, we share with animals the very fact of having bodies—our distinctively human characteristics and endeavors must lie in a realm quite remote from physiological needs and productive activities.[15] Politics alone, she insists, evinces our human distinctiveness, hence politics itself must be entirely independent of those sensual, physiological, and material dimensions of us that recall our animal nature.[16]

For the ancient Athenians, liberation from material necessity *did* serve to distinguish citizens from all other persons, and the potential for such independence also set men apart from women; women were viewed as inherently "enslaved" to their bodies in a way that men were not.[17] "The body always wants to be taken care of and to hell with it!" Arendt says in paraphrase of Plato and she simplifies but does not significantly misrepresent him in doing so.[18] Release from bodily demands underlies Plato's scheme of life for the guardian class of his ideal city and is also the only mode in which he thought a philosopher could expect to encounter truth.[19]

This repudiation of the body and of the activities involved with maintaining and satisfying it breeds no small covey of problems for the political sphere as well as to the sphere to which these concerns have been relegated. I shall argue that these problems are of sufficient stature and complexity to constitute a major portion of Western man's political project from the age of classical Greece onward. The core of the matter is this: as Greek citizens sought to free themselves from their explicit ties to nature—by escaping and denigrating involvement with the productive and reproductive work that is an essential part of our species life—they unwittingly set themselves the difficult task of having to contrive a new basis and location for their existence and identity. They not only had to justify their institutionalized exploitation of those who provided for their material needs but had to conjure ideas, pursuits and activities that would eradicate doubts about their very existence as purposeful beings. Moreover, since human beings cannot ever completely abjure or eschew our physiological aspect, attachment to life, or the force of bodily desires and demands, a politics that strives to overcome or deny these things is necessarily rife with tension and contradiction.

What will become even more evident through the exploration of Aristotle's thought is that as politics is *founded* in estrangement from the common problems of common life, it also emerges as it does precisely to supply a *reality* to those men who occupy the political realm and have rejected other realms and endeavors as insufficiently human. Greek citizens sought to resolve their estrangement from life through ideas and practices embodying a human purpose higher than and indifferent to life. These endeavors constituted their "reality" and identity to a degree that allows Arendt to declare that "to be deprived of the public arena of politics is to be deprived of reality."[20] This founding of politics in estrangement from life is also why what Arendt calls "self-disclosure" is so prevalent in her discussion of the motives driving Greek politics. Disclosing the self becomes all-important when the self or self-identity is in doubt. "Proving the very fact of one's existence," as Arendt puts the matter, characterizes the individual and the polis in Greek politics and results precisely from having cast the fact of one's existence into doubt by repudiating the earthly ties, needs and physicality of human life.[21] In short, man's first and longest-lasting collective identity crisis occurred synonymously with his collective endeavor to distance himself from the physical and material dimensions of existence, an enactment that took the institutional form of the polis in ancient Greece.

I am not criticizing Arendt nor the Greeks as she depicts them for asserting and pursuing values pertaining to matters other than bearing and caring for life. It is in the nature of building a culture to develop institutions, rituals, and values, which go beyond mere survival and the activities bound up with survival. The problem is not that the Greeks formulated values other than caring for life. Rather, the problem lies in the extreme dichotomy established between a life of necessity and a life of freedom, between material existence and "fully human existence," between animal being and human being. When these various aspects of our existence and activities are institutionalized as oppositions and/or ordered hierarchically, the result is self-estrangement as well as estrangement from the context within which one lives. Greek men, as Arendt tells the story, stomped the ground that fed them; they formulated an identity of individual and political being that denied a part of itself, that suppressed and violated their connectedness with others and with nature. Of course human beings always *invent* their self-understandings. As Ortega y Gasset remarks, it is one of those intriguing ironies that "human life in its most human dimension [is] a work of fiction."[22] But the men of the Greek polis engaged in this work of invention in a specifically alienated fashion. As he sought to carve for himself a wholly "free" existence, Greek political man attempted to deny the incontrovertible fact that he is inherently a creature of nature and necessity, regardless of the extent to which he displaces the work of appropriating nature and dealing with necessity onto shoulders other than his own.[23] Because this brute fact cannot be overcome, only denied or suppressed, it presents a shadowy yet persistent threat to man's endeavors and self-conception. Without grounding in the material and necessary activities bearing and nourishing them, both individual men and the "collective manhood" of the polis acquire a fragile, restless, anxious or overwrought character. Both the individual and the polis require constant external affirmation of their existence and worth. Both over-reach themselves in an effort to acquire and sustain such validation.

A quite developed and quite explicit expression of these qualities will emerge in the discussion of Machiavelli and Renaissance Italy. There, the need of men and cities to do daring deeds breeds a world of conquest and aggression even more perpetual and bloody than that of the Greeks. Might, manhood, and the fleeting, transitory nature of glory are thickly and explicitly intertwined in Machiavelli's thought. Machiavelli portrays the restless intensity of political man's quest for heroism and power vividly and without apology. But with the Greeks, the attempt to come to terms with and resolve the "lack of grounding" man has created for himself is still fragmentary and in a certain way, highly self-conscious. While classical Greece had its share of bloody conquests, perpetual warfare, and heroic antics, there is in Greek thought an extraordinary degree of awareness of the singular and even perverse nature of the needs giving rise to these phenomena and of the probable futility of ever fulfilling these needs. There is also recorded a strong element of ambivalence about the excesses of aggression redounding from an *agonistic* mode of life.[24] This self-consciousness and ambivalence at times produce experience and thought riddled with qualities of anxiety and exaggeration, hesitation and uncertainty in the midst of assertions about the nature of politics, the greatness of the Athenian polis, or the excellence of an individual. In the texts of Aeschylus as well as Plato, Thucydides as well as Aristotle, one constantly encounters forceful claims followed by equivocation, dramatic solutions to ethical and political dilemmas that clearly do not warrant such easy answers, laudatory or self-congratulatory cries couched in profound doubt, fiery speech and action that border upon nervous agitation or panic.

These qualities—anxiety, exaggeration, and underlying panic—are among those I have suggested pervade Hannah Arendt's writings. There is an evident degree of anxiety in her obsession with the rarified, untainted nature of the political realm; her adamance that true politics must have a space of its own lest it perish; her concern that if man does not "insert himself" into this sphere and excel in word and deed, he will fall into the abyss of oblivion; her strange demand that genuine political action be "free" in the triple sense that it is "free from motive," "free from concern with results," and that it occur in the presence of others who are liberated from necessity.[25] There is something perilously close to pathology in Arendt's attempt to avoid touching and contamination, to situate action in a free space where it touches absolutely nothing—neither intellect or will, neither need nor desire, neither aim nor results.[26] Some extraordinary level of horror at "the natural" shapes Arendt's fierceness about its danger to political life, her insistence that today "the social realm . . . has let loose an unnatural growth . . . of the natural,"[27] and that "the less active we are, the more forcefully will [the] biological process assert itself, impose its inherent necessity upon us, and overawe us."[28] Some nightmarish picture of reclamation by need and the body informs her vexation at the prospect of hunger and poverty driving political and especially revolutionary action such that "freedom [is] surrendered to necessity, to the urgency of the life process itself."[29] Panic and anxiety also appear to drive her concern that we moderns might complacently accept our fate as mortals and seek not to leave gouges and pillars in the annals of political history as proof of our collective existence but come to care only (!) for life, work, beauty, knowledge, or a just social order. That modern cultures and progressive movements within them foster pursuit of these or even more limited collective and individual aspirations is a matter deeply disturbing to her and, she claims, is anathema to the true man and the truly political.

Through these overwrought formulations, Arendt offers a glimpse of what I have already intimated is a persistent, albeit protean, feature of Western and especially ancient Greek political thought and practice. Arendt's anxieties and striving toward paradoxical purities are stronger than those of the Greeks' (and she exaggerates Greek political motives in this regard), but this undoubtedly results from her conviction that the battle has nearly been lost. "There is perhaps no clearer testimony to the loss of the public realm in the modern age than the almost complete loss of concern with immortality."[30]

If the obsessive qualities of Arendt's personal pedagogic mission can be distinguished from the more accurate elements of her depiction of classical politics as fragile, anxious, and overwrought, she will have provided a useful inroad to this work. What Arendt lacks in grace and accuracy may be compensated by her honesty, her unapologetic attachment to a politics of manly deeds liberated from concern with life and the lives of others. If the following chapters reveal that the Greeks formulated these themes in slightly less extreme and desperate terms, it may have only been because they felt their values to be less imperiled.

Notes

1. Hannah Arendt, *The Human Condition* (Chicago: University of Chicago, 1958), pp. 36, 37.

2. Ibid., pp. 35–45, 60–62.

3. Ibid., p. 51.

4. Ibid., pp. 18–19; "The Concept of History," in *Between Past and Future* (New York: Viking Press, 1954), pp. 41–44.

5. *Human Condition*, p. 19; "What is Freedom?" in *Between Past and Future*, pp. 154–155.

6. *Human Condition*, p. 19.

7. Ibid., p. 22.

8. Ibid., p. 35.

9. Ibid., p. 53.

10. Ibid., p. 58.

11. Clearly, neither the slave nor the "barbarian" live in isolation; both have some semblance of community, and while slaves suffer from being unfree, "barbarians" do not.

12. For a similar and almost equally sanguine view of the "non-human" status of all noncitizens in ancient Athens, see J. Peter Euben, "Political Equality and the Greek Polis," in *Liberalism and the Modern Polity*, ed. Michael McGrath (New York: Marcel Dekker, 1987). "By nature, circumstance, and function, [foreigners, women, children and slaves] required masters, rulers, and permanent moral tutelage, all of which were inappropriate in the political arena where men were peers and equals. . . . People who by nature or circumstance were unfit for public life, or who chose to live a private life, were deprived of the opportunity to become fully human . . ." Euben, like Arendt, identifies the human with the capacity to distinguish oneself ("biog-

raphy") and the nonhuman with enslavement to necessity ("biology"). "[Political life] alone permits men to live as equals, free, under no master but the law, giving them opportunity for biography as well as biology." p. 214.

13. *Human Condition*, p. 37.

14. If it is not obvious, Arendt's insistence that dealing with material necessity is what identifies us with other animals stands in direct opposition to Marx's claim that the human mode of dealing with material necessity (through production) is precisely what distinguishes us as a species. In the *German Ideology*, Marx states simply, "men can be distinguished from animals by consciousness, by religion or anything else you like. They themselves begin to distinguish themselves from animals as soon as they begin to *produce* their means of subsistence." *Marx-Engels Reader*, p. 150. For Arendt's explicit critique of Marx, see Arendt, *Human Condition*, Chapter III.

15. *Human Condition*, p. 37. See also Euben, "Political Equality and the Greek Polis," *op. cit.*, p. 214. "For the Greeks the household . . . was concerned with the physical survival of the species, with reproduction and subsistence, what Aristotle called 'mere life.' Because men shared such necessities with all other species, these qualities could hardly be definitive of their humanity and must therefore be inferior to what was. What *was* definitive of human life was political."

16. It is significant that Arendt denies the close connection between politics and war associated with the Greeks by most classical scholars, that she calls war (and violence in general) "pre-political." These moves do not accord easily with the usual picture of the Greek citizen-warrior and would seem to have everything to do with her interest in identifying politics as that which alone distinguishes man from animal. In war, of course, this distinction can become extremely difficult to sustain. See Arendt, *Human Condition*, p. 31, and *On Violence* (New York: Harcourt Brace, 1969).

17. In the Greek polis, says Arendt, "hidden away were the laborers who 'with their bodies minister to the bodily needs of life' (Aristotle's *Politics*) and the women who with their bodies guarantee the physical survival of the species . . . The fact that the modern age emancipated the working classes and the women at nearly the same historical moment must certainly be counted among the characteristics of an age which no longer believes that bodily functions and material concerns should be hidden." Arendt, *Human Condition*, pp. 72–73.

18. Interview of Arendt in Melvyn Hill, ed. *Hannah Arendt: The Recovery of the Public World* (New York: St. Martin's Press, 1979), p. 305. While there is truth in Arendt's characterization of Plato's view of the body, she also oversimplifies his often tortured attempts to settle the problem of the body. For a fuller discussion of Plato and Socrates on the body, see my " 'Supposing Truth Were a Woman?': Plato's Subversion of Masculine Discourse," *Political Theory* (forthcoming 1988), and Arlene Saxonhouse, *Women in the History of Political Thought*, chapter 3.

19. *Phaedo* 65, 81, trans. H. Tredennick, in E. Hamilton and H. Cairns, eds.,*The Collected Dialogues of Plato* (Princeton: Princeton University Press, 1961) and *Phaedrus* 258e, trans. R. Hackforth in *Collected Dialogues of Plato*. Both dialogues hereafter cited simply by name.

20. Arendt, *Human Condition*, p. 199.

21. Ibid.

22. Jose Ortega y Gasset, "Man the Technician" in *History as a System and Other Essays toward a Philosophy of History*, trans. H. Wegl (New York: Norton, 1962), p. 108.

23. Aristotle, of course, attempts to reconcile man's "nature" with man's place in the natural order. See chapter three, pp. 33–34.

24. See, for example the "Melian Conference" in Thucydides *The Peloponnesian War*, trans. J. H. Finley (New York: Modern Library, 1951) pp. 330–37 (hereafter cited as *Peloponnesian War*) and Aeschylus' *Oresteia* for extremely self-conscious discussions of the ignoble motives sometimes underlying forays into battle and the individual and political tragedies that ensue from these forays.

25. Arendt, "What is Freedom?", p. 151.

26. Ibid. p. 152.

27. Arendt, *Human Condition*, p. 47.

28. Arendt, *On Revolution* (New York: Viking Press, 1963), p. 53.

29. Ibid. p. 54. This fear of being consumed by the life process, by natural necessity and the body, is so exaggerated in Arendt that one cannot help but speculate upon the extent to which it was shaped by the experience of being a female intellectual prior to the days of the "second wave" women's movement. The same theme is so heavily accentuated in de Beauvoir's premovement feminist treatise and, in a different way, in Shulamith Firestone's early manifesto for women's liberation that the point seems impossible to ignore: no woman avoids patriarchal identification of woman with body and of freedom with escape from the body. If this identification is accepted rather than interrogated, a woman who has somehow pried herself loose from the "bodily realm" is going to bear even more dread than her male counterpart about this realm's capacities for reclamation.

30. Arendt, *Human Condition*, p. 55.

3

Aristotle:
The Highest Good for Man

AMONG STUDENTS OF POLITICAL THEORY, Aristotle is probably best known and most appreciated for his insistence upon the naturalness of human political association. "Man is by nature an animal intended to live in the polis," he declares at the beginning of his lectures on politics."[1] The terms of this utterance—man, nature, animal, polis and political—will be subjected to critical scrutiny in this chapter, primarily through analysis of Aristotle's account of the origins and nature of the polis and the oikos in Book I of the *Politics*. The questions around which this analysis revolves are three: What are the features of man and of the polis that so perfectly suit each other and only each other? Why must men be members of a political community to be complete as men and what is it about others in the population that does not require this membership? What is the character of the politicalness Aristotle takes to be man's natural *métier*?

I

An appropriate place to begin an interpretation of Aristotle's *Politics* is with that which most bothered Hannah Arendt about his account of the polis: "he tentatively assumed that at least the historical origins of the polis must be concerned with the necessities of life."[2] For Aristotle indeed attempts to derive the polis from the "prepolitical" associations of household and village, even as he seeks to establish the polis as a transcendent and self-sufficient association. The polis emerges out of household and village but comes into existence to serve entirely different ends. This seemingly paradoxical construction occurs in the opening passages of the *Politics*:

> When we come to the final and perfect association formed from a number of villages which were formed from a number of households,

32

we have already reached the polis—an association which may be said to have reached the height of full self-sufficiency; or rather, we may say that while it *grows* for the sake of mere life, it *exists* for the sake of a good life.[3]

Aristotle's problem is a thorny one: from associations formed to meet basic human needs, he wants to derive the "naturalness" of an association whose essence lies in transcendence of necessity. While it is a problem his own metaphysics of nature has set for him, he hardly attempts to resolve it rigorously: "every polis . . . must have [itself] the same quality as the earlier associations from which it grew."[4] Having mentioned without exploring or elaborating their "similar quality," Aristotle then returns to assert their teleological relation: "the polis is the end or consummation to which the [household and villages] move, and the 'nature' of things consists in their end or consummation."[5] But right on the heels of—and not altogether compatible with—their teleological relationship comes an assertion of *hierarchy* as the most significant aspect of the relationship between *oikos* and *polis:* since "lower things always exist for the sake of the higher," Aristotle, with Arendt, insists that as far as members of the polis are concerned, household life exists for the sake of the "good life."[6]

In Aristotle's account, the polis is the "higher thing," the end or consummation of other associations, because the polis and the polis alone can imbue these associations and their constituent activities with "self-sufficiency."[7] After naming the polis the "final and perfect association"[8] *because* it is self-sufficient he adds:

Again, the end or final cause is the best. Now self-sufficiency is the end and, so the best. From these considerations, it is evident that the polis belongs to the class of things that exist by nature and that man is by nature an animal intended to live in a polis.[9]

Aristotle's ontological grounding of both the polis and man's politicalness in "nature" requires brief consideration of the significance of this term for him. Although Aristotle was himself an innovative theorist of nature, his rudimentary understanding of the term issues from the Ionian philosophers of the 6th and 7th centuries B.C. for whom nature "never meant the world or the things which go to make up the world, but always something inhering in these things that make them behave as they did . . . the principle in virtue of which things behave as they do."[10] Despite its many permutations, the whole of Greek natural science "was based on the principle that the world of nature is permeated or saturated by mind."[11] The intelligence or logic of objects and phenomena found in nature was the same intelligence or logic that established human purposes or guided the best human constructions, e.g., a good polis.[12] The omnipresence of "mind" in nature is thus the basis of Aristotle's portrayal of the *natural* aspect of human convention: at its best, human activity develops in accord with nature, not separately from or at odds with it.

From this account it should be clear that when Aristotle claims the polis exists "by nature," the stakes are both higher and lower than they would be within the definition of nature issuing from the modern tradition of natural science, a definition that does not ordinarily include in its purview such things as political organization or the institution of slavery.[13] They are high insofar as Aristotle must establish the logic or inherent rationality of the polis as the only genuine human habitat since the polis can be explained and vindicated by no other means. On the other hand, given the tendency of the Greek conception of nature to imbue "what is" with rationality, Aristotle need not search too far to locate the sources and dimensions of the polis as *the* human association. A kind of crude positivism operates here: Aristotle sees elite men spending their days in the political realm and concludes that the political realm is man's natural *métier*, much as positivist social scientists today speak of man's inherently acquisitive, self-interested, or competitive nature.

What confounds Aristotle, however, is the problem of deriving an apparently transcendent organization from the immanent or need-related institutions of household and village. What is the precise relationship between these two kinds of organization and how is an organization unconcerned with material necessity born out of associations devoted to it? How is it possible to assert the naturalness of an association that one is simultaneously trying to distance from needs and necessity? Here is the way Aristotle scholar Ernest Barker attempts to resolve the difficulty:

> The state is natural because it develops from natural associations. But it would be wrong to think it is only natural because they are natural and because it grows from them. It is natural in itself, as the completion, end or consummation of man and man's development . . . If we could imagine a state coming into existence directly or immediately, without the preceding stages of the household and the village, it would still be natural, in virtue of completing and perfecting man and his development.[14]

The problem with Barker's explanation is that it eclipses Aristotle's concern to establish the polis as self-sufficient, as *the* association making life "desirable and lacking in nothing," and as the *culmination* of all prior or lower associations. In his effort to make Aristotle coherent, Barker too easily dismisses the teleological aspect Aristotle ascribes to the oikos-village-polis development and emphasizes as part of what makes the polis "natural." Nor does Barker really probe the content of the political nature Aristotle ascribes to man, a nature that Aristotle claims only the polis can draw forth to perfection. Barker simply endorses Aristotle's attempt to make man's political nature and the polis' natural status explain one another:

> The polis thus fulfills the whole nature of man, and especially the higher part of his nature; and that is why it has reached 'the height of full self-sufficiency' containing as it does, in itself . . . all the resources necessary for full and complete human development. Thus fulfilling the whole nature of man, the polis is particularly and specially "natural" in the sense of the word which means the final and perfect condition of ultimate development.[15]

In addition to its tautological aspects, Barker's interpretation simply does not resolve the questions raised by Aristotle's formulation of the nature of the polis and its relationship to other associations. Why does Aristotle both seek a teleological relation between the polis and oikos and fail to discern one? Why is the naturalness of the polis and man's political nature only asserted over and over again, never really *shown*? Why does the polis and the polis alone fulfill man, what is insufficient about the prior associations, and what is it about man that is fulfilled in the polis? What is the connection between manliness and the polis? Especially since from other Aristotelian works and other passages in the *Politics*, one learns that Aristotle imbues only men and only *some* men with a political nature, a deeper exploration of the self-sufficiency of the polis and of man's political nature is required to discover how men and the polis are constitutive of one another.

In the first chapter of the *Politics*, Aristotle explains that the distinctive nature of the polis can be ascertained "by considering analytically the elements of which a polis is composed."[16] One would, therefore, expect Aristotle to begin with the study of an individual, proceed to a study of relationships, and proceed from there to a study of institutional associations. This is precisely what he does except that Aristotle cannot start with just any member of the population; while the polis exists for the perfection of man's political nature, this perfection or this nature does not extend to all men, let alone all individuals. What if such an analysis were begun with one of the noncitizens, especially with one of those not "fully human" creatures who are not "of" but only "for" the polis—a male slave or a woman? Using Aristotle's inductive mode of analysis, such beginnings would generate either a morass of confusion or devastatingly revolutionary conclusions. Aristotle escapes this quandary via a formulation of the relation of social "parts" to social "wholes":

> We may now proceed to add that the polis is prior in the order of nature to the family and the individual. The reason for this is that the whole is necessarily prior to the part. If the whole body be destroyed, there will not be a foot or a hand, except in that ambiguous sense, in which one uses the same word to indicate a different thing, as when one speaks of a "hand" made of stone. . . . All things derive their essential character from their function and their capacity; and it follows that if they are no longer fit to discharge their function, we ought not to say that they are still the same things, but only that, by an ambiguity, they still have the same names. We thus see that the polis exists by nature and that it is prior to the individual, in the sense that not being self-sufficient when they are isolated, all individuals are so many parts all equally depending on the whole which alone can bring self-sufficiency.[17]

On a superficial reading, it would seem that Aristotle is here claiming nothing more for the "natural" and "whole" status of the polis than that it embodies and fulfills man's material and spiritual need for community. But if we press hard on this passage, and consider it in light of other passages already examined, we may extract a doctrine of a slightly more pernicious order.

Recall that the polis is "higher" in the order of human things than the necessary activities of human existence and that the latter activities are performed only so that the polis may exist as it does. From the perspective of those providing the material requisites of life, however, the polis may be viewed as *superfluous* to the needs of "mere life"—household and village alone provide for these needs. Yet in the passage above, Aristotle pronounced the polis the "whole" of which all other activities, creatures, and associations are the "parts." Moreover, this entity, which exists for non-necessary reasons and which, on a material level at least, has a parasitic relation to the realm of necessity, is the only thing that can provide its "parts" with any meaning, purpose, or function. Without this curious "whole," a man is not really a man but a "poor sort of being," a beast or a god, or something else travelling under the name of a man.[18] Similarly, without the polis, Aristotle argues, slaves, women, and artisans perform their work "without function," thus have no "essential character," and may as well not exist. Clearly in the absense of slaves, artisans, wives, and male citizens the polis cannot exist at all, yet Aristotle precisely reverses this and says that it is only through the polis that the "parts" of the polis exist and gain meaning. Why does he do this? In asking this question, we are still laboring over the

problem of what constitutes the "self-sufficiency," hence the superiority, hence the "naturalness" of the polis.

Before this question can be resolved, we need to draw forward the
other thread with which this exploration began and the other route
Aristotle takes in his effort to establish the naturalness and self-
sufficiency of the polis. This is the claim that man's nature is *political*.
We have just seen that the polis does not arise "naturally" nor from
necessity, that is a purely conventional and materially "superfluous"
entity. The polis is in the most literal sense artificial—an artifice of the
men who create and occupy it. Yet Aristotle calls it natural and insists
that a man cannot experience being a man unless he has a polis,
unless he is in the company of others like himself who are also
estranged from their physiological and mortal existence. Somehow,
the polis fulfills the incomplete man, fills the void, gives him meaning, makes a man a man. Conversely, if the polis is destroyed, a man
ceases to be a man. But if the polis is in a deep sense artificial,
unrelated to necessity, mere life, the sustenance and maintenance of
life, then so must be man's political nature. Even if this did not follow
logically, we would have begun to suspect it by virtue of the fact that
political man requires being surrounded by his peers and removed
from his source of sustenance and maintenance in order to come into
his own *as* a man. Only through the artifice of the polis and through
distance from the oikos can Aristotelian man experience himself as
real.

Where Aristotle tells us man is most at home, we see him most
estranged from life; what Aristotle posits as an association most in
accordance with nature appears as the most glaringly conventional of
institutions; and what Aristotle pronounces self-sufficient looks to be
either parasitic, utterly dependent, or superfluous. Yet living and
acting within a polis is all that can imbue a man with manhood, all
that can bring him to a state in which "life is desirable and lacking in
nothing."[19] In this very quest for self-sufficiency, Aristotelian man
defames and banishes the activities that initiate, constitute, and
sustain his existence. Man's political nature is rooted in self-repudia-
tion, in a drive toward alienation, toward forgetting of his desirous
and mortal self. Man's political nature is fulfilled by doffing his
animal being and donning an artificial self, a self which is only at
home in an artificial realm.

We need to know what it is that men, and only certain men, lacked
prior to the polis. And we need to know why those Aristotle excludes
from polis membership do not suffer from this lack. It appears that
there may be something in the "mastering of necessity" itself that
renders the man destined for the polis empty, degrounded, and

purposeless, a malaise that can only be resolved through the status and activities of the polis. Therefore, we now turn to an exploration of Aristotle's account of the realm of necessity, the oikos, or as Arendt calls it, the "prepolitical."

II

In his discussion of the social structure of the ideal polis, Aristotle remarks:

> In the state, as in other natural compounds, the conditions which are necessary for the whole are not organic parts of the whole system which they serve. The conclusion which clearly follows is that we cannot regard the elements which are necessary for the existence of the state . . . as being parts of the state.[20]

The political relevance of this distinction between "necessary conditions" and "parts" of the state is generally thought to lie in Aristotle's discussion of citizenship: "The truth is that we cannot include as citizens all those who are 'necessary conditions' of the state's existence."[21] But there is a second, and for our purposes, quite important aspect to Aristotle's distinction and that is the *instrumental* relation he is attempting to establish between inhabitants of the realm of necessity and citizens of the polis.

There is a double aspect to this instrumentality. First, the realm of necessity is posited as nothing more than a means for supplying the material requisites of the citizens. Secondly, individuals involved with necessity are literally regarded as "instruments for the purpose of life, the sum of which is 'property.' "[22] In the first book of the *Politics*, Aristotle engages in elaborate and what has sometimes been viewed as "humanistic" justification for this perspective and we shall eventually need to examine these passages.[23] But it is Arendt who sets aside matters of justice and justification to put the Aristotelian conclusion sharply:

> Because all humans are subject to necessity, they are entitled to violence toward others; violence is the prepolitical act of liberating oneself from the necessity of life for the freedom of the world . . .

> The "good life" as Aristotle called the life of the citizen, therefore was not merely better, more carefree or nobler than ordinary life, but of an altogether different quality. It was "good" to the extent that by having mastered the necessities of sheer life, by being freed from labor and work, and by overcoming the innate urge of all living creatures for their own survival, it was no longer bound to the biological life process.[24]

The themes are familiar: politics, as an aspect of the "good life," is of an altogether "different quality" from other kinds of life. It takes place independently of—in Arendt's formulation, over and against—the "biological life process" and "innate human urges." Not merely distance from but contempt for the realm of necessity, contempt which serves as an implicit justification of violence and domination there, emerges as a fundamental ingredient of a properly constructed political realm. The biological life process and the urge of all living creatures to care for their survival are construed as not simply irrelevant but anathema to the cultivation of man's "true" nature.

"In all cases where there is a compound," Aristotle states, "a ruling element and a ruled can always be traced."[25] This principle he extends to everything, animate and inanimate, individual and collective. The soul itself is divided into ruling and ruled, rational and irrational parts, and the soul also rules the body in a virtuous human being. These hierarchies have a good deal more instrumentality than complementarity about them: "in the world of nature as well as of art, the lower always exists for the sake of the higher."[27] From these ontological claims, Aristotle derives a theory of legitimate rule or domination according to the superiority of *mind*. The supremacy of mind is the basis for phenomena as far-reaching as man's domination of all earthly things, as general as the polis's domination of the oikos and man's rule over woman,[28] and as particular as a specific master's command of his slave.

> The element which is able, by virtue of its intelligence, to exercise forethought, is naturally a ruling and master element; the element which is able, by virtue of its bodily power, to do what the other element plans, is a ruled element, which is naturally in a state of slavery.[29]

While this formulation would seem to pertain primarily to what Aristotle calls "ethics" or the right ordering of the soul, Aristotle insists that "what holds good in a man's inner life also holds good outside of it."[30] Thus,

> if the mind is to be reckoned as more essentially a part of living being than the body, parts of a similar order to the mind must equally be reckoned as more essentially parts of the state than those which serve its bodily needs.[31]

The element "whose virtue lies in its bodily power" is therefore not only the body of every living creature, but the collected body of human beings in service to the polis, namely, slaves, women, and artisans. So concerned is Aristotle to establish the inherent "bodily nature" of creatures such as slaves that he even wades into the dangerous waters of appearance:

> It is nature's intention also to erect a physical difference between the body of the freeman and that of the slave, giving the latter strength for the menial duties of life but making the former upright in carriage and

(though useless for physical labor) useful for the various purposes of civic life.[32]

Aristotle's tendency to absurdity here notwithstanding, this description of the bodily nature of slaves points to the extent to which the institutionalization of the mind/body hierarchy in the social structure ideologically converts those involved with productive and reproductive work into pure Body. From the perspective of men, masters, and the polis, women and slaves stood for the function and identity of the body, and were nothing other than their bodies. Conversely, men of the polis were citizens by virtue of their freedom from or repudiation of bodily concerns. From this posture of repudiation, they constructed and legitimated a social and political order over which they presumed to rule with mind "purified" of body.

Most interpreters of Aristotle's *Politics* regard as his primary justification of slavery the claim that the slave cannot reason well enough to direct his own actions but can think sufficiently well to apprehend reason in a master.[33] This obviously weak argument has overshadowed much more important features of Aristotle's defense of slavery, features that illuminate Aristotle's general view of bodily labor:

> From these considerations, we can see clearly what is the nature of the slave and what is his capacity. We attain these definitions—first, that "anybody who by nature is not his own man but another's is by his nature a slave;" secondly, that "anybody who, being a man, is an article of property, is another man's:" and thirdly, that "an article of property is an instrument intended for the purpose of action and separable from its possessor."[34]

There is a foreshadowing in this passage of what is to come in Aristotle's discourse on oikos life—that it is the *very capacity to work* that renders one vulnerable to being enslaved. Just one chapter later, Aristotle declares: "a man is thus by nature a slave if he is capable of becoming (and this is why he also actually becomes) the property of another."[35] The mere capacity for work contains the potential for "becoming the property of another," for becoming an "instrument" of someone else's needs. Since Aristotle's epistemology and ontology involve imbuing "what is" with rationality, he does not leave this matter at the level of potential. Indeed, the "naturalness" and hence justification of the unfree realm of the oikos depends upon turning the *potential* for alienation inherent in labor into a *metaphysical necessity* and good. Listen again: "a man is thus by nature a slave if he is capable of becoming (and this is why he also actually becomes) the property of another." The lack of freedom associated with work issues less from the fact that it is bound up with nature or necessity than from the institutionalization of workers as the property of nonworkers. Those who evince the capacity for productive and reproductive work are narrowed into such beings as are capable of nothing else and are reduced in the political order to a stratum that exists and performs such tasks only for the good of those who are free.

Since slavery diminishes the capacity of producers and reproducers to formulate their own purposes and protect themselves, Aristotle proclaims them inherently in need of rule and protection, thereby introducing his notion of "rule for the benefit of the ruled," which is the dictum of the master, father, and husband as well as citizens of the polis. All matter requires form, all action needs a guide or principle, and according to Aristotle, if the form or principle is not available from within, it must be supplied from an external source. This is how Aristotle describes procreation (woman provides the "matter," man provides the seed or "principle of growth,"[36]) and the work performed by slaves (who are capable of apprehending reason in another, "though destitute of it themselves"[37]). In his discussion of the wide application of the "ruling for the benefit of the ruled" postulate, Aristotle says:

> What holds good in man's inner life also holds good outside of it; and the same principle is true of the relation of man to animals as is true of the relation of his soul to his body. Tame animals have a better nature than wild, and it is better for such animals that they should be ruled by man because then they get the benefit of preservation.[38]

From Aristotle's discussion of slaves and women, we may deduce that the "superiority" of tame animals lies in their obedience, a quality that depends upon the rule of their minds over their appetites and bodies. Aristotle approves tame animals because they, like men of virtuous nature, have mostly quelled their instincts. Of course, the "tame" were not born that way but were coerced, bribed, and punished into their tame state by man. The "taming" of an animal depends upon making it fear for its own preservation and teaching it through any number of clever, coercive, or barbarous means that its self-preservation lies in the master's hands. The tame are thus in a condition of forced dependence, a condition that, filtered through Aristotle's theory of nature and observational method of inquiry, is then rendered as their essential nature. In this way, the "second nature"—the learned dependence and subservience—of a tame animal, male slave, or woman is presented as its "first nature," its true being and function.

Once man gains control over the bodies of slaves, women, and animals, their minds too must be devoted to the needs of man for it is only through apprehending and fulfilling man's wants that their survival and their place within the "human" structure is guaranteed. In this process of double alienation, i.e., of surrendering self-directed minds as well as bodily instincts and needs to a master, a new creature may indeed emerge—a tame or crippled one. As long as these creatures are deprived of the means of their own self-sufficiency and hence, of their own survival, it may appear "natural" that free men should rule them, extract benefit from them, and protect them. And here, in microcosm, is the essence of Aristotle's formulation of the "natural" relationship between master and slave, husband and family, man and animal, the realm of politics and the realm of necessity. The politics of domination and exploitation are converted ideologically as well as institutionally into what is given and natural.

One reason, then, for Aristotle's concern that men of the polis avoid direct involvement with the realm of necessity pertains to the potential in work for alienation leading to domination, that is, the potential for labor to be appropriated and for laborers to be enslaved. Through the practice of slavery and the subjugation of women in ancient Greece, this potential was actualized in Aristotle's milieu and he treated its actualized state as natural and necessary. The second reason for Aristotle's concern to establish distance between polis and oikos pertains to the elements of violence and domination in the oikos. The significance of this will become clear through an integration of the foregoing discussion of Aristotle's account of man's command over slaves, women, and tame animals with his general philosophy of rule.

Aristotle refines his thesis that all compounds and relations have a ruling and a ruled element with the argument that there is a *best* kind of rule associated with the highest form of ruled elements:

> There are . . . many kinds of both ruling and ruled elements. This being the case, the rule which is exercised over the better sort of ruled elements is a better sort of rule—as, for example, rule over a man is better than rule over an animal. The reason is that a function is a higher and better function when the elements which go to discharge it are higher and better elements.[39]

In this passage, Aristotle at first appears concerned only with establishing or preserving a certain noble sensibility: the best man's duties must be "worthy" of him and he will be diminished in stature if he is surrounded by lowly creatures. This is certainly what is implied by Aristotle's claim elsewhere that while artisans can achieve goodness, the extent and quality of such goodness is limited by the crudeness of their daily tasks.[40] But there is an underside to the notion that "rule is best over the better sort of ruled elements," an implication that the "lower" forms of reproductive and productive activity can contaminate those above them if the master or ruling element draws too close or rules them directly rather than through the mediation of institutions. Aristotle makes this explicit in the metaphysical account of the ruling/ruled doctrine proffered in the *Generation of Animals*:

> And as the Form, is better and more divine in its nature than the Matter, *it is better also that the superior one should be separate from the inferior one.* That is why whenever possible and so far as possible, the male is separate from the female, since it is something better and more divine in that it is the principle of movement of generated things, while the female serves as their matter.[41]

Not only, then, are those bound to nature and necessity unfit for higher things, the higher thing itself is threatened by proximity to or involvement with lower things. The fear, noted in Arendt's thought, of letting the most valued things and activities touch anything else now appears in Aristotle. For him as for Arendt, the public realm must be literally separated and insulated from the realm of necessity. What this implies is the irony that the "best of men" and highest of activities—manhood and politics—are actually extremely fragile, easily threatened or contaminated by the inferior elements supporting them and giving them life. These men who are so superior to all others and who inhabit the most superior association, who determine all matters of right order and justice, must be physically and spriritually sequestered from the contaminating effects of those who "receive the benefit of their rule."

Both Aristotle and Arendt refuse to grant political standing to a realm that provides for the polis and is organized politically, that is, through systematic and institutional relations of power.[42] Yet Aristotle, unlike Arendt, does not sucessfully establish that politics begins only where the force and violence of the "pre-political" ends. His discussion of the oikos is replete with analogies between husband and statesman, slavemaster and monarch;[43] he introduces his discussion of slavery with considerations of justice—a supremely political referent;[44] and he devotes the first section of a work on politics to the nature and structure of the household. Aristotle recognizes that those elements and activities that are mere "conditions" of the polis have a political character and must be dealt with by the political theorist; indeed this is precisely what was insisted upon by Plato, his teacher and predecessor. But Aristotle's strategy in dealing with these elements and activities is to depoliticize them, both ideologically and practically. He spies the politicalness of these relations and then proclaims them natural. He spies their threat to polis life and demands their exclusion from the realm called politics.

Everything under the auspices of the "pre-political" is excluded from politics precisely because its structure and organization is bound up with the violence and inequality inherent in institutionalized subordination. Despite Aristotle's elaborately woven ontology and teleology designed to justify the violence Arendt simply declares legitimate in the realm of necessity, violence it remains. Both Aristotle and Arendt insist that equality and the activities and relations appropriate to equals are the hallmark of genuine political life; where inequalities prevail, there is not politics (speech and action) but violence, nature, force. Moreover, wherever bodies and/or bodily necessity are at issue, inequality and violence are necessarily present. This is explained by Aristotle as consequent to nature's tendency to place the ruling and ruled elements of a compound in different persons and by Arendt with the remarkable claim that human beings are entitled to violence toward others whenever they are trying to master necessity.[45]

All of this results in an extraordinary set of conclusions about politics. For both Arendt and Aristotle, politics is what occurs in refined conversations between male citizens, not in the violence or domination in relations between masters and slaves, men and women, colonized and colonizers—relations both theorists proclaimed "natural" or necessary rather than political. In this view, wherever there is violence or inequality, not politics but nature is at work and wherever there are conversations and negotiations between equals, men are expressing their highest affinity, their true selves, their political nature. The maintenance of this fiction through the "naturalization" of domination and violence in the oikos and through masking the agency that sustains this domination is what necessitates such severe boundaries around the political realm. This is why the "pre-political" must be sharply separated from the public realm, why Arendt is so anxious about the infestation of politics with those activities she considers polluting of the public realm, why Aristotle speaks of those associated with such activities as mean, servile, common or generally in "poor taste" and insists that such people must be exluded from citizenship as mere "conditions" rather than "parts" of the polis.[42]

Thus, even as Arendt and Aristotle struggle to keep the realms of necessity and politics apart, we have peeled back the lid on the realm of necessity to find most of the important politics of polis life going on *there*. The real "dirtiness" in the realm of necessity—the basis of its potential contamination of "public" things—lies in the way it is organized and in the denial of the role of public power in accomplishing this organization. The inhabitants of the unfree realm are "spiteful," "mean," "common," or "bestial," because they are enslaved and dominated, forced into narrow, nasty, servile roles. Aristotle himself sketches a vivid picture of those who are barred from the place where law prevails and virtue is nourished:

> Man, when perfected, is the best of animals; but if he be isolated from law and justice, he is the worst of all. Injustice is all the greater when it is armed injustice; and man is furnished from birth [with arms] e.g., language, which are intended to serve the purpose of moral prudence and virtue, but which may be used in a preference for opposite ends. That is why, if he be without virtue, he is a most unholy and savage being, and worse than all others in lust and gluttony.[47]

Now, no public servant wants to come into contact with such people for they make demands on him, recall the unjust foundation of the political order to him, and confuse his assessment of what is really and truly political. Moreover, if the political and "prepolitical" realms are too proximate, the "slaves to necessity" may grasp the political-ness of their own situation. On the other hand, as long as the public realm maintains a distance of space and concerns from the prepoliti-cal, it is easier to sustain the fiction of the "naturalness" of the oikos-polis relation and the obvious unfitness of oikos inhabitants for anything other than their enslavement.

The other reason that freedom in the polis is cast as so antithetical to necessity pertains to the ideology of work we discerned in Aristo-tle's discussion of the household. His rendering of what is only the potential for alienation inherent in bodily labor as natural, necessary, and actual suggests the basis for the Greek fear of "entrapment" by the body, material life and the natural world. If one uncritically associates the life of a Greek slave or woman with the very nature of productive and reproductive activities, then one has good reason to fear that engaging in this work is a substantial threat to human, free existence. Such work then appears not merely necessary, or at times banal and tedious, but dehumanizing and enslaving in the most literal sense of the words. Since this is precisely the association Aristotle made, the "good life" was posited in dire contrast to all activities pertaining to the procreation and sustenance of life. And, as we shall see, the dread of nature, work, femininity, and enslavement against which the "good life" was pursued is omnipresent in the Greek formulation of political action and political meaning. In other words, this structure of power and ideology about "necessity" shapes not only the lives of those who are bound up with necessity but the nature and content of politics itself. With this in mind, we now turn to Aristotle's formulation of the aims and ends of political life.

III

In his discussion of "political ideals," Aristotle explicitly poses the question, "what is political association for" and links the problem of discerning the *telos* of politics to questions about the *telos* of man.[48] In this regard, Aristotle returns to Plato's identification of the nature of the polis with the nature of the soul yet as he does so, he creates difficulties for himself insofar as he seeks to avoid the profoundly critical conclusions Plato drew about extant political life.[49] In asserting that the "true end . . . for any state . . . of society . . . is the enjoyment of partnership in a good life and the felicity thereby attainable," Aristotle must confront the fact that much of the activity of the Greek polis revolves around war and defense and that these things are not directly constitutive of "partnership in a good life" and "felicity."[50] Moreover, in establishing *eudaimonia* as the telos of man and the polis, Aristotle raises the problem of whether political life itself fulfills this end or whether it is only a means to the higher good of contemplative life. He introduces the problem this way:

> There is one thing clear about the best constitution: it must be a political organization which will enable all sorts of men to be at their best and live happily. But . . . even those who agree in holding that the good life is most desirable are divided upon the issue, "Which way of life is the more desirable? The way of politics and action? Or the way of detachment from all external things, the way . . . of contemplation . . . ?" Here . . . are the two ways of life—the political and the philosophic—that are evidently chosen by those who have been most eager to win a reputation for goodness in our own and previous ages. It is a matter of no small moment on which of the two sides truth lies: for whether individuals or states are in question, it is always the duty of wisdom to aim at the higher mark.[51]

In his commentary on this passage, Ernest Barker suggests that the issue is "whether a state should devote itself to internal cultivation or external aggrandisement."[52] Given the discussion of constitutions organized around war and conquest immediately following the passage, there are clearly grounds for Barker's interpretation. Yet when Aristotle has concluded his critical treatment of militaristic constitutions with the statement that "military pursuits are . . . to be counted good . . . [not as] the chief end of man [but as] means to the chief end," he retains his equivocation about the virtues of a life of action relative to a life of contemplation.[53] He then seeks to recast the problem:

> We must now consider the views of those who are agreed in accepting the general principle that a life of goodness is most desirable, but divided in their opinion about the right way of living that life. One is the

school which eschews political office, distinguishing the life of the individual freeman from that of the politician and preferring it to all others. The other is the school which regards the life of the politician as best; they argue that men who do nothing cannot be said to "do well" and they identify felicity with active "well-doing."[54]

Here Aristotle appears to be trying to compel an answer to the action-contemplation problem through recalling that goodness—with which both rightly practiced action and contemplation are infused—must be active. "Goodness by itself is not enough: there must also be a capacity for being active in doing good."[55] Thus, "felicity should be held to consist in 'well-doing' " and "it follows that the life of action is best, alike for every state as a whole and for each individual in his own conduct."[56] Yet precisely at the moment Aristotle seems to have resolved the dilemma between action and contemplation in favor of action, he snatches away the solution. Contemplation rightly pursued, it turns out, is also a kind of action. In fact, it is the highest sort of action, for it is the most rational and the most god-like.

The life of action need not be . . . a life which involves relations to others. Nor should our thoughts be held to be active only when they are directed to objects which have to be achieved by action. Thoughts with no object beyond themselves, and speculations and trains of reflection followed purely for their own sake, are far more deserving of the name of active . . . As thought in itself may be activity, so activity may exist without relation to others . . . If it were not so, there would be something wrong with God himself and the whole of the universe, who have no activities other than those of their own internal life.[57]

This conclusion, that goodness in action need not involve others, have an aim, nor be visible to observers, is equally applicable to the city and to the individual. "States situated by themselves and resolved to live in isolation, need not be therefore inactive . . . this is also and equally true of the individual human being."[58]

Thus Aristotle finally settles his dilemma by changing—and ultimately collapsing—the opposing terms of the problem. Action and contemplation are not antimonious since contemplation is a form of action. It is the highest form of action because it involves the highest aspect of man's being (mind) in its purest form (disembodied). "The exercise of rational principle and thought is the ultimate end of man's nature."[59] Action that is not pure thought always bears irrational elements—the body carrying out the action and the ambiguities of political space in which the action occurs. Action (other than thought) requires the body, and this drastically lowers the worth and prestige of the activity. Conversely, thought unattached to any object beyond itself is not, in Aristotle's view, subject to the contaminants of body and context and is therefore a higher, better, more god-like form of action. It may aspire to an absolute and pristine self-control and self-sufficiency.

What does this discovery of action in the contemplative life portend for the status and purpose of politics? We have labored over the first book of the *Politics* in which Aristotle declares man to be a political animal, finds man's perfection in the polis, and finds the polis to be the highest form of human existence. In the discussion of the ultimate ends of the polis and the ideal constitution, Aristotle again returns to the "self-sufficient" quality of the polis, this time to elaborate upon the elements which make it so.[60] Yet after he has sought to establish the polis's self-sufficiency in terms of its inclusion of all the elements that make life "lacking in nothing" and after he has named the polis the highest form of human association, Aristotle forthrightly states that political life itself is a *means* to other ends:

> Life as a whole is . . . divided into its different parts—action and leisure, war and peace; and in the sphere of action we may further distinguish acts which are merely necessary, or merely and simply useful, from acts which are good in themselves. The preferences which we give to the parts of life and their different activities will inevitably follow the same general line as those which we give to the parts of the soul and their different activities. War must therefore be regarded as only a means to peace; action as a means to leisure; and acts which are merely necessary, or merely and simply useful, as means to acts which are good in themselves . . . it is true that the citizens of our state must be able to lead a life of action and war, but they must be even more able to lead a life of leisure and peace.[61]

The well constituted polis and political activity itself are thus means to leisure which, in turn, is a means to other high quality pursuits.[62] Anything merely useful, necessary, or bound to practical objectives is a means to the higher good of leisure. The two issues of significance here are the supreme value Aristotle places upon the rational activity of the mind "purified" of body and the antipathy to "the necessary" whose basis we have already explored in the discussion of the "pre-political" realm. So strong is this antipathy, this concern to free genuinely human pursuits of all connection to the animal order, the body and the necessary, that Aristotle ends up ascribing a lower value to political action and deliberation than he seemingly had intended. The aim of the polis is no longer politics; the "good life" is no longer synonymous with political life. This conclusion emerges in its sharpest form in the *Ethics*:

> We occupy ourselves with action in order that we may have leisure, and we make war in order to enjoy peace. The activity of the practical virtues

is shown in political or military affairs, but our action in such affairs must be held to be unleisured action. Military action is entirely so . . . but the action of the statesman too is unleisured action.[63]

Political life and political action, proffered in the opening passages of the *Politics* as the highest good for man, ultimately emerge as instrumental things, tainted as they are by necessity and the body. Action itself, which Aristotle set out to valorize, is so difficult to dissociate from the body that he ends up turning against it: as the body is an instrument of the mind, so action becomes an instrument of its "opposite," even through convoluted efforts to preserve the category of action as an honorable one.

At this point we may note the parallel difficulty Hannah Arendt has when she is grappling with the problem of political action. She, like Aristotle, is sure that "goodness" by itself is of little value, that it must be "active" if it is to have any meaning in the world.[64] What is remarkable about her extensive discussion of the *vita activa* in *The Human Condition* is that she does not offer a single concrete instance of genuine action, either in ancient Greece or in our own times. She does insist that "a life without . . . action . . . is literally dead to the world";[65] that acting, "in its most general sense means to take an initiative, to begin";[66] that action is all that can reveal our human distinctiveness;[67] that action more than any other activity requires the presence of others and that acting in isolation is a contradiction in terms;[68] that action "always establishes relationships and therefore has an inherent tendency to force open all limitations and cut across all boundaries,"[69] and that genuine political action must be free from motives and free from concern with results.[70] Moreover, political action must never be for or about life or any aspect of material existence; its function or ethos is self-disclosure, never usefulness.[71] True political action is not force or violence and it is not speech alone although it must be accompanied by speech if it is to be grasped and recorded for posterity.[72]

These are the stipulations on political action and the litany of what it is not according to Arendt. But what is it? What counts as a political act? Why, if the Greek polis was the most perfectly formed "political space" in Western history, can not even one example of Greek political action be extracted from Arendt's works? The answer to this question is similar to the reasons Aristotle ended up treating political action as a means to higher ends although Arendt makes the matter even more extreme. Her theoretical formulation of action has rendered action impossible. She takes the Greek repudiation of the body and material life so far that despite her idolatry of political action, she eliminates the very possibility of it. For action requires not just thought and words but a body, and Arendt refuses the body entry into politics. She has not misread Aristotle in this regard, but has simply taken his position to its logical, if slightly absurd, extreme. Yet Aristotle, too, fails to say exactly what it is that citizens of the polis *do* other than take turns ruling each other and even this he regards as *instrumental* activity, a means to the ends of leisured life in which necessity plays no part. Aristotle, too, ultimately hushes the activity of the polis in the course of his attempt to establish the polis as the highest human association. Aristotle, too, founders on the problem of "body-less action" as a consequence of his identification of manhood with mind's mastery of the body and necessary separation from it.

In the end, the supreme advocate of political life turns away from politics, indeed from community itself, to establish the highest good for man. Aristotle's construction of manhood justifies and reinforces the structure of domination and elite composition of the polis while ironically, subverting the value of the polis as a realm of activity.

Notes

1. *Politics* I.ii.9, trans. Ernest Barker (Oxford: Oxford University Press, 1946). Hereafter cited as *Politics*.

2. Arendt, *Human Condition*, p. 37.

3. *Politics* I.ii.8.

4. Ibid. I.ii.8.

5. Ibid. I.ii.8.

6. Ibid. I.ii.7.

7. For Aristotle, self-sufficiency (from the Greek *autarkeia*) connotes an ethical condition as much as a material one. In the *Nicomachean Ethics* I.vii [trans. J. A. K. Thomson (Middlesex, England: Penguin, 1955), hereafter cited as *Ethics*)] where the term is explored most fully, Aristotle explains that the "final good" is thought to be self-sufficient. "Now by self-sufficient we do not mean that which is sufficient for a man by himself, for one who lives a solitary life, but also for parents, children, wife, and in general for his friends and fellow citizens . . . the self-sufficient we now define as that which when isolated makes life desirable and lacking in nothing; and such we think happiness to be." As Barker notes in the *Politics*, self-sufficiency "may be understood to mean the possession of such material resources and such moral incentives and impulses, as make a full human development possible, without any dependence on external help, material or moral." (*Politics*, note B, p. 8).

8. *Politics* I.ii.8.

9. Ibid. I.ii.9.

10. R. D. Collingwood, *The Idea of Nature* (Oxford: Oxford University Press, 1960, 1st edition, 1945), pp. 44–45.

11. Ibid. p. 3.

12. "Every entity, animate and inanimate, represents a specialized local organization of this all-pervading vitality or rationality, so that a plant or

animal . . . participates in its own degree psychically in the life process of the world's 'soul' and intellectually in the activity of the world's 'mind,' no less than it participates materially in the physical organization of the world's 'body.' " Ibid. p. 4.

13. Admittedly there are many social scientists, even in the post-behaviorist era, who try to reduce human affairs to the principles of natural science but the reverse is rarely the case: few contemporary nature scholars consider their purview to be limitless.

14. Barker, *Politics*, note 2, p. 5.

15. Ibid. note B, pp. 7–8.

16. *Politics* I.i.3.

17. Ibid. I.ii.12–14.

18. Ibid. I.ii.9.

19. *Ethics* I.iii.7.

20. *Politics* VII.viii.1.

21. Ibid. III.v.2.

22. Ibid. I.iv.1.

23. For Aristotle's "humanism" on the slave issue, see Barker, *Politics*, pp. lvii-lviii and S. R. L. Clark, *Aristotle's Man: Speculations Upon Aristotelian Anthropology* (Oxford: Clarendon Press, 1975), pp. 106–107, 211.

24. Arendt, *Human Condition*, pp. 31, 37.

25. *Politics* I.v.3.

26. Ibid. VII.xiv.9; I.v.6; *Ethics* I.xiii.

27. *Politics* VII.xiv.10.

28. For Aristotle, man's rule over woman derives not merely from his superior mental capacities but from the fact that insofar as she is engaged in reproductive activity, woman cannot, even abstractly, shed her bodily existence. She is in this way enslaved to her body, a "bodily creature," and thus inherently inferior to those whose prevalent feature is mind. Arendt quite explicitly reduces women to bodily existence. In ancient Greece, she argues, "hidden away were the laborers who with their bodies minister to the needs of life and the women who with their bodies guarantee the physical survival of the species. . . . The fact that the modern age emancipated the working classes and the women at nearly the same historical moment must certainly be counted among the characteristics of an age which no longer believes that bodily functions and material concerns should be hidden." *Human Condition*, pp. 72–73. But it is not only anti-feminist or masculinist thinkers who make this move. Both Simone de Beauvoir [*The Second Sex*, trans. H. M. Parshley (New York: Random House, 1953)] and Shulamith Firestone *The Dialectic of Sex* (New York: Bantam, 1976) cast women as inherently enslaved to their bodies through reproduction and both regarded avoidance or elimination of natural reproduction as the absolute prerequisite to women's liberation.

29. *Politics* I.ii.2.

30. Ibid. I.v.7.

31. Ibid. IV.iv.14.

32. Ibid. I.v.10.

33. Ibid. I.v.6–8.

34. Ibid. I.iv.6.

35. Ibid. I.v.8.

36. *Generation of Animals* I.xx, trans. A. L. Peck. Loeb Classical Edition (London: Heinemann, 1942), hereafter cited as *Generation of Animals*.

37. *Politics* I.v.8.

38. Ibid. I.v.7.

39. Ibid. I.v.2–3.

40. Ibid. VII.ix.3.

41. *Generation of Animals* II.i (emphasis added).

42. *Politics* VII.viii.1–9.

43. Ibid. I.vii.1.

44. Ibid. I.v.1.

45. Arendt, *Human Condition*, p. 31.

46. Ibid. I.xi.5–6.

47. Ibid. I.ii.15.

48. Ibid. VII.i.1.

49. Ibid. VII.i.11.

50. Ibid. VII.ii.17.

51. Ibid. VII.ii.5–8.

52. Barker, *Politics*,, note 2, p. 284.

53. *Politics* VII.ii.17.

54. Ibid. VII.iii.1.

55. Ibid. VII.iii.7.

56. Ibid. VII.iii.7–8.

57. Ibid. VII.iii.8–9.

58. Ibid. VII.iii.9–10.

59. Ibid. VII.xv.8.

60. Ibid. VII.xiii–ix.

61. Ibid. VII.xiv.12–13.

62. *Scholē* is the term translated as "leisure" and it is contrasted not with activity but with occupation (*ascholia*) and recreation (*anapausis*). *Scholē* is pursued for its own sake (unlike occupation and recreation) and is itself activity, the highest form of activity insofar as it is engaged with the part of the soul which possesses the rational principle, and especially the speculative dimension of that part. The activity of leisure is *diagoge* or "cultivation of the mind." *Scholē* is spent in *diagoge* (*Politics* VIII.iii.6) and *diagoge* is pursued in and during *scholē* (VIII.ii.8). Barker, *op. cit.* Note GGG, p. 323–324.

63. *Ethics* X.vii.6–7.

64. Arendt, *Human Condition*, pp. 73–78.

65. Ibid. p. 176.

66. Ibid. p. 177.

67. Ibid. p. 176.

68. Ibid. p. 188.

69. Ibid. p. 190.

70. Arendt, "What is Freedom?," *Between Past and Future*, p. 151.

71. Arendt, *Human Condition*, p. 208.

72. Ibid. p. 176.

4

The Greek Body: All-Too-Human and Super-Human

> The female always provides the material, the male
> provides that which fashions the material into shape;
> this is the specific characteristic of each of the
> sexes: that is what it means to be male or female
> —Aristotle[1]

THE ANCIENT ATHENIAN RELATIONSHIP to the body is more complex and equivocal than Aristotle's and certainly Arendt's depiction would suggest. Not only do the implications of the attempt to repudiate the body extend beyond the tensions and contradictions in Aristotle's political thought just examined, but as anyone having the slightest familiarity with antiquity knows, repudiation, denial, or disdain for the body is hardly the whole story of Greek culture. Ancient Greece is renowned not only for its literary achievement, political innovation, and artistic genius, but for its cultivation and celebration of bodily beauty, strength, and skill. It is also marked by an apparently lively culture of male homosexuality and, of course, by glorification of daring and accomplishment in battle. In this chapter, these two, apparently paradoxical estimations of the body—disdain and glorification—will be drawn into relationship with one another and the importance of this relationship for the designated boundaries and pursuits of manhood and politics will be developed.

I

We have already considered one way in which the Greeks spurned the body. Nietzsche states it succinctly: "labor is a disgrace because existence has no value in itself."[2] This attitude was extended to

53

reproductive labor as well. Again Nietzsche: "and as a father admires the beauty and the gift of his child but thinks of the act of procreation with shamefaced dislike, so it was with the Greek."[3]

In addition to the denigration of "necessary" activities and the assignment of them to noncitizens, there was another level on which the Greeks expressed contempt for and dread of the body. In modern terms, it might be called "sexual repression" but this is misleading in the same way as are discussions of the Greek concern with "moderation" that lift the term from its very immoderate Greek context.[4] For by anyone's account, Athens in its "golden age" was a highly sexual culture, and the frequent literary references to the virtue of containing sexual desire surely were a direct response to this overflowing, omnipresent sexuality. Even as sexual exhuberance pervaded the air, art, drama, and polis, it was cast by most poets and philosophers as a serious threat to individual and collective strivings toward greatness. Hence, individual resistence to sexual impulse was regarded as a virtue, and collective repression was frequently articulated as a necessity for a polis seeking eminence over others.[5]

The Greek political concern with suppressing carnal or physiological cravings was not limited to sexuality. Resistance to other "base desires" and endurance of bodily deprivation were touted as political, ethical, and military virtues and were treated by the philosophers as a necessary precondition for success in the search for truth.[6] In the *Republic,* Cephalus notes with relief that he is of an age where sexual urges no longer plague and distract him from virtue and piety.[7] Socrates commends himself in the *Phaedo* for achieving relative indifference to bodily comforts, desires, and satisfactions.[8] Aristotle devotes an entire book of the *Ethics* to the virtue of "continence" in all of its potential applications.[9] Plato, of course, takes the concern with ridding individuals of bodily cravings to its pinnacle when he designs the living conditions for the guardian class of his ideal city and when, in both the *Republic* and the *Symposium,* he attempts to completely sublimate sexual desire into a passion for wisdom.[10] And Xenophon defines "lack of self-control" as the inability to hold out against "hunger, thirst, sexual desire and long hours without sleep."[11]

In many of his discussions of the body, Plato draws upon Orphic doctrine in which the body was pictured as the soul's prison.[12] E. R. Dodds notes that for Plato and some of his contemporaries, the body was also conceived as a tomb "wherein the psyche lies dead, awaiting its resurrection into true life, which is life without the body."[13] Indeed Socrates' ironic show of eagerness, in the *Crito* and the *Phaedo,* to be a soul liberated from the body, would seem to corroborate Dodds' claim.[14] Dodds attributes the Greek "horror of the body" to the importation of "shamanistic beliefs . . . interpreted by the Greeks in a moral sense [such that] the world of bodily experience inevitably appeared as a place of darkness and penance."[15] In Plato's words, "the corporeal is heavy, oppressive, earthly and visible. So the soul which is tainted by its presence is weighed down and dragged back into the visible world . . . or the invisible, and hovers about tombs and graveyards."[16] Darkness, murkiness, prisons, tombs and wombs are metaphors for the body's relationship to mind or soul and are also the terms connoted by *megaron*, the Greek word for the interior of the house, the women's chambers.[17] Here we begin to see the multitude of associations with the body against which manliness is constructed.

Small capacity for suppression of bodily needs and desires not only rendered a man "unfree" in the eyes of the Greeks, but explicitly cast his masculinity into doubt. Then, as now, women were viewed as less able than men to control their emotions.[18] According to K. J. Dover, women were also seen as more prone to drinking, uncontrollable panic, grief, and sexual desire.[19] Dover concludes that Greek women were not only thought to be more lustful than men, but to enjoy sex more and to be incapable of resisting sexual temptation.[20] Much of Dover's evidence is drawn from Greek drama, but Aristotle corroborates him on most of these points.[21]

For the Greeks then, femininity, animality, incontinence, and enslavement to the body were cut from the same fabric. A real man is independent of the realm of necessity, of constraints by others, and of the needs and desires of his own body. As Alvin Gouldner puts the obverse case,

> to be constrained, although inevitable for man, is in the Greek dramatists' view to make him more of an animal and less of a human being. This is suggested by the frequent use of the "net" image, especially by Aeschylus. To be entrapped is to be caught like a beast.[22]

For the ancient Athenians, women were the creatures quintessentially trapped by and within the body. Not only were women viewed as relatively incontinent by comparison with males, even the acquired virtue of continence would not enable them to shed their bodily nature during their childbearing years. Thus, on both a moral and physiological level, women appeared to be in a natural and permanent state of entrapment.[23] In this regard, women come to represent the extreme of man's fears for himself and his freedom. Since humanity is defined against animality, women threatened this self-conception to the extent that they were counted as members of the human species. Woman's apparent inability to escape her physiological or "animal" nature establishes her as an omnipresent challenge to a conception of the human being as transcending animality. In this regard, Sophocles' quip, "a modest silence is a woman's crown,"

cited approvingly by Aristotle, and Thucydides' remark in the Peri-
clean funeral oration, that woman's greatest glory is to be "least
talked of among men," each take on an interesting hue.[24] For speech-
lessness on the one hand and invisibility or absense in human
discourse on the other are the traits not of persons but of animals.[25]

The Athenian male concern with overcoming the demands of the
body may well provide an explanation for a "paradox," which has
long bothered some classical scholars. It is a fact that the position and
status of women were much "worse" in the "school of all Hellas"
during its "golden age" than for example, in Sparta at the same time
or in Athens during the Homeric age. That an otherwise so "enlight-
ened" people could regard and treat their women so abysmally has
baffled many students of Athenian culture and politics and has, led
them to some rather extraordinary feats of apologia.[26] Yet it should
now be evident that it was precisely the sharpness of the Athenian
conception of manhood that bore with it a necessary degradation and
oppression of women, a denial of the status of "human" to women.
To the extent that women were viewed as part of the human species,
they would recall to men the species' animal or "natural" aspect.
Alternatively, women could be denied fully human status and remain
the somewhat less threatening repository of the "lower elements" of
existence. Seen in this context, Aristotle's infamous characterization
of women as "deformed males" bears significance as more than
incidental misogyny.[27] Aristotle does not merely posit the general
inferiority of women but describes them as "incomplete beings," their
thinking as "inconclusive," and the female state in general as a
condition of "deformity and weakness."[28] Women are also depicted as
"matter" in need of the "form" only men can supply.[29] Women are
therefore not merely lesser humans than men but less-than-human,
malformed, and ill-equipped for the human project, creatures in a
gray area between beast and man.

The Platonic dualism of "being" vs. "becoming" also reveals Greek
man's conception of the threat posed to his freedom by nature and by
the nature he ascribed to women. In politics and philosophy, man
strived toward Being (a state occupied by the gods and all immortals)
and to escape the mire of Becoming. Becoming is a condition Socrates
describes as a "barbaric bog," a turn of phrase conjuring a foreign,
dark, murky place where the potential for entrapment is very high.[30]
These symbols of immanence are also those frequently attached to the
natural world and the feminine. Becoming, Nature, and Woman are
thus linked to one another and appear to stand for danger and
subversion in the mind of Greek man. His fear of *falling into* this
barbaric bog was addressed through heroic political and military feats
and through zealous pursuit of rational truth.[31] The fear of *being pulled*

into this state was dealt with by casting nature and necessity as contaminating, as matter in need of form, and above all, as subject to man's mastery.

For the Greeks as for us, then, misogyny and the battle with external nature were two sides of the same coin even though, by contemporary standards, the ancient antagonism to nature is quite subtle. Two surviving fragments of Semonides of Amorgos make explicit the connection between misogyny and the construction of nature as hostile and requiring man's mastery. In one, Semonides expounds against the female gender at length, associating various types of women with different animals. In the other, Semonides portrays man as a helpless victim of divine caprice and the unpredictability of the natural world.[32] Taken together, these fragments convey rational and virtuous man as pitted against the animal, vengeful, and irrational, whether in the guise of nature or of woman.[33]

Fear of feminine envelopment appears in many other Greek literary discussions of women and nature. Phillip Slater notes that a particular focus for this fear was the issue of sexual contact with women.[34] The prevalence of male homosexuality for which the Greeks are infamous adds to the evidence Slater draws from literature. Yet envelopment is a relatively passive threat compared to the animated desire to thwart man's projects, which the Greeks attributed to both nature and women. Nietzsche captures one angle of this fear:

> In this feeling of shame [regarding labor and slavery] is the hidden unconscious discernment that the real aim needs these conditional factors but that in the need lies the fearful and beast-of-prey-like quality of the Sphinx, Nature, who in the glorification of the artistically free culture-life, so beautifully stretches forth her virgin body.[35]

Even this formulation, in which nature/woman eternally lurks in the shadows, waiting to snare man and swallow up his freedom and accomplishments, does not convey the extreme antagonism between male and female, civilization and nature, freedom and femininity contained in the Greek ethos and practice of manhood. Euripides may capture it best: in an unidentified fragment, he performs the same equation of woman and nature noted in Semonides and depicts woman's very existence as a testimony to the gods' hatred of mankind. She is "a more terrible thing than the violence of the raging sea, the force of torrents, or the sweeping breath of fire."[36]

II

Still, the dread of woman and her enveloping body, the denigration of labor and reproduction, and the dread of desire and bodily need comprise only half the story of the Greek regard for the body. The

Greeks also celebrated the body as an artifact of beauty, an athletic marvel, and the supreme instrument of war. Gymnastic was a vital part of citizen education, the athletic games were one of the highest moments in Greek *paideia*, and heroic performance in battle was an unparalleled means of achieving recognition by fellow citizens. Thus, even as they expressed dread and contempt for the body in so many ways, ancient Athenians also glorified strong or beautiful (male) bodies and honored them with praises, prizes, and affection.

These two, apparently antimonious, aspects of the Greek regard for the body are intimately related and rooted in a common source. The simultaneous repudiation and celebration of the body is linked in the quest to surpass human limits in pursuit of individual and collective glory. The body was not appreciated in its 'everydayness'—indeed, this was the level on which it was despised. Only in its most spectacular performances and heights of beauty was it praised, and this appreciation is directly related to the effort to transcend the body's routine capacities and suppress its routine needs. This valuation of the body also designates it as an *instrument* serving a good higher than its own satisfaction or sustenance, just as the realm of bodily activity serves the polis. The "body" of the polis (the oikos) and the body of man are viewed and treated as necessary but inferior and degrading aspects of human existence. Both bodies represent a feature of life establishing our kinship with other animals and holding the potential for individual or collective enslavement. Both appear to pose a persistent threat to man's desire for freedom. Thus, the ideal Greek man's approach to his own body was one of eternal vigilance and concern with transcendence, with mastering himself or imposing the "form" of the most rational part of his soul upon the "matter" of his body. Freedom, ethical goodness, and excellence of action lie precisely in this alienation, this wielding of the body as an instrument of the mind. Plato and Aristotle make this point repeatedly in their discussions of the proper relation between body and soul.[37]

In the collective dimension of the head-body relation, i.e., the polis-oikos relation, we have seen that the threat to freedom represented by the oikos pertains to the way it is organized, to the fact that those who occupy this realm are in a structural condition of domination. Similarly, we saw the contortions involved in Aristotle's effort to construe oikos inhabitants, especially slaves, as "matter in need of form," bodies in need of an external guiding principle or master. The form-matter paradigm was the rationalization for the rule of master over slave, man over woman, and above all polis over oikos—the polis gave meaning and direction to all its "parts" and "conditions" just as the master gives meaning to the existence of the slave.[38] In fact, of course, those engaged in productive and reproductive work are not the unformed or subrational "material" Aristotle proclaims them to be. They are not mere matter nor the natural "instruments" of others but structurally enslaved, systematically dominated servants of the citizens of the polis.

Now we can also grasp the contortions in viewing and treating one's own body this way, that is, we can grasp what these formulations of manhood did not only to those who were its servants but to those who wore its mantle. The Greek man performs an act of deformation when he seeks to deny bodily needs and desires on the one hand, and pushes his bodily capacities beyond their limits on the other. Both political and individual glory hinge on precisely this construction of physicality—fighting, denying, or transcending necessity and nature in order to realize man's "nature" as a political being. This alienation and the concommitant effort to surpass human and ecological limits is the heart of the Greek glorification of excellence in action known as *aretē*.

The Greek notion of *aretē* has been treated extensively by nearly every serious student of Greek culture, drama, politics, and philosophy; it is the expression of ultimate achievement for the Greeks and captures what many moderns most admire about the classical period in Western civilization. Rather flatly translated as "excellence," when this term is placed in the context of Greek standards and accomplishments, it conjures all the manly courage, striving, aesthetic aspirations and efforts at surpassing limits that are the distinctive glory of the Greeks. This is not the place to offer a comprehensive account of *aretē* in Greek culture nor consider the many kinds of accomplishment it signified; we shall be concerned only with its relevance for politics, political action and Greek manhood as they have been explored thus far.

Classicist Werner Jaeger describes *aretē* in politics this way:

> the real test of manly virtue was victory in battle—a victory which was not merely the physical conquest of an enemy, but the proof of hard-won *aretē*. This is exactly suited by the word *aristeia*, which was later used for the single-handed adventures of an epic hero. The hero's whole life and effort are a race for the first prize, an unceasing strife for supremacy over his peers.[39]

Aretē is greatness, it is excellence, it is virtuousity of performance, and above all, it is superiority. In Maurice Bowra's account:

> The great man is he who, being endowed with superior qualities of body and mind, uses them to the utmost and wins the applause of his fellows because he spares no effort and shirks no risk in his desire to make the most of the gifts and to *surpass* other men in his exercise of them.[40]

Bowra's description makes immediately evident a relationship between the cultivation of *aretē* and the *agonistic* or highly competitive feature of Greek public life. In the words of still another classical scholar, "nothing defines the quality of Greek culture more neatly than the way in which the idea of competition was extended from physical prowess to the realm of intellect, to feats of poetry and dramatic composition."[41] Phillip Slater also remarks upon the raw competitiveness coursing through Greek culture:

> The Greeks used to stage contests in anything that offered the bare possibility of a fight—beauty (male, of course), singing, riddle-solving, drinking, staying awake. *Nothing seemed to have meaning to the Greeks unless it included the defeat of another.*[42]

It is Aristotle, however, who gives this fierce and pervasive competitiveness a philosophical basis: "actions cannot be good and outstanding unless the doer himself has a degree of preeminence over others as great as a husband has over his wife, or a parent over his children or a master over his slaves."[43] In short, *aretē* is expressed neither through simple virtuousity nor by the usefulness of an act but by the explicit defeat of rival claims to a particular arena of glory.

Alvin Gouldner notes that *agathos* and *aretē* retain their militaristic overtones—their overarching concern with victory over a completely demolished rival—even when invoked for "higher" ethical or aesthetic purposes.[44] Jaeger corroborates this, not only with his claim that the Greeks believed that the real test of manly virtue was victory in battle, but with his etymological note that "in the city state, courage was called manliness, a clear reminiscence of the Homeric identification of courage with manly *aretē*."[45] While it is no news that the Greeks were highly competitive and that they were obsessed with war, a consideration of these matters in light of the earlier discussion of Aristotle's construction of the polis raises two questions: how are *agathos* and *aretē* expressed in political life? And what relation do they bear to the qualities of manhood and politics explored in Aristotle's thought?

Recall that in Hannah Arendt's view, public action is the only means men have of proving that they exist, of establishing the reality of their presence on earth. A life without action, she claims, "is literally dead to the world; it has ceased to be a human life . . . with word and deed we insert ourselves into the human world and this insertion is like a second birth."[46] I have already suggested why Greek men would find the very fact of their existence precarious and in need of certification. It is striking only that Arendt does not find the obsession with proving one's very existence through political action—making this the point of political action—a strange one.

Hanna Pitkin certainly does and indeed ridicules Arendt's account of Athenian political life with the suggestion that Arendt's ancient Greeks look like "posturing little boys":

"Look at me! I'm the greatest!" "No, I am! Look at me!" And then . . . we discover that the little boys are rather anxious and fearful as well, uncertain not merely of their own value and courage, but even of their own existence: "Look at me! Tell me I'm better than you! Tell me I'm big and brave! Tell me I'm real!" And isn't it ultimately a false assurance they seek? "Tell me I'll live forever! Tell me I have no body and cannot die, that I am more than human!" Of course they feel unreal and unsure of themselves, poor fools: they have left their bodies behind somewhere in the hopes of transcending death . . . Unable to face their mortality and physical vulnerability, the reality of being merely human, the men [Arendt] describes strive endlessly to be superhuman and, realizing that they cannot quite achieve that goal, require endless reassurance from the others in their anxious delusion.[47]

The trouble with Pitkin's marvelous account is that she judges this caricature to be relevant to Arendt and to Arendt's interpretation of Aristotle and Greek political life, but not to Aristotle or the Greeks themselves. Yet Aristotle quite explicitly relates political action to man's need for awe and recognition in the eyes of his peers and to a concern with mitigating the ephemeral nature of action and life. In the *Ethics*, he identifies "honor" in connection with "the good" as the goal of political life, "yet . . . honor is felt to depend more on those who confer it than on him who receives it. Again, people seem to seek honor in order to convince themselves of their own worth."[48] Aristotle also makes clear that the singular potential of political action is its contribution to the quest for immortality:

No other human operation has the same permanence as virtuous activities (they are considered to be more persistent even than the several kinds of scientific knowledge); and of these themselves the most highly esteemed are more persistent than the rest, because it is in them that the truly happy most fully and continuously spend their lives: this seems to be the reason why we do not forget them.[49]

Aristotle locates the "permanence" of great action not in its effect on political life or history but in the fact that the act itself is "not forgotten"—it is witnessed and remembered by others. Thus Arendt exaggerates very little in finding the assertion of individual existence and the quest for immortality to be the essential motives of Greek political action. Aristotle would not appear to quarrel with her insistence that "without a space of appearance and without trusting in action and speech as a mode of being together, neither the reality of one's self, of one's own identity, nor the reality of the surrounding world can be established without doubt."[50] In both Aristotle's and Arendt's account, Greek man grasped his existence through acting politically and could not know that he existed unless others acknowledged his action by bestowing honor upon him. "Denial of honor due," says Jaeger of the classical Athenians, "was the greatest of human tragedies."[51] Failing to receive honor for great deeds did not merely diminish the glory of the activity but threatened man's sense of self at the deepest level. According to Jaeger, Greek man "estimated his own worth exclusively by the standards of the society to which he belonged. He measured his own *aretē* by the opinion which others held of him."[52]

More significantly for the nature of political life, this recognition and honor by one's peers could not be shared with another and still serve the purpose of asserting and affirming one's existence. For a man to achieve recognition, hence existence, he had to obliterate the greatness and thereby the existence of some other man or men. Manhood itself appears to have been predicated upon the shortage of available existences. "As *aretē* is man's only weapon against oblivion," the diminished *aretē* of another was the only means of asserting one's own *aretē* and existence.[53] The *agonistic* nature of Greek politics was thus not a mere component or consequence of the quest for manhood through action but part of the bedrock of this quest, a necessary feature of its foundations.

Arendt's invocation of *aretē* as a weapon against oblivion returns us to the larger issue of immortality in the Athenian culture of manhood. Clearly, the Greeks' obsession with immortality derived in part from their severe denigration of existence-related or mortal things. Antagonism to mortality—expressed through domination and devaluation of the people and activities involved in the sustenance of life—is naturally accompanied by the valorization of immortality; the one produces the other. Seen from a slightly different angle, the Greek pursuit of immortality does not embody, as Arendt implies, the simple and understandable desire to be extraordinary or godlike, but rather, the ultimate attempt to transcend the body, to be freed from its constraints, liberated from its requirements and limitations.

Another and slightly more subtle source of the concern with immortality appears to have rested in a desire to preserve or freeze the moment of recognition gained through political action. The achievement of immortality is the only thing that can bring to an end the otherwise ceaseless striving for recognition whose basis we have already explored. In this respect, the achievement of immortality signifies the victory of Being over Becoming in political life, a place where this victory is very difficult to achieve. Yet, there is an ironic twist to the philosophical problem most fully developed by Plato. The victory of Being over Becoming through political action remembered by posterity is not synonymous with the discovery of Reality as opposed to Appearance. Rather, action itself, Arendt insists, *establishes* or creates a reality—the reality of the individual actor and the reality of the political world—in contrast with the "unreal" or natural world of rhythms, cycles of birth, decay, and death. Peer recognition of action freezes an action in time and becomes the very identity of the actor. A man is known by and for, *as*, his memorable actions. The Greek obsession with immortality thus appears in part as a response to the transient and "achieved" quality of manhood, the fact that manhood can only be acquired through action recognized by others and that this recognition is always fleeting. Pindar's well-known victory ode for an athlete is an example of Greek self-consciousness about this matter:

> He who wins, of a sudden, some noble prize
> In the rich years of youth
> Is raised high with hope; his manhood takes wings
> He has in his heart what is better than wealth
> But brief is the season of man's delight.
> Soon it falls to the ground; some dire decision uproots it.
> —Thing of a day! Such is man; a shadow in a dream.[54]

If *aretē* is the only means to establishing that one exists, the achievement of immortality is the only way of insuring that one's existence will persist, even during one's lifetime. For immortality is based upon the aquisition of fame—distinguishing oneself amongst one's peers—and lasting fame itself insures that one did not just exist while doing the deed but continues to exist over time.

Providing for survival, making or producing things, desiring or creating, tending the growth of young ones or cultivating the well-being of a community have all been cast aside as possible bases of existence or identity—they are not "fully human." Hence the need for fame in order to know that one is real, the need to defeat another in order to assert one's own importance, the need to invent and protect a reality in order to have one. The reality of daily existence—of need and necessity, of bodies and mortality—has been banished from the polis; identity can only be gained through battle to create a new reality and to prove that one exists within it.

The kind of politics to which these concerns with fame, victory, eminence, and surpassing human limits gives rise is well-known to any who have even the slightest familiarity with Greek political history. No Greek author captures the driven and striving character of this culture better than Thucydides. Through a speech ascribed to a Corinthian, he offers this description of the Athenians:

> They are adventurous beyond their power, and daring beyond their judgement and in danger they are sanguine. . . . They make a plan; if it fails, they think they have lost something; if it succeeds, this success is nothing in comparison with what they are going to do next. It is impossible for them either to enjoy peace and quiet themselves, or to allow anyone else to do so.[56]

Despite his admiration for the Athenian spirit, Thucydides himself perceives the overwrought and dangerous character of such an ethos. When men live this way, they live in a world of their own—at odds with the natural world and with the larger political and social world in which their "reality" is situated. They do indeed pursue and perceive their own acts, and the meanings and understandings they attach to them, as constitutive of reality. Thus, when the tide turned against the Athenians, they had neither the resiliency nor the strength to weather it well. With the Spartans in Attica for a second time and Athens gripped by the plague, the Athenians turned on Pericles, accusing him of having led them into a war they claimed they never wanted. Pericles responded:

> I have not changed: it is you who have changed. A calamity has befallen you, and you cannot persevere in the policy you chose when all was well: it is the weakness of your resolution that makes my advice seem to have been wrong. *It is the unexpected that most breaks a man's spirit* . . .[56]

The problem of political adaptability and its relation to manhood will be explored in detail in the chapters on Machiavelli. For now, we may simply note that "creatures of a day" not only pursue glory restlessly and constantly, but that this very pursuit deepens and widens the degrounded nature of an already alienated politics. The "unexpected," even when it arises from within the political realm, is either fought off as an enemy or succumbed to in defeat because the alienated political actor has lost his capacity to see or move beyond himself. Driven by all that he has repudiated and banished, striving for an existence entirely dependent upon peer recognition of his acts, compelled to conquer for identity, he is trapped in a trajectory of his own making that renders him supremely unadaptable and ultimately, incapable of being fulfilled. He cannot live with others nor with his own needs but only against them, against himself.

III

I have argued that the Greek constructions of manhood and politics, especially as expressed through Aristotle's political thought, are integrally constitutive of one another. Both the conception and the practice of Greek manhood and politics involve such profound estrangement from all that is entailed in man's physiological aspect and from external nature that politics itself gains a bearing of anxiety, insecurity, and restless desire for mastery. I have also suggested that this politics is not merely problematic but oppressive and danger-ous—oppressive to those off of whom it lives and dangerous to those whom it preys upon outside its boundaries. We do not need Freud to tell us that what is suppressed and oppressed does not go away but in its crushed or shadowy form continues to threaten and poison its surroundings. Women, slaves, workers, man's own bodily aspect, and the natural world within which he lives—all are subjugated and denigrated through a politics of domination, a politics through which man gains his manhood as a form-giving creature. But the subjugated "matter" lives on: it is the substance of man himself and continues to haunt and threaten his deeds, words, self-conception and politics. The supremacy of Mind cannot win this battle, although it has been summoned for precisely this purpose: to kill the claims of the body and the body politic. Disembodied mind is a weapon in the hands of Western political man, designed to make him victorious in the battle with chosen enemies as well as with nature and those tied to the natural, with his own desirousness and with external provocateurs of his desires. In Norman O. Brown's intonation,

> the external enemy is (part of) ourselves, projected; our own badness, banished. The only defense against an internal danger is to make it an external danger: then we can fight it; and are ready to fight it, since we have succeeded in deceiving ourselves into thinking that it is no longer us.[57]

Notes

1. *Generation of Animals* II.iv.

2. "The Greek State," *The Complete Works of Friedrich Nietzsche*, p. 4.

3. Ibid., p. 5.

4. See Aristotle's *Ethics* II and III.

5. *Ethics* III.x; VII.iv,xi,xiv; see K. J. Dover, "Classical Greek Attitudes to Sexual Behavior," *Arethusa* 6, no. 1, pp. 64–65.

6. See, for example, Plato's *Phaedo* 65a–d and Aristotle's *Ethics* VII.xiv. For a more indepth exploration of Plato's and Socrates' formulation of the relationship between eros and philosophy, see my "Supposing Truth Were a Woman?': Plato's Subversion of Masculine Discourse."

7. *Republic* 328C–329C, trans. A. Bloom (New York: Basic Books, 1968), hereafter cited as *Republic*.

8. *Phaedo* 64–67.

9. *Ethics* VII.

10. *Republic* 457–62 and *Symposium* 209, trans. M. Joyce, in *The Collected Dialogues of Plato*, hereafter cited as *Symposium*.

11. Cited in Dover, "Classical Greek Attitudes to Sexual Behavior," p. 64.

12. *Cratylus*, 400c.

13. E. R. Dodds, *The Greeks and the Irrational* (Berkeley: University of California Press, 1951), p. 152.

14. *Apology* 40d–41c, trans. H. Tredennick, in *Collected Dialogues of Plato*, hereafter cited as *Apology*; *Phaedo* entire, esp. 66–68c.

15. Dodds, *The Greeks and the Irrational*, p. 152.

16. *Phaedo*, 81d.

17. Arendt, *Human Condition*, p. 71.

18. *Ethics* IX.xi; *Phaedo* 60a–b.

19. Dover, "Classical Greek Attitudes" p. 64; see also Dover's *Greek Popular Morality* (Oxford: Oxford University Press, 1974).

20. Dover, "Classical Greek Attitudes" p. 65; see also Dover's *Greek Homosexuality* (Cambridge: Harvard University Press, 1978).

21. *Ethics* VII.v; VII.vii.

22. Alvin Gouldner, *Enter Plato* (New York: Basic Books, 1965) p. 37.

23. This was further compounded by the fact that woman's unique role in the reproductive process—pregnancy and lactation—was ideologically extended to encompass the entirety of reproductive work, thereby making her responsible for all the labor involved with infants and children. She thus appeared "trapped" by her body not only because of its physiology, but because the product of pregnancy was assigned wholly to her and reproductive work thereby became the entirety of her identity. For a more fully developed analysis of this phenomenon, see Clark and Lange, *The Sexism of Social and Political Theory*, and my "Reproductive Freedom and the 'Right to Privacy': A Paradox for Feminists."

24. *Politics* I.xii.11; Thucydides, *Peloponnesian War* II.vi., p. 109.

25. Valerie Hartouni drew my attention to the way the injunction to silence establishes a connection between women and animality.

26. See, for example, C. M. Bowra, *The Greek Experience* (New York: Mentor, 1957), pp. 38–39 and H. D. F. Kitto, *The Greeks* (Edinburgh: Penguin, 1951), pp. 219–36. Both of these popular introductory volumes on Greek culture and politics offer truly stunning accounts and apologies for the situation of Greek women. The opening lines of these discussions are indicative of the level and quality of rhetoric that follows. Kitto begins with a distasteful mix of pomposity and misogyny: "Most men are. interested in women and most women in themselves. Let us therefore consider the position of women in Athens" (p. 219). While no less derivative in approach, Bowra is more somber: "A society which cherishes . . . a heroic ideal is not always easy or happy in its treatment of women" (p. 38). Happily, there are a few recent exceptions to this misogynist and apologetic tradition of scholarship on the glory that was Athens. In addition to Sarah Pomeroy's *Goddesses, Whores, Wives and Slaves: Women in Classical Antiquity* (New York: Schocken, 1975) and other recent works by feminists, there are scholars not focused solely upon women who nonetheless analyze them intelligently, e.g., Seth L. Schein, *The Mortal Hero* (Berkeley: University of California, 1984).

27. *De Anima* II.iii, trans. R. D. Hicks (Cambridge: Cambridge University Press, 1907), hereafter cited as *De Anima*.

28. Ibid. IV.vi; V.i.

29. *Generation of Animals* II.i.

30. *Republic* 533d.

31. It is *dialectic*, Socrates says in the *Republic*, that lifts the soul up and away from the muddy swamps in which shadows are mistaken for real figures, where becoming and appearance are everywhere and being is nowhere to be found. 532a-d.

32. Cited in Marilyn Arthur, "Liberated Women: The Classical Era" in Bridenthal and Koonz, eds., *Becoming Visible: Women in European History* (Boston: Houghton Mifflin, 1977), p. 65.

33. See Mary Lefkowitz's brief but intriguing interpretation of Semonides in *Heroines and Hysterics* (New York: St. Martin's Press, 1981), pp. 71–73.

34. *The Glory of Hera* (Boston, Beacon Press, 1968), pp. 81–82.

35. Neitzsche, "The Greek State," p. 6.

36. Cited in Arthur, "Liberated Women," p. 73.

37. See, e.g. Aristotle, *Politics* I and *Ethics* VII; Plato *Republic* VI.

38. In the *Generation of Animals* II.iv, Aristotle states, "the female always provides the material, the male provides that which fashions the material into shape; this is the specific characteristic of each of the sexes: that is what it means to be male or female." Hippocrates, of course, is the source of much of Aristotle's thinking on these matters and is himself quite an ideologue on the subject of gender. Hippocrates depicts man as giving form and function to everything about women, right down to the nature and duration of her orgasms during intercourse. *Hippocratic Writings*, ed., G. E. R. Lloyd (Harmondsworth, England: Penguin, 1978), see especially pp. 317–20.

39. *Paideia: The Ideals of Greek Culture*, trans. Gilbert Highet (Oxford: Oxford University Press, 1974; 1st edition, 1939), Vol. I, p. 7.

40. C. M. Bowra, *The Greek Experience*, p. 33.

41. M. I. Finley, *The World of Odysseus* (New York: Viking, 1954) p. 73.

42. Slater, *The Glory of Hera*, p. 36, emphasis added.

43. *Politics* VII.iii.

44. Gouldner, *Enter Plato*, pp. 12–13.

45. Jaeger, *Paideia*, pp. 6–7.

46. *Human Condition*, p. 176.

47. "Justice: On Relating Public and Private," paper presented to the 1979 Conference for the Study of Political Thought, pp. 35–36. (A condensed version appears in *Political Theory*, vol. 9, no. 3 (1981).

48. *Ethics* I.v.

49. Ibid. I.x.

50. *Human Condition*, pp. 207–8.

51. Jaeger, *Paideia, Volume I*, p. 9.

52. Ibid. p. 9.

53. *Human Condition*, p. 207.

54. Cited in Kitto, *The Greeks*, p. 174.

55. *Peloponnesian War* I.iii., p. 70.

56. Ibid. II.vii., p. 60., emphasis added.

57. *Love's Body* (New York: Vintage, 1966), p. 162.

Renaissance Italy

Machiavelli

5

Machiavelli: From Man to Manhood

Mᴀᴄʜɪᴀᴠᴇʟʟɪ'ꜱ ᴜɴᴅᴇʀꜱᴛᴀɴᴅɪɴɢ ᴏꜰ ᴘᴏʟɪᴛɪᴄꜱ stands in sharp contrast to that of Aristotle. Machiavelli makes no grand claims for the exalted nature of man, he does not cast political life as the whole of life, he is infamous for having divorced politics from ethics and for distinguishing the virtues of the political man from virtue itself. In the tradition of political theory, Machiavelli is unique by dint of his passionate devotion to political *action*. He loved the subject matter of political theory—politics itself—to a degree unparalleled by any other theorist of equal repute. Ironically, the consequence is that through five hundred years of interpretation, Machiavelli has probably been more maligned and disparaged than any of his fellows in the tradition of political theory. In fierce and uncompromising fashion, Machiavelli pierced to the quick of Western politics and the men who comprise it; weaker hearts have rebelled.

Above all, Machiavelli reincorporated into political thought that which we watched the Greeks try to eliminate—the body. For Machiavelli, politics is a visceral, earthly, flesh and blood affair. His is a politics seething with irrepressible drives and urges, a politics that transpires on earth and through the body. There are no unchanging "forms" or spiritual ideals in Machiavelli's political world, no ultimate telos that man fulfills, no gods to whom he pays homage with his political activity. Politics is not an aesthetic ideal, but life itself.

However, the particular constructions of body, desire, and need in Machiavelli's politics are profoundly gendered. The life in which this politics is situated is the life of men bent upon control and domination, the life of communities ruled by those who care for ruling and the expansion of their power above all else. Similarly, while "necessity" figures largely in Machiavelli's musings on politics, this necessity too is narrow and one-sided, signifying for Machiavelli the limitations and dangers to one's quest for power and, conversely, the spur to greatness—it has little to do with daily, concrete human needs.

Machiavelli's sharply gendered view of human beings and politics lead him to subvert some of his own understandings about the political world. Despite his attunement to the intricacy and complexity of political life, he often urges the political actor to use the bluntest of instruments and force in this realm, advice that secures fleeting victories at best and more often increases the actor's vulnerability to threatening and incomprehensible forces (*fortuna*). Similarly, Machiavelli's commitment to demystifying the political world is thwarted by his own reification of power's consequences in the character of *fortuna*. This chapter and the next explore the ways in which these tensions in Machiavelli's work grow out of his devotion to and development of an ethos of manhood.

For Machiavelli, politics emerges from what he takes to be the nature of man *and*, develops men into creatures of true manliness. In contrast to the Greeks, this development does not involve bringing man's nature to "perfection" through political life, but transforming, overcoming, or harnessing to specifically political purposes a number of the unwieldy qualities he perceives as indigenous to man. For Machiavelli, men are the raw material of politics and require a form superior to that which naturally inheres in them if political life is to flourish and if they are to achieve individual and collective glory. This superior form embodies the Machiavellian ideal of manhood that, in turn, provides the shape of Machiavellian politics. Moreover, for Machiavelli, politics always bears the limitations of the transformative possibilities for man's nature. Machiavelli harbors no illusions about the usefulness of a political theory based upon "men as they might be" rather than men as they are or can be.

We begin, then, with a close inspection of the nature of "unmodified" Machiavellian man. Here it will be evident that while Machiavelli has much to say about "human nature" and identifies human beings as creatures of the natural world, his exploration of human nature is based upon a very particular kind of man. From the beginning, Machiavelli assumes men to be alienated from themselves and their surroundings, driven by a kind of random desire for power and conquest, inherently short-sighted and frustrated in their aims and ambitions.

I

Machiavelli's writings are replete with remarks about man's nature. Most of his political "advice" begins from or culminates in statements about one or more immutable characteristics of man. Thus, for example, when discussing Scipio's failure to quell rebellion in his troops, Machiavelli concludes, "this came from nothing else than not fearing him, because men are so restless that if the slightest door is opened to their ambition, they at once forget . . . all love for a prince."[1] Enumerating the difficulties of political innovation, Machiavelli cautions, "men don't really believe in anything new until they have had solid experience of it."[2] His teachings to the would-be leader of an insurrection are capsulated in the doctrine, "men are driven by two things: love and fear."[3] Nowhere, however, does Machiavelli offer a comprehensive portrait of man's nature. Rather, his ruminations on this subject are scattered throughout his writings and are synopsized only in the repeated declaration, "the nature of man is everywhere and always the same."[4] Thus, we must elicit a composite drawing of Machiavellian man from the diverse and partial testimony Machiavelli offers throughout his literary and political works.

We begin with Machiavelli's appreciation of man's animality. In contrast with the many political theorists who arrive at a definition of man by distinguishing him from other animals, Machiavelli suggests a very close and by no means unfortunate kinship between man and beast. Most familiar in this regard is chapter eighteen of the *Prince* in which he praises ancient allegory for its frequent depiction of the apprenticeship of would-be princes to Chiron, the centaur.[5] The mythical creature who is half-man, half-beast, is the symbolic figure of perfection in the *Prince*, a book of teachings and models for political success. On a first reading, it would seem that the most effective political actor is he who draws closest to his animal nature. On the other hand, the discussion of Chiron and the "lion and fox" allegory that follows might be read as an attempt to distinguish the nature of animals from the nature of man. Identifying man as a "creature of law" in this discussion, Machiavelli appears to make this distinction explicitly:

> You need to know, then, that there are two ways of fighting: one according to the laws, the other with force. The first is suited to man, the second to animals; but because the first is often not sufficient, a prince must resort to the second. Therefore, he needs to know well how to put to use the traits of animal and man.[6]

However, several matters contradict the seemingly clear opposition between man and beast put forth in this passage. First, Machiavelli never treats politics as something that has a nature independent of the men who generate it. Thus, insofar as successful political action requires the qualities of beasts, it is because bestial creatures have constructed the political conditions facing political actors. Seen in this light, the reference to man as one who fights according to law appears ironic, as a statement of what most people *think* men are, while the nature of politics suggests, indeed proves, quite otherwise.

We need not rely upon subtle methods of interpretation for this point. For once Machiavelli proceeds to expound the details of a prince's political education at the hands of Chiron, the human "half" of man's character drops from sight. The human qualities upon which political success depends are *worked into* the animals Machiavelli chooses as worthy models for political actors. The fox is selected for his clever scheming and sharp wits, the lion for his brute strength. The fox represents what is traditionally considered the distinctly human element of the man-beast amalgam. The fox's talents are also insufficient for precisely the reason man's are: while he harbors the cunning needed to avoid entrapment, he lacks the raw force necessary to frighten and fight an enemy.

There are many other passages in the *Prince* and the *Discourses* in which Machiavelli likens men of a certain character or condition to beasts. The following remarks on liberty are only one example:

> What great difficulty a people accustomed to living under a prince has later in preserving its liberty, if by any accident it gains it. . . . And such difficulty is reasonable because that people is none other than a brute beast which, though of a fierce and savage nature, has always been cared for in prison and slavery. Then if by chance it is left free in a field, since it is not used to feeding itself and does not know the places where it can take refuge, it becomes the prey of the first one who tries to chain it.[7]

Even these instances of Machiavelli's use of analogy to establish man's proximity to the rest of the animal world do not yet plumb the depths of Machiavelli's radical assessment of man *qua* animal. For a full sense of this assessment, Machiavelli's literary endeavors are more revealing than his explicitly political writings. Particularly interesting in this regard is his allegorical poem, *The Golden Ass*.[8]

In one of the several vignettes contained in *The Golden Ass*, the narrator has stumbled into a strange forest where he is greeted by a beautiful woman leading a large flock of wild and domestic animals.[9] The shepherdess explains to Machiavelli that he has come to a netherworld from which he cannot escape and is doomed by order of her queen (Circe) to become a member of her flock. "In the world," she explains, "these animals you see were men like yourself."[10] She then shows him that the "men" of this habitat were not arbitrarily transformed into particular animals; instead, each was given the body of the creature his nature most resembled in his human life.[11] Moreover, the "transformation" is not complete; the animals retain some generic human characteristics as well as some of the specific idiosyncrasies each had in his particular life as a man.

Before the hapless protagonist of the story is transformed into animal shape, the shepherdess brings him to her abode for several days where he shares her food, her bed, and gains acquaintance with the strange world into which he has fallen. The story concludes with a tour of the grounds where the tame animals reside permanently and the wild ones rest at night. In this setting, Machiavelli muses on man's place in the animal world. His survey of the barnyard scene begins with a description of the animals who have lost or abused their respective virtues. Instead of graceful or magnificent, these creatures appear pathetic and helpless:

> I saw a lion that had cut his own claws and pulled his teeth through his own counsels, not good and not sagacious. A little further on some injured animals—one having no tail, another no ears—I saw standing blockish in utter quiet. Then I saw an ass in such poor condition that he could not carry his packsaddle much less anything more . . . I saw a hound that kept sniffing at this one's muzzle and that one's shoulder as though he were trying to find his master . . . A stag I saw that was in such great terror, turning his course now here now there, such a fear of death he had.[12]

In short, the human individuals who so closely resembled these beasts had, in their humanness, done a kind of civilizing violence to their natures. By breaking the bounds and balance of their natural animal virtues, they incapacitated or mutilated their most useful instincts and rendered worthless or self-destructive their natural abilities. The *genuine* ass is revealed as more noble, able and useful, as well as happier, than the man in ass's clothing.

The rest of the poem is a deeper exploration of this theme. The narrator wishes to speak with one of the animals and for this purpose, the shepherdess chooses a huge, filthy hog bathing in a mud wallow. She also grants Machiavelli the power to remove the hog from this setting and return him to his human shape if the hog so desires. When Machiavelli greets the hog with this offer, it is vehemently refused and the hog offers a lengthy sermon about the superiority of his life as a beast to the life of man. It is in this speech that Machiavelli offers his most thorough account of man's bungled relationship with his own animal nature.

"We," proclaims the hog, "seek the climate friendly to our way of life, as Nature who teaches us commands." On the other hand, man goes "exploring one country and another, not to find a climate either cool or sunny but because your shameful greed for gain does not confirm your spirit in a life sparing, law-abiding and humble."[13] Similarly, the hog explains contemptuously, animals are generally stronger than men, purer of spirit (having received a "richer gift of hearts invincible, noble and strong") and purer of motive:

> Among us are done bold deeds and exploits without hope of a triumph or other fame, as once among those Romans who were famous. In the lion you see a great pride in a noble deed, and at a shameful act a wish to blot out its memory.[14]

Furthermore, the hog continues, "there are animals among us who would die before enduring the life of slaves, or be robbed in any way of their liberty."

The most poignant aspect of this harangue is reserved for the final verses. "How hapless you are above all other earthly creatures!" this section begins. Animals are in every way "closer friends to Nature." While every animal is born "fully clad," man alone is born "devoid of all protection."[15] Animals always have one or more very keen senses, while man's are relatively dull. And where nature does provide men with some things potentially advantageous such as hands and speech, she sends a curse along with them—"ambition and avarice, with which her bounty is cancelled."[16] The poem concludes,

> To how many ills Nature subjects you at starting! Yours are ambition, licentiousness, lamentation and avarice . . . No animal can be found that has a frailer life, and has for living a stronger desire, more disordered fear or greater madness. One hog to another causes no pain, one stag to another; man by another man is slain, crucified, plundered. . . . If any among men seems to you a god, happy and rejoicing, do not believe him such, because in this mud I live more happily; here without anxiety I bathe and roll myself.[17]

Machiavelli presents man as a creature who lives by desire rather than need, a creature with few innate tools for living other than his wits, and even these are a mixed blessing, often turning on him because they are placed in the service of his appetites and ambition. Man lives in a state of extreme vulnerability—without hide or scales— and he begins his life in tears and utter helplessness. He rarely seeks a habitat compatible with his needs but "often into an atmosphere rotten and sickly, leaving a healthful climate [he] shifts [him]self."[18] He does not find his way about the world easily nor in self-beneficial ways, and knows not by instinct even "what any plant is, whether harmless or injurious."[19] He has little capacity for dissimulation and flexibility in the interest of "pursuing his own well-being and avoiding distress."[20]

In short, hardly a single feature of man is "natural" or makes him fit to live in the natural world. Yet Machiavelli, unlike so many other political thinkers, does not therefore conclude that man lives above nature in a higher, better world. The conundrum of man is precisely that he, like all other animals, must cope with nature and his own needs but is severely ill-equipped and ill-tempered for doing so. Prior to the modern age, most political theorists conceived of politics as the activity that sets man apart from beast and issues from the former's intelligence, will, and capacity for conscious action. For such theorists, politics is the highest expression of man's superiority over animals. Machiavelli turns this formulation on its head: man is a poor sort of being and constructs a political world out of his poverty—his vulnerability, passion, and precarious bearing in the natural world. Whatever its prospects for individual or collective glory, Machiavelli insists that politics emerges from and in accord with man's weakness rather than from his superiority.

In the *Golden Ass*, Machiavelli depicts man as a creature who is highly alienated both from himself and from nature. Because of this alienation, *within* nature, man has no dignity and little chance of survival. Ironically, man seeks to resolve the ill effects of this alienation by means that drive it further, that make him even less "at home" in his world, and that make his existence anything but commodious, self-subsistent or peaceful.

II

If Machiavelli were pressed to capture in a word that feature of man least shared by other animals and most salient as a political quality, inarguably the word would be "ambition." "What province or what city escapes it? What village, what hovel? Everywhere Ambition and Avarice penetrate."[21] These "two furies sent to dwell on earth"[22] are the source of nearly all that man does or creates, especially that which is destructive or self-destructive. "If they had no existence, happy enough would be our condition . . . [but they] deprive us of peace . . . set us at war . . . and take away from us all quiet and all good."[23] Ambition and avarice never arrive anywhere alone but bring their necessary companions, Envy, Sloth, and Hatred, who in turn are always accompanied by Cruelty, Pride, and Deceit.[24] Machiavelli considers ambition an utterly ineradicable feature of individuals and of the human condition as a whole: "when man was born into the world, [ambition] was born too."[25] And in the *Discourses* he says, "whenever men cease fighting through necessity, they go to fighting through ambition, which is so powerful in human breasts that whatever high rank men climb to, never does ambition abandon them."[26]

Machiavelli does not have moral objections to the drive he has labelled ambition; indeed, he considers it the spark and fire of political life. But he does identify a number of problems created by ambition, problems that together comprise the framework upon which his entire political theory is built. Machiavelli begins his political theorizing from the assumption that man's craving for power is boundless, his interest in domination unquestionable, his need to control a given. However, while Machiavellian man is insatiably appetitive and restless, this energy and ambition is polymorphous in character—it has no particular object and by itself is not political. "Nature has made men able to crave everything but unable to attain everything."[27] Even Hobbes did not cast men as so voraciously and indefatigably desirous; the boundless quest for power in Hobbesian man has its root in self-preservation whereas for Machiavelli ambition is its own engine. Joseph Mazzeo captures the unbounded and unfocused nature of Machiavellian man's ambition in a comparison with Dante:

> Machiavelli, like Dante, sees man as driven by infinite desire, but the infinite goal and the ladder to it have disappeared. The enormous energies which Dante had seen as focused on the infinite, Machiavelli sees as unleashed in the world. . . . In Machiavelli, man appears in fundamental conflict with his universe for he is hopelessly incontinent . . . desirous . . . ambitious, yet his survival depends upon some degree of renunciation and restraint.[28]

In Machiavelli's view, the ubiquitous, polymorphous character of ambition is useless in its raw form for man's survival as well as for political projects. Indeed, much of his political thinking is concerned with the means of harnessing man's random quests for power to the project of Italy's redemption.

A second and related problem with the kind of ambition Machiavelli considers indigenous to man pertains to the competitive, individualistic elements it insinuates into human community. One cannot pursue one's own desires without making others fear for the status of their aims. "Every man hopes to climb higher by crushing now one, now another . . . To each of us another's success is always vexatious, and therefore always . . . for another's ill we are watchful and alert."[29] Such a mentality is more than a mere consequence of ambitious activity. Rather, the fearful or defeated condition of another is instrumentally essential to one's own success. Machiavelli makes this explicit in a discussion of the battles for power between plebians and patricians in ancient Rome:

> Desire for defending its liberty made each party try to become strong enough to tyrannize over the other. For the law of these matters is that *when men try to escape fear, they make others fear and the injury they push away from themselves they lay on others, as if it were necessary to either harm or be harmed.*[30]

Yet a third problem with ambition is that while "it is very natural and normal to wish to conquer,"[31] ambition interferes with the achievement of its own end. Even when ambition is "joined with a valiant heart"[32] or is rewarded "only in those who seek support by public [as opposed to private] means,"[33] its individualistic root remains a problem for politics and for man. The constructive possibilities of politics, a strong, rightly ordered and regenerative state, are at odds with the life energies of politics—individual striving, appetitiveness, and quests for glory. Furthermore, the nature of ambition undermines other qualities required for the achievement and maintenance of power, qualities such as analytical keenness, effective political judgement, and a right measure of subtlety and patience. Machiavelli even suggests that political ambition and political judgement have an inverse relation: "as men lessen in vigor as they grow older, [they] improve in judgement and prudence."[34] Ambition blinds men, thereby subverting the promise of their aspirations.[35]

Finally, if ambition is the eye through which men view their world, they will inevitably see it differently from one another and differently according to their constantly shifting ambitions. "As men's appetites change, even though their circumstances remain the same, it is impossible that things should look the same to them, seeing that they have other appetites, other interests, other standpoints."[36] The problem ambition creates for accurate perception and judgement is more active, more practical, than the familiar debilitation of truth by subjectivity. If men unselfconsciously view the world through the prism of their desires, they conceptually locate themselves and these desires at the center of a universe that actually has quite a different axis or no axis at all. They fail to see the "poison lurking underneath a pleasing policy" and they deceive themselves generally about the difference between appearance and reality.[37] The result is men vigorously acting in a world they understand insufficiently to be effective. They act according to a zealous passion for power rather than out of concern with realistic possibility, need, public or even private good.

However aware Machiavelli is of the problems and perils of ambition, he establishes it as the central dynamic of political life. Ambition, whether of a political or nonpolitical sort, is Machiavelli's way of talking about man's unbounded "will to power," his drive not simply to experience himself as a being of power but to have power over others. Even when ambition is collectivized, it is rooted not in the good for a community but in a community's drive for power and domination. It is this impulse toward mastery and conquest that Machiavelli locates as the essence of man's uniquely human nature, and that gives all shape and bearing to political life.

What we are seeing in this creature driven and plagued by ambition is the development of a particular kind of man first uncovered in ancient Greek political life. As I argued in the chapters devoted to the Greeks, once man alienates his head from his body, once he conceives of the body as something to be mastered, once he institutionalizes that conception in the organization of social life, he is set upon a course in which he strives to conquer, master, dominate, or control all that threatens his precarious freedom from the body. The head that is separate from the body and subjugates the body is threatened and spooked by what it has suppressed, and it must be eternally vigilant in sustaining its "achievement." The mastery is never complete, never final, and the amorphous drive for power at the center of Machiavelli's conception of man is at least in part a consequence of this dynamic.

III

One of the most striking features of the distorting effects ambition has upon perception and judgement is formulated by Machiavelli as a tendency to reify gaps or failures in one's own understanding of the world. An excessive emphasis upon appearances—a confusion of appearances with reality—is one manifestation of this reification. A man "blinded by ambition" is too caught up in his own desires to perceive what lies underneath superficial appearances. But by far the most extreme expression of this reification is that which Machiavelli joins with his predecessors in denoting as *fortuna*. A full discussion of *fortuna* will be reserved for the next chapter. At this point, I want only to suggest the extent to which *fortuna* is constituted by the limitations of man's understanding of the world and his place within it— limitations spurred by his excessive ambition.[38]

While Machiavelli often portrays *fortuna* as a goddess with mind, will, and intentions of her own, he also declares that *fortuna* is nothing other than man's inadequate grasp of his circumstances. The former is how Machiavelli knows most men regard *fortuna* while the latter is his own view of her existence. Machiavelli's most explicit discussion of the relationship between subjectivity and *fortuna* occurs in a letter to Piero Soderini.

> I believe that as Nature has given each man an individual face, so she has given him an individual disposition and an individual imagination. From this it results that each man conducts himself according to his disposition and his imagination. On the other hand, because times and affairs are of varied types, one man's desires come out as he had prayed they would; he is fortunate who harmonizes his procedures with his time, but on the contrary he is not fortunate who in his actions is out of harmony with his time and with the types of its affairs. Hence it can happen that two men working differently (in different circumstances)

come to the same end, because each man adapts himself to what he encounters. . . . Thus because times and affairs in general and individually change often, and men do not change their imaginings and procedures, it happens that a man at one time has good fortune and at another time bad.[39]

Here Machiavelli portrays *fortuna* as a function of the relative *fit* between a given man's temper and actions on the one hand and the conditions under which he is acting on the other. Machiavelli thereby solves the enigma that inspired this meditation, i.e., how both Hannibal and Scipio, with their very different temperaments and methods, each achieved political and military success. Their different methods were suited to their respective circumstances. "One of them with cruelty, treachery and lack of religion . . . the other with mercy, loyalty, and religion . . . got the same effect . . . [and] won countless victories."[40] Machiavelli concludes the letter to Soderini:

And certainly anyone wise enough to understand the times and the types of affairs and to adapt himself to them would always have good fortune, or he would protect himself always from bad, and it would come to be true that the wise man would rule the stars and the fates.[41]

Machiavelli has thus punctured the mysticism and superstition of his age through a brazen confession: men call *fortuna*, "fate," or "providence" that which they fail to comprehend or control and these things are therefore actually problems or figments of mind, not some external agency. He issues the same theme in the *Discourses*:

Many times I have observed that the cause of the bad and of the good fortune of men is the way in which their method of working fits the times, since in their actions some men proceed with haste, some with heed and caution. Because in both of these methods men cross the proper boundaries . . . in both of them they make errors.[42]

And in the *Prince*, Machiavelli links the problem of flexibility and fortune more closely to the problem of ambition considered earlier:

No man, however prudent, can adjust to . . . radical changes [in circumstances] not only because we cannot go against the inclination of nature, but also because when one has always prospered by following a particular course, he cannot be persuaded to leave it. . . . If only he could change his nature with time and circumstances, his fortune would never change.[43]

Machiavelli does not limit this understanding of *fortuna* to individual experiences of her. Because ambition penetrates "every province . . . every hovel" and because ambition results in rigidity of method and shortsightedness about circumstances and consequences, to this impulse Machiavelli ascribes the rise and fall of whole cities and empires. While gains and losses of power are perceived by the ignorant as due to the mysterious vicissitudes of *fortuna*, the true cause is ambition—its blinding effects on judgement, on the selection of appropriate political methods, and the formation of political goals. In one of his soliloquies in the *Golden Ass*, Machiavelli muses:

> That which more than anything else throws kingdoms down from the highest hills is this: that the powerful with their power are never sated. From this it results that they are discontented who have lost and hatred is stirred up to ruin the conquerors; whence it comes that one rises and the other dies; and the one who has risen is ever tortured with new ambition and fear.[44]

Similarly, in the "Tercets on Ambition," Machiavelli establishes unleashed ambition as the cause of every shift in the winds of *fortuna*. "From [ambition] it results that one goes down and another goes up; on this depends, without law or agreement, the shifting of every mortal condition."[45] Law and agreement, we recall from Machiavelli's "lion and fox" discussion in the *Prince*, are the forms of struggle conventionally viewed as "appropriate to man." But Machiavelli has made clear that the most prominent feature of man—the raw drive for power—makes a farce of this account of human conduct and politics. Man has his own peculiar animalistic nature, whose drive and *raison d'être* is ambition. Ambition renders him a creature *in* but not *of* the jungle, a creature who has both more and fewer tools for his own survival than any other animal, a creature who eternally complicates the means of his own existence, and stands in awe and bewilderment at the problem he makes for himself.

IV

For Machiavelli, the cultivation and exercise of *virtù* is the one hope men have of redressing the vulnerability resulting from their infinite passions, scarce natural endowments, and incompatibility with their environment. *Virtù*, like *aretē*, connotes active excellence yet it differs in significant ways from the Greek notion. In Machiavelli's account, man's excellence is measured against his natural inadequacies. Where the problem is poor judgement, *virtù* is keen insight; where laziness or idleness would prevail, *virtù* is energetic activity; where men would incline toward cowardice or effeminacy, *virtù* is courage and willingness to risk life. *Virtù* is an expression of freedom where any kind of enslavement threatens, strength where weakness is commonplace, action where inertia or passivity reigns. In short, the common quality in the diverse applications and meanings of *virtù* in Machiavelli's writings is *overcoming* and this is what distinguishes *virtù* from *aretē*. While *aretē* entails strain and striving, this effort was viewed by the Greeks as a movement toward the perfection or consummation of man's nature. *Virtù*, on the other hand, entails a struggle against man's natural self-indulgence, unfocused passions, laziness or passivity. Strain and exertion are common to both, but one is a struggle toward perfection while the other is a secular quest for rectification of man's limitations *vis à vis* his goals.

Virtù is required to channel amorphous passions—especially ambition—into worthwhile, often public, aims. *Virtù* turns greed for gain into calculating, albeit spirited, plans for enlarging one's power. As Machiavelli repeats tirelessly, it is not enough to want something very badly, one must have the correct combination of discipline, patience, foresight, cunning, and strength to achieve one's ends, and this composite is *virtù*.[46] *Virtù* is also required to temper the excesses of powerful, passionate men; the best example of this dimension of *virtù* is drawn from Machiavelli's favorite pair of antagonists, Hannibal and Scipio. There was a danger, Machiavelli says in the *Discourses*, that each of these characters would bring about their own ruin by virtue of the very qualities that yielded their successes: Hannibal through making himself too much feared and Scipio by being too well loved. "From either one of the two courses can come difficulties great enough to overthrow a prince: he who is too eager to be loved gets despised; he who too much endeavors to be feared . . . gets hated."[47] *Virtù* saved each from these extremes:

> [One] cannot keep exactly the middle way, because our nature does not allow it, but . . . must with extraordinary *virtù* atone for any excesses, as did Hannibal and Scipio. . . . It does not much matter which method a general practices, if only he is able to impart a good flavor to either way of behaving . . . in either one there is defeat and peril if extraordinary *virtù* does not correct it.[48]

From this passage it is evident that contrary to the claims of many of Machiavelli's interpreters, *virtù* and ambition are by no means synonymous in his writings.[49] In fact, only when ambition is converted into desire for public glory does ambition cease to rival *virtù* and instead join forces with it. In all of his remarks about ambition, Machiavelli never links it with *virtù* yet the quest for fame and glory are expressly cast in terms of *virtù*. In his pastoral for Lorenzo de'Medici, Machiavelli concludes his litany of praise, "and by no means as something less excellent [virtuous] appears your natural desire for gaining fame that will make your glory evident."[50]

The road from individualistic ambition to public pursuit of glory is no easy one. In this task, *virtù* is called upon for two quite distinct and ultimately conflicting purposes. First *virtù* must supply the keenness of insight into conditions and farsight about consequences ordinarily hindered by man's ambitious nature. Second, *virtù* fosters a bold and determined approach to gaining one's ends. The first matter is an often neglected aspect of Machiavelli's conception of *virtù*. While *virtù* is most commonly associated with action (and finds its supreme expression there), effective action is predicated upon a thorough understanding of what Machiavelli calls "the times" and, as we have seen, this understanding is most elusive to the mind of men driven by ambition. In addition to developing the capacity for perceiving "opportunity,"[51] *virtù* of insight and foresight entails the excerise of patience and the inglorious work of establishing and maintaining solid foundations and fortifications.[52] The *virtù* of overcoming man's natural short-sightedness involves obtaining a long and accurate view of things and planning or ruling accordingly. It involves remedying diseases of state in their early stages, waging a war one does not have to wage in order to prevent one later where there would be less advantage, and seeing opportunity in what appears to others as chaos or seething social corruption.[53] In this regard, *virtù* is the reclamation of all the powers of vision and subtle uses of strength that ambition diminishes.

The problem is that such reclamation is nearly impossible and never absolute. Repeatedly Machiavelli laments that "men are more attracted by immediate than by remote events,"[54] and that even men of great *virtù* are incapable of understanding their circumstances and suiting their actions to the times. In this mood, Machiavelli's advice and formulation of *virtù* turns one hundred eighty degrees: be blunt, be bold, seize your world and impose yourself upon it. When *fortuna* (bewildering or antagonistic circumstances) is upon you, be impetuous and audacious. The famous lines bear repeating: "It is better to be impetuous than cautious . . . [fortuna] is the friend of young men because they are less cautious, more spirited, and with more boldness master her."[55]

As far as possible, then, one must know and work with the times and in this regard, *virtù* is historical knowledge, appreciation of patterns and cycles in human affairs, construction of political and military foundations, and intense, penetrating vision. But then the *virtù* of will, strength and boldness takes over; force and firmness of purpose gain an importance rivaled only by the flexibility and caution Machiavelli counsels as virtues when there is space, time and capacity for them. "Many times one achieves with impetuousness and audacity things that could never be achieved by ordinary means."[56]

Thus *virtù* not only involves both physical and mental strength, there are two sorts of each of these and they are ultimately in conflict with one another. In action, the importance of building foundations, carefully constructing conditions, and altering one's methods when the shifting winds call for it is overwhelmed by the call for unequivocal, bold, brute attack. In intellection, the *virtù* of insight and foresight is at odds with the *virtù* of a single-minded and opportunistic perspective. Utterly antagonistic to the open, searching mind needed to apprehend one's world is the mentality required for *virtù* in action where the bold exercise of will requires a relatively narrow, calculating, instrumental rationality. In the latter, contemplation has no place at all, and deliberation is relevant only in the most superficial—militaristic or strategic—sense of the term; what is wanted is a mind attuned solely to the relation between its aims and the opportunity to achieve them. Not only must such a mind avoid external distractions, it must hush all the inner sentiments, doubts, and conflicts that would subvert the fixity of its purpose and means of achieving it. As Jerrold Seigel remarks, "it [is] indecisiveness to which audacity is most strongly opposed, and this links it most closely to the necessity which creates *virtù* in Machiavelli's mind: both are opposites of choice and *virtù* dissolves in the realm of choice."[57]

Indecisiveness is only the extreme expression of what Machiavelli perceives as subversive of *virtù*. Any mental moves that deflect focus from a chosen goal will amount to assaults on the *virtù* of a mind intent upon this goal. Reason itself, unless tethered firmly to the task at hand, weakens a man's control over his world.[58] Undisciplined reason is no more trustworthy in Machiavelli's account than in Hobbes's. Harnessed to a purpose, however, reason becomes as powerful a force as physical might in shaping the world according to one's desires. "Force and fraud," Machiavelli's two pistols of politics, are simply different elements of the same medium. Neither is a mode of working *with* one's circumstances; both comprise the activity of imposing form on matter, or combatting another form (generally mysterious and in the guise of *fortuna*) with one's own. To this end, the mind must be cleared of all that makes it "soft" or "effeminate"; not only moral considerations but deep, reflective thought itself must be suppressed. Only as the mental equivalent of an invading army can the mind be marshalled as a force adequate to the task of conquering the unknown.

One can see this *virtù* of mind modelled in the very character of Machiavelli's own writing. Machiavelli's literary style is famous for its starkness and definitiveness—a situation is either "this" or it is "that," one must do either "a" or "b." This either/or, black and white motif Federico Chabod calls "a perfect formal expression of a mode of thought which is always based upon the precept that *virtù* in a politician consists entirely in making prompt and firm decisions."[59] No one is more aware than Machiavelli of the subtleties and nuances in the conditions of political action and relationships. Yet Machiavelli insists that descending into the depths of these subtleties and nuances portends disaster for political men. What one cannot be sure of, one must never pause before but, rather, bludgeon or overwhelm. Mental *virtù* entails suppression of the distinctly human reaches and byways of thought and brings man closer to being an animal driven by fear or voraciousness. As Felix Gilbert puts the matter, "man's control over his world depends on his attaining a level of instinctiveness where he becomes part of the forces surrounding him."[60]

Instinctiveness is indeed the characteristic Machivaelli looks to *virtù* to supply but he neither expects this to yield absolute control over one's world nor believes that such instinctiveness results in blending into surrounding forces. For Machiavelli makes clear that even in actions of the greatest *virtù*, man remains at odds with his world and controls only what he strongarms, what he imprints with his own form. *Virtù*, in the sense of boldness and courage, impetuousness and audacity, does not bring the actor in line with the times but rather, signifies his determination to shape the times rather than pander to them or mix with them. *Virtù* of this sort involves courage, risk, and acting in an occupied space. It is, as Machiavelli says repeatedly, the opposite of relying upon time or *fortuna*.[61] It is also the opposite of relying upon others or upon institutions not of one's own making.[62] In this regard, *virtù* embodies a quest for control, for mastery of one's surroundings, but such control and mastery are achieved only to the degree that all manifestations of power other than one's own are subdued. This kind of *virtù* has nothing to do with bringing one's actions and intentions into accord with one's surroundings, with what Machiavelli has designated as *fortuna*, and it therefore intensifies the battle with *fortuna*. *Fortuna* and *virtù* remain locked in permanent combat; the war between the sexes is, for Machiavelli, *the* paradigm of politics.

What is becoming clear is that Machiavelli's comprehension of the complex nature of the political realm—complexity rooted in boundless human potentialities as well as limitations—is failed by the kind of actor he inaugurates into this world. Machiavelli urges control and mastery where he knows they are ultimately impossible, he counsels blunt domination of circumstances that he has revealed as nuanced and shifting. The *virtù* of bold action is at odds with Machiavelli's understanding of the fluid, nuanced and strongly contextual nature of political life. This kind of *virtù* is realized through shows of determination, firmness, and lack of equivocation. One must adhere to the path one carves and make events or *fortuna* flow around it—if that were possible.

Hence, while *virtù* is posed as a remedy to the alienation and relative powerlessness to which man's amorphous drive for power has given birth, it actually intensifies this alienation as well as the distance between everyday life and the realm called politics. Not only does the cultivation of *virtù* increase the intensity of struggle between political actors, it increases the extent to which the political realm is an arena of battle among the few for power over the existence of the many. Moreover, the domination of certain elements and forces, which is entailed in the exercise of *virtù*, increases the mysteriousness and dangerousness of that which is dominated or suppressed. To this matter we now turn.

V

As we approach Machiavelli's thinking on the subject of that which mysteriously undermines or threatens man's intentions in the political realm, we are once again confronted with his brilliance of insight subverted by his ultimate attachment to manliness. For Machiavelli is one of the few theorists of politics to have recognized the power borne by that which is oppressed, power generated by the very act of oppression, power that must be perceived and addressed by any successful political actor. Machiavelli saw in stark political terms what Freud would many centuries later put forth in refined psychological language: what is dominated, suppressed, or repressed does not disappear or die but takes on a life of its own in an underworld, eternally threatening and dangerous to that which has sought to lock it away. Yet even as Machiavelli so perceptively explores this phenomenon in political life, he turns his back on its implications and ultimately seeks to overcome it, despite the futility of this attempt. The language of "form" and "matter" permeating Machiavelli's political discourse is a perfect example of this self-subverting twist in his thought.

Before we explore Machiavelli's form-matter paradigm, a brief etymological digression is in order. "Matter" and "material" stem from the Latin *mater*, which, in turn, derives from the Greek *ule*. The Greek and Latin terms both signify "mother" as well as "matter" and the Greek term also signifies "wood," "forest," "timber," "stuff of which a thing is made," and "trunk of a tree." From this array of meanings two possible explanations for the mother-matter connection suggest themselves: (1) Man perceives wood or forests as matter for his enterprises in a similar way as he regards mothers, i.e. as "the stuff of which a thing (an artifact or a child) is made." This corresponds especially to Aristotle's account of the reproductive process in which woman supplies/is the material for conception and man supplies/is the principle or seed; (2) If mothers and women are ideologically synonymous in patriarchal culture, then matter signifies women generally, not just mothers. In this case, *mater*'s multiple meanings reveal a more general facet of man's relationship to women and his genderization of the world: women are perceived as material for his use, service, or imposition of form and conversely, wherever man sees the possibility of imposing his form in the world, he sees himself (man) against "the other" (woman). In other words, woman-matter-mother is set up in opposition to man-form-father and the former not only exists for the use of the latter but is seen as given shape and purpose by it.

The significance of this for Machiavelli's work emerges clearly when we recall that the Italian *virtù* comes from the Latin *virtùs* and the root of both words, *vir*, means "man." *Virtù* connotes manly activity, as "virtuoso" signifies a great and accomplished man and "virility" a potent and powerful man. For Machiavelli, the two definitive expressions of *virtù* are the act of giving form (*forma*) to matter (*materia*), especially in founding a city-state, and the act of defeating or outwitting *fortuna*. Both are supremely gendered constructions, of course, and both involve a construction of manliness that entails not mere opposition to but conquest of woman.

On close inspection, Machiavelli's "form-matter" model of political action and political foundations is both revealing and deceptive with regard to his understanding of the nature of political life. It reveals that all Machiavelli's talk of the importance of flexibility in a political actor does not attenuate his conviction that one can only overpower events and circumstances one does not understand by forcefully assailing them, imposing one's form upon them.[62] However one translates the famous passage in chapter twenty-five of the *Prince*, Machiavelli's stance here is clear: *fortuna* is to be cuffed and mauled, beaten or raped, anything but handled respectfully, gingerly or flexibly.[63] *Virtù* opposes itself to what *fortuna* represents in this case— the fluidity of setting and circumstance a man faces. Machiavelli calls this battle the imposition of form upon matter and portrays it as the sexual conquering of woman by man.

The deception lies in the fact that what Machiavelli calls *fortuna* or "matter" does not have the passive qualities either term evokes but instead embodies a different kind of power than the one available to man or used by him when he is exercising *virtù*. *Fortuna* and "feminine power" *appear* mysterious, capricious, intangible, and utterly subversive to man if he does not effectively guard and prevail against them. Machiavelli repeats this theme tirelessly in his political, dramatic, and literary works. In "How a State Falls Because of a Woman," he concurs with Livy: "Women have caused much destruction, have done great harm to those who govern cities, and have occasioned many divisions in them."[64] The hero of *Mandragola* is a man who has lost all interest in his worldly pursuits for love of an unavailable woman.[65] One of Machiavelli's lesser known plays, *Clizia*, is also a study of the corrupting effects of love on a man and of the indefatiguable power of a woman intent upon preventing a man from his desire. In this play, Nicomaco, the old man smitten by his adopted daughter, is described by his wife as a man who was "serious, steadfast, cautious . . . spending his days in dignified and honorable pursuits."[66] But "since this infatuation for that girl has got into his head, his farms are going to ruin, his business ventures fail, everyone has given up respecting him and makes a game of him."[67] Even though Nicomaco is master of his home and has all the social and economic power his wife lacks, it is she who wins the battle to get him away from the girl after whom he lusts. In the middle of the play, Machiavelli explains why:

> He who once angers a woman
> rightly or wrongly, is a fool if he believes,
> to find in her, through prayers or laments, any mercy.
> When she enters upon this mortal life
> along with her soul she brings
> pride, anger, and disregard of pardon.
> Deceit and cruelty escort her
> and give to her such aid
> that in every undertaking she gains her wish;
> and if anger harsh and wicked
> moves her, or jealousy, she labors and watches;
> and her strength mortal strength surpasses.[68]

Still another example of Machiavelli's identification of women's enormous capacity for subversiveness arises in "Balfagor: The Devil Who Married." This work has as its central theme the question of whether wives are the cause of their husbands going to hell.[69] Predictably, the tale ends with an answer in the affirmative and along the way Machivaelli also muses upon the difference between male and female power and the ability of the latter to undermine the former.

In none of these depictions of women's power is the power at issue a political or institutional sort. Women did not have such power and Machiavelli never assumes that they did.[70] But it is female power— mysterious, seductive, vengeful, cunning, associated with the impenetrable and unpredictable ways of Nature—that Machivelli calls "matter" or *fortuna* elsewhere in his writings. While many interpreters of Machiavelli regard *fortuna* and "matter" as passive entities, obstacles rather than direct threats to men's interests, this misreads what Machiavelli is saying about women and about all the elements of man's universe he does not understand and control.[71] *Fortuna* and female power not only conspire to undo men but are also the very things man is acting against, in an effort to master, control or escape.[72] He must avoid being bewitched by them as well as being thrashed by them; again, we glimpse the extent to which the enemy man perennially fights within himself. When Machiavelli expounds on the perils of love, it is not the power of women *qua* women that is so deeply threatening but the passions a man feels toward them, his experience of being in thrall to his needs, that make ruins of the rest of his life and undermines his institutional power over women. It is self-mastery that is preeminently endangered. Since he has fallen in love with Lucretia, Callimaco complains in the *Mandragola*, he cannot sleep, eat, or return to his work in Paris.[73] Not Lucretia but his own lust has undermined his self-mastery.

The other way Machiavelli speaks of female power—as vengeful, surreptitious and elusive—is also a mirrored image of man's inadequacies. It represents the unknown and incomprehensible against which man is powerless to prevail. To women and to *fortuna* are ascribed whatever powers and abilities men experience themselves as lacking.[74] Machiavelli makes this clear each time he chastises a prince or a people for blaming upon *fortuna* what is actually caused by their own paucity of ability, by their own lack of *virtù*.[75] But to know this intellectually, while partially demystifying "female power," does not vitiate that power, and Machiavelli's concern is with the strategies of battle between male and female, *virtù* and *fortuna*, not with the origins or deep structure of the contest.

The stakes in this battle are both freedom and manhood. The man who succumbs to or attempts to rely upon *fortuna* sacrifices both.[76] Conversely, men and states whom Machiavelli calls "effeminate"— without fortifications, discipline, energy, *virtù*—are the first to fall to the blows of *fortuna* and womankind.[77] "Female power" must be confronted directly and with no moves toward reconciliation; avoiding dependence upon *fortuna* is a theme Machiavelli repeats as often as he argues the need to fortify against her unpredictable blows.[78] *Fortuna* must be deciphered and paralleled in some instances, bludgeoned in others, and the real man must be able to do both. Says Robert Orr,

> Boldness . . . is the one advantage of character that men hold permanently over *fortuna*. Up to a point, we have to fight her with her own female weapons—variety, flexibility, effectiveness. But we hold an additional weapon, which, if we did but know it, can be made an ace. She is a woman but we are men, able to move with speed, which carries with it a certain quality of determination, and even some negligence of consequences.[79]

Virtù is the paradigmatic symbol of manhood; exercised to its fullest, it rids a man of all softness in himself and all dangers of being enveloped, overcome, or seduced by the goddess who would undo or enslave him. The acquisition of *virtù* is also the acquisition of freedom. But what an expensive and precarious freedom it is! Instrumental in its essence, *virtù* storms everything in its path and quells even other dimensions of the actor, dimensions that come to haunt him in the guise of *fortunà* and female power. All but the aim become tools or obstacles in the pursuit and expression of *virtù*.[81] Everything in the field and vision of the virtuoso is rendered either as an oppposing force to be squelched or as matter upon which form must be imposed.[82]

Recall from whence the man of *virtù* has come. Naturally, polymorphously, desirous and ambitious, *virtù* shapes these drives into public, political ones and focuses man's cravings upon glory and public power. Ill-suited for and uncomfortable within his habitat, Machiavellian man seeks to resolve his vulnerability by commandeering his surroundings, reshaping them under his own auspices, stamping his world with his own projects and purposes. Limited in rationality and foresight by his boundless desires, *virtù* focuses his mind more intently upon the means and opportunities for achieving them and inspires him to boldly seize these opportunities. Intellectually and physically, man must become fierce, resolute, and in a sense, one-dimensional, if he is not to be overwhelmed by his weakness in the world. Freedom in the sense of *virtù* has peace as its antagonist or enemy, the sacrifice of collective sociability and security as its cost.[83]

We have come full circle: from Machiavelli's depiction of man as a poor specimen of animal, through the perils of harnessing man's ambitious nature, to the development of the man of *virtù* who rekindles the animal in himself and acts as one who is either hunted or hunting—swiftly, deliberately, without regard for convention, ethics, or the general order of things, except insofar as they are instrumentally useful for his purposes. Yet there is something very curious about Machiavelli's cultivation of this "magnificent animal." Humankind, after all, does not live in a jungle, nor, if one reads its annals, does it strive to make civilization in the image of the wilderness. Yet the man of Machiavelli's making, poised for political action, is meant to view his world in just these terms. Put the other way around, conditions of political necessity, the conditions that demand and nourish *virtù*, are meant to be a human version of the conditions a wild animal faces and, as will become clear in the next chapter, the human version is a profoundly disturbing one.

Notes

1. All Machiavelli citations are from *Machiavelli: The Chief Works and Others*, trans. A. Gilbert (Durham, N.C.: Duke University Press, 1965) and are cited by work and page number. *Discourses* III–21, p. 478.

2. *Prince* 6, p. 26.

3. *Discourses* III–21, p. 477.

4. Ibid. I–58, p. 315; I–11, p. 226; III–43, p. 521.

5. *Prince* 18, p. 64.

6. *Prince* 18, p. 64.

7. *Discourses* I–16, p. 235.

8. While this poem derives its title and even some of its fanciful structure from Lucius Apulieus' classic tale of the same name, Machiavelli clearly wrote the piece for his own pedagogical and comical purposes; the *content* of his poem bears almost no resemblance to the tale told by Apulieus.

9. Following the structure of Apulieus' allegory, the narrator of the story is the author himself but transformed into an ass. Since Machiavelli's poem is the story of how this transformation comes about, the narrator is actually an ass recounting the experiences that befell him while he was still of human form.

10. *Golden Ass*, p. 754.

11. Thus, as Machiavelli is first introduced to the various sorts of fierce animals in her brood, the shepherdess says: "at the first entrance are the lions . . . with sharp teeth and hooked claws. Whoever has a heart magnanimous and noble is changed . . . into that beast, but few of them are from your city . . . If anyone is excessive in fury and rage, leading a rude and violent life, he is among the bears in the second house . . . He who delights in good cheer and sleeps when he watches by the fire is among the goats in the fifth troop." Ibid. p. 765.

12. Ibid. pp. 767–69.

13. Ibid. p. 771.

14. Ibid. p. 771.

15. Ibid. p. 772.

16. Ibid. p. 772.

17. Ibid. p. 772.

18. Ibid. p. 771.

19. Ibid. p. 770.

20. Ibid. p. 770.

21. "Tercets on Ambition," p. 735.

22. Ibid. p. 736.

23. Ibid. pp. 735–36.

24. Ibid. p. 736.

25. Ibid. p. 735.

26. *Discourses* I–37, p. 272.

27. Ibid. p. 272.

28. Joseph Mazzeo, "The Poetry of Power" *Review of National Literatures: Italy, Machiavelli 500* vol. I, no. 1, p. 40.

29. "Tercets on Ambition," p. 737.

30. *Discourses* I–46, p. 290, emphasis added.

31. *Prince* 3, p. 18.

32. "Tercets on Ambition," p. 737.

33. *Discourses* III–28, p. 493.

34. Ibid. II-Preface, p. 323.

35. "The ambition of men is so great that when they can satisfy a present desire they do not imagine the ill that will in a short time result from it." Ibid. II–20, p. 383.

36. Martin Fleischer, "A Passion for Politics: The Vital Core of the World of Machiavelli," *Machiavelli and the Nature of Political Thought*, Martin Fleischer, ed. (New York: Atheneum, 1972), p. 132.

37. *Prince* 3, p. 54.

38. This is not the only source of *fortuna's* existence, but it is an extremely important one and explains especially her centrality in political life.

39. *Letters*, pp. 896–97, emphasis added.

40. Ibid. p. 896.

41. Ibid. p. 897.

42. *Discourses* III–9, p. 452.

43. *Prince* 25, p. 91.

44. *Golden Ass*, p. 762.

45. "Tercets on Ambition," p. 736.

46. Thus, the French armies, for all their passionate zeal, lacked *virtù*, and ended up, in Machiavelli's words, "less than women." Without discipline, plan, and method, passion is worse than useless. *Discourses* III–36, p. 510.

47. *Discourses* III–21, p. 478.

48. Ibid. pp. 478–79.

49. See, for example, Friedrich Meinecke, *Machiavellism: The Doctrine of Raison d'État and its Place in Modern History*, trans. D. Scott (London: Routledge, 1957). Plamenatz denies ambition a place in the elements which make up *virtù* but even Plamenatz does not go far enough in probing the relationship between the two qualities. See "In Search of Machiavellian *Virtù*," *The Political Calculus: Essays on Machiavelli's Philosophy*, A. Parel, ed. (Toronto: Toronto University Press, 1972).

50. "A Pastoral: The Ideal Ruler," p. 98. Fame and glory do not occupy the same kind of place in Machiavelli's thought and Renaissance culture that they did in ancient Greece, but a place they certainly had. And as for the Greeks, fame was linked by men of the Renaissance to possibilities for immortality. In the "Discourse on Remodeling the Government of Florence," Machiavelli links political founding, giving form to matter, fame, glory and immortality with one another: "No man is so much exalted by any act of his as are those men who have with laws and institutions remodeled republics and kingdoms . . . No greater gift, then, does Heaven give to a man [than] . . . that of giving you power and material for making yourself immortal, and for surpassing in this way your grandfather and father's glory," p. 114.

51. "I remember having heard the Cardinal de Soderini say that among the reasons for praise permitting anyone to call the Pope and the Duke great was this: they are men who recognize the right time and know how to use it very well." From "On the Method of Dealing with the Rebellious Peoples of the Valadichiana," p. 162.

52. Thus Machiavelli calls for standing armies (never mercenaries) and insists "a prince should never turn his mind from the study of war; in times of peace he should think about it even more than in war times . . . this is the

only art for a man who commands and it is of enormous *virtù.*" *Prince* 14, p. 55 and see *Discourses* I–40, p. 284.

53. "Truly, if a prince is seeking glory in the world, he should wish to possess a corrupt city, not to ruin it wholly like Ceasar, but to reform it like Romulus. Truly the Heavens cannot give a greater opportunity for glory, nor can men desire a greater." *Discourses* I–10, p. 223. See also I–11, p. 225.

54. *Prince* 24, p. 88.

55. *Prince* 25, p. 92.

56. *Discourses* 6, p. 26.

57. Jerrold Seigal, "*Virtù* in and Since the Renaissance," *Dictionary of the History of Ideas,* ed. Philip Wiener (New York: Scribners, 1973–1974) Vol. 4, p. 482.

58. Recall Machiavelli's assault on reason in the *Golden Ass.* Felix Gilbert also remarks, "to Machiavelli, animals possess the pristine genuineness which in man is weakened by reason." *Machiavelli and Guicciardini* (Princeton: Princeton University Press, 1965), p. 197.

59. Federico Chabod, *Machiavelli and the Renaissance,* trans. David Moore (New York: Harper and Row, 1965), p. 128.

60. Gilbert, *Machiavelli and Guicciardini,* p. 197.

61. *Prince* 3, p. 17.

62. *Prince* 18, p. 66.

63. *Prince* 25, p. 92.

64. *Discourses* III–26, pp. 488–89.

65. *Mandragola* pp. 778–80.

66. *Clizia* pp. 835–36.

67. Ibid. p. 836.

68. Ibid. p. 847.

69. "Balfagor: The Devil Who Married" pp. 869–77.

70. Machiavelli is more honest in this regard than some of the later historians of the Renaissance. Burckhardt asserts that "perfect equality" prevailed between men and women of the period. He has contributed heavily to the myth of the Renaissance as a "feminist epoch." Women were so far advanced in the Renaissance, says Burckhardt, that there was no need for feminism—they were "beyond feminism." Jacob Burckhardt, *The Civilization of the Renaissance in Italy,* trans. S. G. C. Middlemore (Vienna: Phaidon Press, 1890) pp. 203–206. Joan Kelly-Gadol challenges this position in "Did Women Have a Renaissance?" in R. Bridenthal and C. Koonz, eds., *Becoming Visible: Women in European History* (Boston: Houghton Mifflin, 1977).

71. See, for example, Leonardo Olschki: "*Fortuna* is the passive and *virtù* the active forces of political action." *Machiavelli the Scientist* (Berkeley: University of California Press, 1945), p. 38; and Anthony Parel who agrees with Olschki in "Machiavelli's Method and His Interpreters," *The Political Calculus,* p. 10.

72. Lest it seem that I have made too much of the female symbolism in *fortuna* and of Machiavelli's other references to gender, let Machiavelli speak for himself: "Certainly the man who said that the lover and the soldier are alike told the truth. The general wants his soldiers to be young; women don't want their lovers to be old . . . Soldiers fear their commanders anger; lovers

fear no less that of their ladies . . . Soldiers pursue their enemies to the death; lovers, their rivals . . . Equally in love and war, secrecy is needed, and fidelity, and courage. The dangers are alike and most of the time the results are alike." *Clizia*, p. 829.

73. *Mandragola*, pp. 780, 784.

74. There are two levels on which this projection of power occurs. First, as I have already argued, man tends to reify in the guise of *fortuna* the consequences of action which misfires; and second, femininity embodies a number of human powers that are eschewed by "manly" men—sensitivity, perceptiveness, receptivity, nurturance. Both of these dimensions of Machiavelli's account of female power are further elaborated in chapter six.

75. *Prince* 24, p. 89; *Discourses* II–30, p. 412.

76. Similarly, any man who loses to or is ruled by a woman is protrayed by Machiavelli as a slave and a wimp. Such are the characters of Nicia in *Mandragola*, Nicomaco in *Clizia*, and Balfagor in "The Devil Who Married."

77. *Discourses* I–7, pp. 210–11; and *Prince* 19: "What makes the prince contemptible is being considered changeable, trifling, effeminate, cowardly or indecisive; he should avoid this as a pilot does a reef and make sure that his actions bespeak greatness, courage, seriousness of purpose and strength . . . he lays down decisions not to be changed." P. 68.

78. *Prince* 6, pp. 25, 26 and 10, p. 42. *Discourses* III–31, p. 498.

79. Robert Orr, "The Time Motif in Machiavelli," *A Passion for Politics*, p. 204.

80. In Neal Wood's view, "*virtù* represents the principle of freedom" in Machiavelli's writings. "Machiavelli's Humanism of Action," *The Political Calculus*, p. 46.

81. Plamenatz, "In Search of Machiavellian *Virtù*," p. 176.

82. *Prince* 20, p. 79.

83. This is not too high a price, however, for one's "humanity" and "manhood" according to Neal Wood:" Whoever behaves, ceases to act . . . not only is he reduced to being the creature of his own uncontrolled impulse but also he may be readily enslaved by the manipulation of tyrannical power seekers. Those who place themselves in thralldom to *fortuna*, by ceasing to act lose their freedom, and in a very significant way endanger their manhood and their humanity." "Machiavelli's Humanism of Action," pp. 46–47.

6

Machiavelli: Manhood and the Political World

THE DRIVE TOWARD DOMINATION constitutive of Machiavellian man issues partly from an alienation from the body first articulated in Greek political philosophy. In the previous chapter, we saw how this drive shapes and complicates man's posture on earth, especially his endeavors in collective life. These perspectives may now be drawn into an exploration of the purpose, characteristics and ethos of Machiavellian politics.

In the course of this exploration, some earlier themes will recurr: the need for perceptual clarity thwarted by unbridled desire; the reification of gaps or failures in perception as *fortuna* or female agency; the ultimate call to conquer what cannot be fathomed. But we will also witness the way in which politics itself removes man further and further from concrete "reality," the way politics comes to transpire in a realm of appearances, as a game, as theater. While Machiavelli seeks to root politics in the body and in "life," the male bodies and lives in which he roots it produce a politics distant from and threatening to life and the body. As with the Greeks, Machiavellian politics issues from aspects of alienated man that create and sustain a struggle "above" the cultivation and concerns of life. Politics becomes its own cause, its own glory, its own pernicious and bloody battle for manhood and freedom. This frenzy in which political men are ensnared also casts its curse upon all that is outside the official purview of politics, whether men, women, children or external nature.

I

Machiavelli opens the *Discourses on the First Decade of Titus Livius* with a problem seemingly quite peripheral to issues of politics and

96

power: in what kind of climate and terrain should a city ideally be established?[1] This discussion at first appears either anachronistic or trivial—perhaps Niccolo's own particular manner of warming up his pen for a lengthy treatise on infinitely more complex and demanding subjects. But the paradox Machiavelli sets forth in the discussion of geographical considerations turns out to be a major theme in the 500-page symphony that follows.

> Because men act either through necessity or through choice, and because *virtù* appears greater where choice has less power, it must be considered whether for the building of cities it would be better to choose barren places, in order that men, forced to keep at work and less possessed by laziness, may live more united, having because of the poverty of the site slighter cause for dissensions . . . Such a choice would without doubt be wise and most useful if men were content to live on their own resources and were not inclined to govern others. . . . Since men cannot make themselves safe except with power, it is necessary for them to avoid such barrenness of country and to establish themselves in very fertile places, where, since the richness of the site permits the city to expand, she can both defend herself from those who assail her and crush whoever opposes himself to her greatness.[2]

Men perform best and are least self-destructive when their activities are dictated by genuine and pressing need, but they have other inclinations making governance by external nature impractical. They require collective power, both for satisfaction of their own desires and for defense against omnipresent predators with similar desires. Machiavelli establishes the need for this kind of power as the prime mover in the formation of political communities.

> Cities built by men native to the place [arise] . . . when the inhabitants, dispersed in many little places, perceive that they cannot live in safety. . . . Hence . . . they unite to dwell together in a place chosen by them, more convenient for living in and easier to defend.[3]

The problem is that men are not naturally inclined toward building the collective power they require. Man's ambitious nature leads him to grasp for wealth and dominion via methods that do not necessarily engender nor sustain virtue, strength or community. Thus, in Machiavelli's view, ambition and slothfulness are frequent companions; men will take whatever appears to be the easiest road to their gainful ends. This also means that prosperous societies are frequently ridden with corruption; instead of enjoying or safeguarding their luxury and tranquility, men will incessantly and invidiously seek to augment it in their own personal or partisan favor.

Because men are "not content to live on their own resources" and are always "inclined to try to govern others," natural necessity is an inappropriate remedy for individual and collective laziness, decadence, and corruption. The power derivable from abundant resources rightly employed is essential for defense and attack, for success in domestic as well as international affairs. Thus, in order to reduce the evils arising from the prosperity prerequisite to power, Machiavelli calls for an arrangement of laws that will "force upon [a city] those necessities which the site does not."[4] Such a city, Machiavelli says,

> should imitate wise cities placed in countries very pleasant and fertile and likely to produce men lazy and unfit for all vigorous activity. They, to forestall the losses which the pleasantness of the country would have caused . . . have laid such necessity for exercise on those who are to be soldiers that through such an arrangement better soldiers have been produced there than in those countries that are naturally rough and barren.[5]

In formulating law as mitigating the corrupting effects of prosperity, it is clear that law has quite a different place in Machiavelli's political metaphysic than it does in the liberal tradition. While we are accustomed to regarding law as that which liberates us from nature (from the "state of nature" in Hobbes's and Locke's accounts) and yields civilized society, Machiavelli looks to law for the replication within society of the demands of a life lived in constant struggle with nature. Law supplies necessity and thus compensates for, rather than gives birth to, civilized existence:

> Men never do anything good except by necessity . . . Where there is plenty of choice and excessive freedom is possible, everything is at once filled with confusion and disorder. Hence it is said that hunger and poverty make men industrious and laws make them good.[6]

Again, it is from the wilderness that Machiavelli has drawn what he considers an essential ingredient of man's individual and collective well-being. Necessity is the food that keeps animals sinewy and strong, active and alert; ease renders them fat and sleepy, destined to dependence or death and no little contempt. But for humans, the manufacture of necessity in society entails a good deal more than constructing constraints against ease or imposing conditions in which body and brain are routinely exercised. Yet even rigorous laws and military discipline are insufficient stays against the fragile character of individual and civic *virtù*. Deliberate and at times contrived construction of conditions of necessity is the only sure guarantee against the decay or corruption of a polity.

Prosperous, libertine polities are utterly unimpressive to Machiavelli. Equally unappealing are tyrannies, whether they are achieved on the foundations of a rich or poor economy, a rebellious people or a resigned one. It is individual heroic *virtù* and collective civic spirit that breeds a polity worth having and a political world worth exhausting oneself within the ceaseless turmoil indigenous to it. Such spirit and involvement are utterly dependent upon the existence of conditions—real or apparent—that *demand* them. "As long as necessity forced the Veientians to fight, they fought most savagely, but when they saw the way open, they thought more about fleeing than fighting."[7] Necessity makes a city strong where its absense "would make her effeminate or divided."[8] Indeed, Machiavelli posits necessity as the impetus for all great human accomplishment:

> The hands and tongue of man, two most noble instruments for making him noble, would not have worked perfectly or brought human actions to the height they have reached if they had not been urged on by necessity.[9]

"Necessity makes *virtù*," Machiavelli declares forthrightly[10] and when it does not do so directly, as in a situation where one either battles gloriously or is destroyed, it does so in more roundabout fashion, by giving rise to an entire culture of competitiveness, covetousness and very rapid pace.[11]

There are resonances here of the relationship between the cultivation of *aretē* and the *agonistic* nature of Greek public life. Intense competition for glory and success is certainly one aspect of Machiavelli's appreciation of the dependence of *virtù* upon necessity. But *virtù* is more than accomplishment, more than excellence in deed—it is also vitality, largeness of purpose, and fierce determination in the face of adverse conditions. Necessity's nurturance of *virtù* is a central concern for Machiavelli because of its role in the development of political *strength* and *power*. This is most apparent in his praise of the "tumults of Rome" chronicled by Livy. In the chapter title of this discussion, Machiavelli declares that "the discord between the people and the Roman Senate made that republic free and powerful"—free because the people had to exercise their freedom in order to maintain it and powerful because the ceaseless discords and quests for power within the city made the people into citizen-warriors of the strongest sort imaginable.[12] Forced daily to fight for their civic status in order to maintain or enhance it, plebians and patricians alike contributed to the enormous strength and vitality of the Roman state. Necessity unifies and focuses ambition and it cultivates vigor where its opposite threatens. "That kingdom which is pushed on to action by energy or necessity will always go upward."[13]

Ambition generates striving, striving breeds competition, competition nourishes *virtù*, the existence of *virtù* intensifies man's experience of scarcity, narrowed options or necessity. Yet, as has already been intimated, Machiavelli does not find the need for conditions of necessity in politics satisfied through this chain of social-psychological reaction. Particularly in building civic *virtù*, political and military leaders must often construct the *appearance* of necessity in order to muster forces conducive to political success. *Perceptions* of circumstances as well as political time and political space all must be manipulated by political actors in the effort to bring necessity into play where it is useful and to disguise it where recognition of necessity by an enemy would be damaging.

In an essay on Machiavelli's concept of *fantasia* ("imagination" or "subjectivity"), K. R. Minogue notes that even necessity, seemingly the most concrete of political imperatives, is a function of imagination, of seeing no options in a situation.[14] It is in this vein that Machiavelli counsels a prudent general to "open to the enemy a road you could close and to your own soldiers close a road you could have left open."[15] He who wishes that a city be stubbornly defended "ought above everything to impose such necessity upon the hearts of those who are going to fight."[16] Concluding this discussion, Machiavelli approvingly cites a Volscian leader's speech to his soldiers: "Come with me, not wall or ditch but armed men oppose armed men; you are equal in courage; in the last and chief weapon, necessity, you are superior."[17]

To create the appearance of necessity where it is not actually present, both time and space must be manipulated or distorted. The prince of true *virtù* no more allows himself to be ruled by time than by that of which it is a subset, *fortuna*. Rather, he uses time as a weapon by shortening or lengthening it as needed. The trick in politics is to obtain as much time as possible for oneself, to shorten time for those one wants to force into acting and to lengthen it for those one wants to defeat through their own confusion and delay.[18] Similarly, the successful political actor wrestles with the dimension of political space to create or dismember the apparent nature of political conditions. Because men respond to what is close at hand and to the superficial appearance of things, a wise prince uses this knowledge in his presentation of circumstances to his constituency and to his enemies.[19] Similarly, he capitalizes upon the distortions that spatial dimensions entail, heeding Machiavelli's belief that "so much more at a distance than nearby the things that make a show are feared."[20]

By now, it should be evident that the kind of "necessity" relevant to Machiavellian politics bears little relation to what might be called the "real necessities" of human existence. Even when Machiavelli speaks of necessity as being imposed externally rather than as a condition fabricated by a political leader or imposed through institutions, it is not actual human or social needs but the imperatives of a particular political milieu and particular political goals to which he is referring. Political necessity arises from a conception and practice of politics rooted in the achievement, maintenance, or defense of individual and collective *power*. Political necessity is of an entirely different order from and moves on a different plane than human needs for material well-being, security, or freedom. Under the auspices of political necessity come such things as allying with another state to strengthen one's international position, or expanding one's state in order to fortify its existing power.[21] Thus, imperialism, domestic repression, acts of cruelty by a prince, and elaborate exercises in popular deception all constitute examples of political necessity.[22] True enough that Machiavelli's concern with political necessity stems from his belief that natural necessity, the struggle with nature, makes men strong. But human culture, while at times taking cues from the natural world, does not simply duplicate it; power it was that initially wrested men out of the jungle and into cities and power it is that dictates what political man "needs." Machiavelli calls for contrived conditions of necessity in civilization in order to push man past a tendency to recline into satisfaction of material wants or into other private desires. Necessity makes men of *virtù* out of mere men.

The political world Machiavelli analyzes is therefore one in which artificial necessity starts the dynamic of political events and the imperatives of success in the established political system perpetuate this dynamic. The basis of politics is the slight satisfaction men get from what they have and the concommitant need to defend themselves against other men who would prey upon them. From this arises the "necessity" of developing individual and collective power as well as the need to foster apparent "necessity," which will nourish and sustain that power. But once this world is operating at full pitch, it generates demands or necessary actions of its own accord: omnipresent striving, competitiveness, and power struggles issue a set of imperatives to any individual or state that would survive let alone gain in such a world. Not that the individual or state actually "need" the offerings or rewards of this struggle but that if one partakes of the rewards of that world at all, these imperatives become that by which one operates.

The manufacture of necessity intensifies the problems, discussed in the previous chapter, of accurately perceiving or assessing political conditions or "the times." The manipulation of time, space, and general conditions in order to make "necessity" appear or disappear according to one's strategy results in a perpetual distortion of the setting in which political judgement and political action occur. The construction of the appearance of necessity is a process of substituting appearances for reality and then acting upon those appearances such that they gain a kind of reality of their own. Myths, deceptions and fabrications become a second-order environment for political action and further complicate the actor's struggle with knowing where he is, what time it is, and where he stands in relation to enemies, allies and objectives. Hence, political life is not only several paces removed from human or social "needs" but also from any autonomous political "reality." In Machiavelli's account, politics transpires in the frenzied realm of appearances—a realm in which the political actor is half-blinded by his own ambitions but is also threatened by camouflaged mine fields and false images of insurmountable passes constructed by his adversaries. We move now to a closer inspection of this milieu.

II

One modern interpretation of Machiavelli stands out amidst the massive literature on his thought. This is a reading that casts him neither as political scientist nor philosopher, but as political playwright. According to Norman Jacobson,

> Someone once inquired of Demosthenes, "What is the chief part of an orator?" "Acting," replied Demosthenes. "What next?" "Acting." "What next again?" "Acting!" . . . Were we to inquire of Machiavelli the chief part of his *Prince*, we would undoubtedly receive the identical reply: acting.[23]

For Machiavelli, so this interpretation goes, the political realm is a stage, there is no essential reality more important than appearance, there is real political power in symbolic action and events, in myth, faith, exuberance, good scenes or bad. Moreover, there is no authentic man but only the masks that he wears—predictable and transparent if he is a poor actor-politician and many, varied, and fluid if he is a clever and successful one.

> Machiavelli's . . . new political art . . . is utterly devoid of content, its teaching precisely the opposite of "Be yourself." Its precept is instead "Be your roles." The object is to create a man of a thousand faces, a master performer who eventually does become his roles.[24]

"After all," says Merleau-Ponty in his kindred reading of Machiavelli, "a face is only shadows, lights and colors."[25] And Jacobson corroborates, "in the *Prince*, political art is the capacity of the unique man to transmute words and events into appearance."[26] From Machiavelli's oft-quoted precept, "in general men judge more with their eyes than with their hands . . . everyone sees what you appear to be, few perceive what you are."[27] K. R. Minogue surmises "politics is then, in a deep sense, an exercise in theatricality."[28] Hannah Arendt develops the theatrical aspect of politics discerned by Machiavelli into a metaphysical principle. Genuine politics, she argues, can only occur in a bounded public realm where "appearance—something that is being seen and heard by others as well as ourselves—*constitutes* reality."[29] From Arendt's remark, N. O. Brown concludes that political organization is theatrical organization. "To see through this show, to see the invisible reality; is to put an end to politics."[30]

Arendt's and Brown's characterization of the theatrical dimension of politics is not quite true to Machiavelli whose political world includes, but is not wholly constituted by the realm of appearances. Machiavelli does not give us inauthentic man, pure role-player, and from him reach inauthentic politics, a politics of nothing but roles and "seemings." To the contrary, Machiavelli begins with men who distinctly crave power but must re-order reality, dissimulate, and fabricate appearances to reach their desires. Machiavellian man is a creature of intense subjectivity and identity—he does not blend easily into the roles and forces that political success demands. He climbs into the realm of appearances for purposes instrumental to his real ends or is caught up in the order of appearances because he does not know better. But he cannot possibly hope to succeed in his endeavors if he takes events, conditions, or individuals at face value. Political man must constantly strive to pierce the appearances thrown up by others while creating appearances useful to his own ends.[31] Thus, while Machiavellian politics has a theatrical element, it contains elements the theater does not (unmasking the rest of the world while masking one's own character and plans), elements distinctly at odds with dramatic success (absense of a script), and elements opposed to theater (players whose own underlying desires and intentions dictate their roles).

If the identity between politics and drama is not so complete as some interpreters of Machiavelli have implied, the *role* of drama and especially of appearances does figure largely in his understanding of politics. Machiavellian politics is never quite real, it is never quite about real things. The spur of politics—ambition or the amorphous quest for power—is itself of an ultimately intangible quality and spins a world of unreality. In the Western tradition of "masculine" politics, political life is always at some level a game played by juvenile delinquents, and this is precisely what Machiavelli confesses as he portrays politics in dramaturgical terms. Still, Machiavelli's concern with the problem of appearances in politics is also about that most concrete of political goods—the construction and wielding of political power. That something so ephemeral as contrived appearances could be partly constitutive of something so tangible and determinate as power is not only an intriguing enigma but one that opens up another dimension of Machiavelli's distinctly masculine construction of politics.

The most overt sense in which Machiavelli treats appearances as constitutive of power arises in his discussions of a prince's efforts to frighten an enemy and to win the loyalty or commitment of his own people. In both cases, it is an emotional calculus with which the prince is working, an appreciation and use of the psychology of civic and political behavior. (Calculated manipulation of basic human drives, dreads, and responses is the way we would speak of this matter today.) The primary emotions to which a prince appeals in his constituency have already been touched upon in the discussion of ambition. He works on his subjects' desire for gain and on their insecurity or fear of loss.[32] But he also seeks to inspire them and command their loyalty through appeals to their sense of vengence and hatred on the one hand,[33] pride and dignity on the other.[34] Above all, he works on the precept that "the masses are always impressed by the superficial appearance of things, and by the outcome of an enterprise."[35] He capitalizes on spatial and temporal distortions related to their short memories and short vision; he gives them the appearance of what they want or need, or the appearance of being forced by necessity, in order to obtain what *he* needs from them— whether it be timid obeisance or blood-thirsty citizen warriors. The clever prince arranges and rearranges appearances—his own and that of his surroundings or adversaries—for the purpose of securing or mobilizing power. Religious rituals as well as purely secular proclamations are useful to this end, and Machiavelli bears no scruples about mixing one with the other.[36]

A prince also builds power within his state through careful attention to his reputation. Not what he is but what he seems to be determines the extent to which he is in control of his dominion, and in turn, the extent to which his state is a powerful one.

> What makes the prince contemptible is being considered changeable, trifling, effeminate, cowardly, or indecisive; he should avoid this as a pilot does a reef and make sure that his actions bespeak greatness, courage, seriousness of purpose and strength . . . Any prince who gives such an impression is bound to be highly esteemed, and a man with such a reputation is hard to conspire against, hard to assail, as long as everyone knows he is a man of character and respected by his own people.[37]

Note how quickly Machiavelli moves from the seemingly superficial elements making up a prince's public image to his actual power in the world. In his account, dissimulation is not an alternative to power but a component of it. The lion is powerless without the fox; force may be useless where fraud is indispensable.[38]

Up to this point, I have intimated that however powerful and prominent the realm of appearances in Machaivelli's politics, this realm remains distinct from an order of "objective reality." Yet Jacobson insists that the drama—the superficial appearance of things—is the only relevant matter in Machiavelli's political world. And K. R. Minogue identifies Machiavelli's ontological view of "reality" as "an unstable part of a flux in which everything is dissolved into appearance by being continually construed as the product of imagination."[39] For these thinkers, Machiavelli did not so much discover the role of appearances in politics as that politics *is* the appearances generative of and generated by that realm. "If Machiavelli has a 'philosophic significance,' it is the rejection of any reality behind the one that appears to us."[40] Or again, in N. O. Brown's words, "to see . . . is to see through, to put an end to politics."[41]

What is eclipsed by these interpretations is Machiavelli's repeated insistence that the successful politician must be able to distinguish what *seems* to be the case from what is in fact the situation; he must be able to pierce the order of appearances if he is to work that realm in his own advantage. No one is more ill-fated than a prince who responds to the reputation rather than to the concrete power of another prince,[42] or who makes the error of trying to *be* what he must appear to be.[43] Whether external conditions or his own image are at issue, a prince who is duped by either is bound to fail. Machiavelli advises the political actor to play the game of appearances from outside of its clutches for political phenomena have an "underlying reality" even if few can grasp it and even though false appearances can transmute into power.

Yet this advice, like Machiavelli's advice to fit one's actions or methods to "the times," is ultimately futile, thwarted by the very problem that has made it necessary. The Machiavellian political actor cannot pierce appearances to grasp what lies beneath them because he is not capable of such judgement, because the underlying reality of men questing voraciously and blindly after power is what has given rise to the "game" that is politics. If the political world is full of illusions, political man is also a creature of delusions. Important as it is for him to see through the fabrications thrown up by others, his judgement is cloaked by its own particular burden, its inseparability from the distorting effects of the intentions and passions that focus it. Add to this the tremendous pace of political events making thoughtful inspection of motives, actions and circumstances so difficult, and we have a picture of Machiavelli's political men incapable of the necessary, doomed by the impossible. Ruled by time and conditions distorted and manipulated by all, politics is a race through a riot by half-blind men who must plow through this chaos in order to face and create still more chaos at the next turn. The only means to averting utter victimization in such a world lies in developing and consolidating institutionalized power—power rooted in something more solid than appearances and reputation.

III

The ancient Greek philosophers were interested in power but disdained the quest for power for its own sake. For them, politics was about the good life and power-mongering was a symptom of corruption.[44] The Athenians forfeited their status as the "school of all Hellas" when they declared to the Melians that "the strong do what they can and the weak suffer what they must."[45] After this turning point in Thucydides' history of the Peloponnesian War, the book becomes a self-conscious chronicle of shattered Athenian principles and future prospects. In the Greek view, it is not power that corrupts, but power as the dominant principle of political purpose, organization, and action that is anathema to an understanding and practice of politics as the "good life." Justice, not power, must be the centerpiece of rightly constituted public life.

Machiavelli's view is quite different. Concern with a public or common good is by no means absent from his cares and writings, but politics is rooted in and revolves around quests for power. The common good is dependent upon power, constitutive of power, and lasts only so long as a polity exercises or increases its power. Moreover, for Machiavelli, power is a relevant and exciting issue even when it is detached from a concern with the public good.

The elements comprising political power in Machiavelli's account range from the obvious and uncontroversial to the surprising. Predictably, quantities of resources are significant—money, soldiers, arsenals, and so forth. However, even these goods do not translate into power unless they are effectively ordered and used within an effective order.[46] "Order" is the term Machiavelli most frequently utters in the same breath with power and is his term of praise for a well-regulated collective entity—a city, army, or government. Order signifies a fortress against nature and against a world that will control man if he does not control them. What a man or his state does not control, he does not really have, even if he owns them in a technical sense. This seemingly banal point Machiavelli considers unheeded by most political actors and he returns to it tirelessly. It is the basis of his doctrines that one must occupy rather than merely annex territories one has taken in battle;[48] muster, discipline, and lead one's own armies;[49] avoid alliances with superior powers;[50] and purge or depower disaffected classes or individuals within one's polity.[51] Machiavelli insists that the most common and grievous political error is to rely upon someone or something not entirely under one's own sway.[52]

Similarly, one cannot rely upon anything not stamped with one's own identity, even if it seems superficially suitable to one's purposes. Power, then, is linked centrally to self-sufficiency, autarky, or independence, as well as to stamping one's surroundings with one's own form.

"The man who makes another powerful ruins himself."[53] Power, while it can be distributed in various ways, cannot be shared. What a man does not control is not merely useless to him, it opposes or endangers him. Machiavellian man cannot know what he has not made or does not control, and in their illusiveness, such phenomena become threatening. Thus, albeit via a very different road than the one Aristotle travelled, Machiavelli returns to the ancient conception of autarky as the most valuable political and human good. Machiavelli, however, forthrightly admits something that had to be teased out from under Aristotle's utterances: power always relies on something, is always generated or produced by someone or something other than itself, and it threatens its own foundations whenever it tries to eschew or sever this relation. Aristotle sought to circumvent this dilemma with his "parts/wholes" construction of the polis-oikos relation. Machiavelli confronts more directly the problem of how one establishes the foundations that are the source of power while simultaneously seeking to acquire an autonomous experience and use of the power derived from these foundations. Independence is the goal and articulation of power, yet power is generated through interdependent relations. Power is always obtained from somewhere or something—it is not autoinseminating—yet when power's purpose is more power, it necessarily repudiates or attempts to depower its sources. This is the contradiction at the heart of a masculinist politics in which power becomes its own end and thereby subverts itself.

A prince may seize power without what Machiavelli calls "foundations," but he does not actually have and hold power unless he has such foundations, unless his rule is rooted in the people. This rootedness has its concrete expression in good armies, good laws, and the people's faith, loyalty, and willingness to sacrifice. It is, in fact, a misnomer to call power any manifestation of rule that lacks these foundations; such rule is not power but mere command. And "the first unfavorable weather destroys [such princes]."[54]

While power is drawn from sources outside of those who hold it, it cannot be shared with these sources and they must be denied their status *as* sources. The ruled must be convinced of the need for the ruler while the obverse must be obfuscated.[55] Yet even if this is accomplished, the problem of power's origins in relation to its projects is not resolved. For real power, the power that makes possible political action and success, entails much more than a prince's acquisition of ideological, emotional, and military support from his people. The power of a great state like that of ancient Rome has its basis in empowering and energizing the people themselves.[56] For Machiavelli, the sign of a truly powerful state is not a bold or even notorious prince but a tempestuous people, ever ready to do battle with each other or against an external enemy. But what is the relationship between the power of a vigorous and energetic people and the power of the head of state? The latter becomes partially determined and directed by the former. An empowered body politic exacts this price from the head because it is an assemblage of many bodies who have at least partly recovered their own heads. Control and order are thus both essential and impossible in building power from below.

Consider again Machiavelli's form-matter metaphor of political action. Machiavelli's treatment of political founding, rule, and action as the process of giving form to matter is rooted in the dictum that if you do not strive to make the world in your own image, it will make you. Form-giving is the highest expression of *virtù* where *virtù* is understood as pitting oneself against givens, nature, *fortuna*, or self-doubt. Yet while Machiavelli speaks of form as something that is imposed upon circumstances, entities, or people without form, the fact is that such "matter" always has a form prior to the one imposed upon it by a political actor. (There is no such thing as formless matter.) Thus, form-giving of this sort is an intensely violent act, involving the usurpation of other forms, including the indigenous form of any given "matter," for the imposition of one's own. Even in the "dispersed matter" Machiavelli describes as the material for the rise of Moses, Cyrus, Romulus, and Theseus, a prior form, however impoverished or corrupt, had to be destroyed for the works of these men to be brought into being.[57] "Matter" may be forced to understand itself as formless but when such matter is a people, that understanding is always an ideological act, a conversion in the people's self-understanding at the hands of the aspiring form-giver, much as we saw Aristotle arguing that slaves and women are without purpose or function unless they have masters to rule them and to provide the higher end to which they contribute. Ideologically too, then, there is violence (destruction of old understandings) in the act of form-giving. A people or city must be made to conceive of itself as "matter" in need of form.[58]

If there is violence in this mode of founding, there is also domination inherent in maintaining such a relationship. Machiavelli's "new prince" is not Rousseau's Legislator, meant to remain powerless and exit from the community as soon as his blueprints are operational. To the contrary, a new prince acquires a principality in the interest of gaining, keeping, or using its power for his own ends. The form he imposes upon his "matter" is not absorbed by and perpetuated by the people because it is imposed for his sake, not their's. It is the prince's power (or, in a republic, the power of the state) that is at stake, and he forms his world accordingly. The matter to which he gives form comprises his foundations for power; thus, his relationship to this matter or these foundations never loses its instrumental character.

The form/matter problematic can also be approached through close attention to Machiavelli's use of metaphor and gender pronouns in political discourse. Consider the following passage:

> A republic, being able to adapt herself by means of the diversity among her body of citizens, to a diversity of temporal conditions better than a prince can, is of greater duration than a princedom and has good fortune longer. Because a man accustomed to acting in one way never changes . . . when the times as they change get out of harmony with that way of his, he falls.[60]

Machiavelli, of course, is neither the first nor the last political thinker to refer to a "body politic" as female. But this passage both reveals something about that "innocent tradition" and moves beyond its usual pale. The body of a state is a woman, its head or heads are male. Male (head) gives form to female (body, material, citizenry). The head does not move in accord with the body but has intentions and actions of its own and relates to the body as the executor of its will or as foundations for its strength. The body of a republic, although still stamped with form meant to produce power for external use, tends to have a closer, more organic relationship with its head. A republic has greater longevity than a princedom because it has a relatively less alien relationship to its head. Yes, a republic also suffers from being slower on the uptake and more indecisive than a princedom[61]—bodies are sluggish things in comparison with the pace of heads—but these are disadvantages only in an environment of fierce predators, i.e., where there are other heads seeking to mutilate or subjugate new bodies.

The whole notion of a "body politic" contains a mystification that Machiavelli lays bare even while he perpetuates it. The "body" is not headless without its official head, the "body" is not "matter," the "matter" is not formless. The matter is not inert but substance and sustenance, the source of all power. The matter is mother with her procreative powers ideologically usurped, institutionally denigrated and structurally confined to a menial, prepolitical status.[62] The politics of form-giving seeks to convert the power of the "body politic" into the sustenance of the "head" by means of forced relations of dependence. The prince claims the "body's" power for his own and the presence of many princes makes her incapable of surviving without him. "[A new principality] being the prince's actual *creation*, knows it cannot stand without his friendship and power; therefore it will do anything to maintain him in authority."[63] The body is dependent upon her prince for survival only because there are others like him. She needs him for protection against other princes, but she needs nothing for protection in a world without princes. The omnipresent rapist keeps woman's security in the hands of the individual man bound to protect her. There is no guarantee, of course, that she will not be raped by her protector:

> When the Duke took over the Romagna, he found it controlled by weak lords who instead of ruling their subjects had plundered them. . . . He judged that if he intended to make it peaceful and obedient to the ruler's arm, he must of necessity give it good government. Hence he put in charge Messer Remirro, a man cruel and ready, to whom he gave the most complete authority. This man in a short time rendered the province peaceful and united, gaining enormous prestige.[64]

Because the weak rulers had only bruised and aggrieved the body, the Duke, when he took her over, brought in a true savage to beat her into submission. But, however much terror such cruelty may instill in a people, it does not inspire genuine loyalty from them and does not therefore empower the prince.[65] So, the story of the Duke's dealings with Romagna continues:

> Then the Duke decided there was no further need for such boundless power, because he feared it would be a cause for hatred. . . . And because he knew that past severities had made some men hate him, he determined to purge such men's minds and win them over entirely by showing that any cruelty which had gone on did not originate with him but with the harsh nature of his agent. So . . . one morning . . . he had Messer Remirro laid in two pieces in the public square with a block of wood and a bloody sword near him. The ferocity of this spectacle left those people at the same time gratified and awestruck.[66]

At this point the people have been rendered submissive, grateful, and loyal, conditioned to view themselves as a body requiring the protection and guidance of a strong head. What plunder by weak masters could not accomplish, thorough brutality by a strong prince achieved. This Machaivelli condones despite his insistence that the primary desire of the people is "not to be oppressed."[67] Or perhaps it is because of this characteristic: merely wanting "not to be oppressed" cannot stand up to the pursuit of power by men of real *virtù*. Just as the corrupt priest in the *Mandragola* declares that "good women can be bamboozled because they are good,"[68] a self-sufficient people can be transformed into the *material* of an ambitious prince's design.

In addition to the violence and domination inherent in the form/matter relation, the prince must constantly suppress certain features of his own creation. A people empowered by good laws, *virtù*, energy or purpose, will burst the bounds of the form externally and instrumentally imposed upon it. Thus a prince must strive for a kind of order and static quality in his dominion that is unnatural or inimical to the nourishment of power, and at odds with the perpetuity of a regime.

Machiavelli's Polybian view of historical cyclicality offers further insight into this problem. For what Machiavelli casts as providential or naturalistic cycles of political renewal and decay turns out to be rooted in the tensions between political power and political order, between the form given to a polity and the tendencies of its "matter" to burst the bounds of this form. Two of Machiavelli's many references to the cyclical history of political regimes are of interest here. The first occurs in the *History of Florence*:

> In their normal variations, countries generally go from order to disorder and then from disorder back to order . . . from good they go down to bad, and from bad rise up to good. Because ability brings forth quiet; quiet, laziness; laziness, disorder; disorder, ruin; and likewise from ruin comes order; from order, ability, from the last, glory and good fortune.[69]

In the *Discourses*, Machiavelli offers a more political account of these historical cycles. He explains, according to abuses of power, the shifts from a princedom to tyranny, to aristocracy, to plutocracy, to popular government, and then back to monarchy.[70] Naturalistic as Machiavelli's descriptive terms for these cycles may be, there is nothing organic about them. What he makes clear in this discussion is that as a form of government nourishes the power from within that a prince requires, either the prince or the people begin to abuse, resist, chafe against or outgrow that form. A man or state requires foundations for power but these foundations are in a real people who potentially have as much ambition, skill, and power as that which would appropriate their power. The more of this potential that can be tapped, the more powerful becomes the state and the more endangered its structure *as* a state. Machiavelli cites Rome as an example of a state that played this tension to the extreme: only through continuous expansion could Rome avoid tearing itself apart over the conflict between an enormously energetic and powerful people and the external form this power was designed to fulfill.

The form-matter paradigm of political order thus entrenches the problem of political rigidity raised in the previous chapter. On one hand, order is a *sine qua non* of political foundations: a prince gains foundations and power through instilling order in a people, an army, or state institutions. On the other, this kind of order is at odds with the inherent fluidity or flux of human affairs. Machiavelli posits order as that which will fortify a state against the sweep of time and the flow of events. Yet order cannot move a polity toward synchronization with the backdrop, context, and real nature of political events; rather, it is a bulwark against losing control to or over these things. Order is a strategy for defeating political alienation with political power. Yet it drives man further away from himself and from any possible reconciliation with the conditions he created that require this overlay of power onto confusion, mystery, and chaos. Order is Machiavelli's masculine response to fluidity and change, a response that intensifies man's myopia, inflexibility, and need for self-sufficiency, all of which were what originally produced a threateningly incomprehensible world.

Paradoxically, Machiavelli's formulation of order both provides the state with the power it needs and undermines its capacity for functioning within, rather than against, its context and sphere of activity. Order, like other forms of renitence, is what brings a state to power and what dashes it against the rocks when circumstances change. Order, like other means of control through force, fights *fortuna* successfully only through resisting her with force, but it can be undermined by the myriad other kinds of power she has. Order is a bulwark against a chaotic world, but when the chaos is man-made, order turns out to be the source of the cycles of political rise and fall that Machiavelli sometimes casts as exogenous. When an order has exhausted its own interiors, it becomes a wall that is as imprisoning to those within as it is a fortress against external adversity.[71] Order, in Machiavelli's sense of the term, can be the cause of political decay as well as political success; order is an external form imposed upon matter that responds to it but does not absorb it. Order answers to a need for control but does not address or resolve from whence the need for this kind of absolute control came.

IV

Fortuna was treated briefly in the previous chapter but the foregoing discussion of power and order invites a more thorough assessment. As noted earlier, Machiavelli invokes *fortuna* in a variety of ways for a variety of purposes, but these may be divided into two general sorts.[72] One has already been mentioned and will be elaborated further: *fortuna* represents the limitations of man's perceptual and predictive wisdom—she is the reified consequences of the shortsightedness resulting from his ambition. The other is the more familiar version of *fortuna*, the one most frequently developed in modern interpretations of Machiavelli, which locates him firmly in an age of superstition. In this portrayal, *fortuna* is a vengeful goddess who supplies luck to the undeserving, sudden calamity to the strong, and jealously undermines man's reach for glory. Brief consideration of this depiction of *fortuna* will reveal it to be nothing more than the popular face of the first version.

While references to *fortuna* as a capricious goddess are scattered throughout Machiavelli's works, they are presented synoptically in his "Tercets on *Fortuna*."

> She turns states and kingdoms upside down as she pleases; she deprives the just of the good that she freely gives to the unjust. This unstable goddess and fickle deity often sets the undeserving on a throne to which the deserving never attains. She times events as suits her; she raises up, she puts us down without pity, without law or right . . . And this aged witch has two faces, one of them fierce, the other mild; and as she turns, now she does not see you, now she beseeches you, now she menaces you.[73]

Fortuna made Castruccio Castracani mortally ill just when he was ready to consolidate his victories and secure great power for himself.[74] *Fortuna*, "never satiated," caused ceaseless and pointless discords in sixth-century Italy.[75] *Fortuna* punished Benedetto Alberti for trying to do good among the many who were wicked.[76] Although *Fortuna* treated Machiavelli himself cruelly,[77] he also spoke of her as his only possible redeemer.[78] In these and countless other instances, *fortuna* seems to stand in a simple and uninteresting way for the element of luck in human affairs and to date Machiavelli as a superstitious believer in supernatural deities. *Fortuna*, he says, in the famous chapter of the *Prince* devoted to her, "is the mistress of one half of our actions," leaving only half, or perhaps less, to our own responsibility.[79]

The first blow to this reading of *fortuna* comes in the "Tercets on *Fortuna*" where Machiavelli carefully distinguishes "Luck" and "Chance" from *fortuna*. Luck and chance are not synonyms for *fortuna* but part of her palace decorations; they sit "above the gates of her palace . . . and are . . . without eyes and ears."[80] Now eyes and ears are the very things with which *fortuna* is richly endowed—if man's senses rivalled hers in acuity, he would never run afoul of her, he would see as carefully and as far as she does, and her power would be dismantled. Moreover, *fortuna's* palace contains not merely one wheel dictating who is to be cast down and who raised to glorious heights, but "as many wheels are turning as there are varied ways of climbing to those things which every living man strives to attain."[81] The problem then becomes the familiar one: a man chooses a path and succeeds on it for a while when *fortuna* suddenly "reverses its course in mid-cycle."

> And because you cannot change your character nor give up the disposition that Heaven endows you with, in the midst of your journey *fortuna* abandons you. Therefore, if this he understood and fixed in his mind, a man who could leap from wheel to wheel would always be happy and fortunate.[82]

The refrain is the same as that in Machiavelli's letter to Soderini: the man who could change his ways in accordance with the changing times would be master of his actions and his fate, completely unfettered by *fortuna*. She is thus the amalgamated consequences, a reified expression of the effects of man's rigidity and subjectivity in a world that moves more quickly and divergently than his own understanding and capacity to adapt to it.

Still, one might argue that even these "many wheels" indicate a kind of determining structure, prior to and autonomous from man's own actions and creations. But in the "Tercets," Machiavelli declares that it is "Laziness and Necessity which whirl [these wheels] around;" the former "lays the world waste" while the latter "puts the world in order again."[83] This is no small confession on Machiavelli's part. He has devoted an entire poem to the fantastic and arbitrary ways of a deity only to proclaim in the midst of it that her substance is wholly human, that she is moved entirely by ourselves. Machiavelli has made clear that laziness can be averted through the construction of necessity and that cyclicality in politics results from a very specific practice of political organization wherein form is imposed upon matter for purposes of producing power for a ruler. *Fortuna* is thus the shadow side of man's single-minded devotion to perpetuating his power, with all the inflexibility and tendency to undercut power's sources that this devotion entails. *Fortuna* is the consequence of man's pursuit of a political aim or construction of a political order that strives to convert context into dominion by means of domination.

Fortuna embodies the Machiavellian actor's alienation from his context or political environment. She is a figment of culture ideologically conceived as anthropomorphized nature. *Fortuna* is the seemingly naturalistic aspect of the political realm—the "new jungle" that man must fight in the "civilized" political world he has made. She is the setting within which he acts, and she is also the enemy with whom he eternally wrestles. Yet she differs profoundly from the jungle with which savage man struggles because her power derives from man's thought and activity, not from his essential needs, let alone from some autonomous existence of her own.

Just as Machiavelli casts cycles of political decay in natural or supernatural terms when their root is wholly conventional, so *fortuna* is portrayed as a natural or supernatural element of politics when she is a product of the peculiar effects of Machiavellian man in action. Man's struggle for survival in the political world is shaped by the institutionalized forms of competition, power, and action originating from his ambitious and overwrought nature. But as these institutions come to appear "natural," his alienated condition comes to appear as his "nature," and his battle with *fortuna* comes to hide the truth that it is a struggle with his own individual and collective shadow.

V

Neal Wood has suggested that "Machiavelli's politico is cast in the mold of the warrior" and that war is the paradigmatic scenario for expression of *virtù*.[84] Wood's insight is accurate enough, but he fails to stretch its implications toward an even more fundamental feature of Machiavellian politics: politics is utterly dependent upon the presence of an enemy, it is at all times a fight, and dissolves when opposition is not present or is too weak to inspire consolidated struggle.[85] This is why Machiavelli insists that peace always give rise to laziness, decadence, or a state of effeminacy.[86] Politics manifests itself only when necessity is present and politics is experienced only as against something or someone. Thus, the frequent observation that Machiavellian political thought is relevant only to kill-or-be-killed circumstances is actually the wrong way of putting the matter.[87] For Machiavelli, the apparent or actual existence of a kill-or-be-killed environment is the precondition for politics as well as the *raison d'être* of politics. This is not merely to say that "politics is struggle" for, in Machiavelli's account, struggle without an end is as corrupting of *virtù* and political life as is idleness or passivity. "The vigor that in other countries is usually destroyed by long peace was in Italy destroyed by the cowardice of those ceaseless wars . . . from 1434 to 1494."[88] Rather, it is to say that politics only appears when there is something to conquer, overcome, ambush, or resist. Wars, Machiavelli writes in the *History of Florence*, are not for purposes of peace but for the enlargement of power and thus necessarily entail resolution through total conquest rather than truces or compromises.[89] Peace, besides being an intangible good, is the death of politics.[90] War, by contrast, presents what Wood calls "the archetypal battle between *virtù* and *fortuna*," a battle, of course, which is itself the archetype of Machiavellian politics and political action.[91] Wood elaborates:

> [War is the contest] between all that is manly, and all that is changeable, unpredictable, and capricious, a struggle between masculine rational control and feminine irrationality. War is the supreme test of man, of his

physique, of his intellect, and particularly of his character . . . As the tide of battle changes adversely, as the peril mounts, and as the sands of time run out, at such unnerving moments, the *virtù* of the captain is on trial. His character, his self-confidence, strength of will, fortitude and courage, become of greater importance than his brains and bodily strength. Cunning and prowess of arms will be of no avail where there is a failure of nerve. Against overwhelming odds, the leader must often discard his carefully prepared battle plan and rally his forces by a determined and audacious improvisation.[92]

If war is the archetype of the political, Wood adds, then nonmilitary political situations always contain characteristics of war, and success in these situations requires the abilities and sensibilities of the warrior. "The model of civic life is always military life, the model of civic leadership is always military leadership."[93] Certainly most of the terrain we have travelled thus far corroborates this interpretation. Machiavelli's concern with necessity, with order, with constructing and piercing appearances, and with mustering *virtù* to battle with the unknown all have their ultimate expression in combat and derive from the requisites of military battle.

How can we have come to this pass? Politics, whose very etymology is rooted in the Greek association for the "distinctly human," has become one with the activity least distinguishing us from the rest of the animal kingdom. According to Arendt, war is "prepolitical;" according to the classical liberals, it is the "state of nature," prior to or outside the bounds of civil society. And by almost all accounts, war is the phenomenon against which politics' meaning and purpose is juxtaposed. Even Clauswitz's infamous declaration that "war is the continuation of politics by other means" is trumped by Machiavelli's literal collapse of the distinction between war and politics.

Our initial encounter with Machiavellian man revealed a creature neither glorious nor powerful; he lived uncomfortably in his habitat and experienced himself as uncontrolled and without control over his world. He craved everything and comprehended too little of himself and his surroundings to pursue his desires with much dignity or success. Politics developed this man but it also reflected and entrenched this nature. Political life intensified the struggle against his nature and gave it a new arena; it also raised the stakes for a good many of his shortcomings. In politics, man must project himself everywhere—he must strive for control or be ruined by his vulnerability; he must attack or be overrun by all the forces within and without that he inadequately understands. Cowardice, effeminacy, pandering to the demands of the body, peace, otherworldly cares, apathy, idleness, and irresoluteness are all anathema to this effort. Political man must re-form himself by reducing all tenderness, vulnerability, and inclinations toward peace, and by overcoming bodily cares such that the body is reduced to an instrument, a foundation for his power. The body's mortal and easily injured character as well as its incessant demands for food, rest, sex, and absense of pain must be supplanted with a single-minded treatment of the body as potential strength. The head, with its boundless yearnings, has larger and higher purposes for the body than its mere satisfaction. As the body becomes martyr and servant to the head, body and head also become alien to one another. Politics demands this alienation of body and head, but it also demands the power of both. Politics is not for bodies, but it does not dispense with them, Plato notwithstanding.

As political man tries to make himself hard and determinate, he wars against softness, flexibility, vulnerability, and equivocation everywhere—within, without, in mind, body, citizen, polity, and nature. Yet he gives a new power to these things as he tries to purge them from his being, his surroundings and his creations. They constantly conspire to steal his manhood or *virtù* from him through *deception*, through *seduction*, or through *satisfaction*. These correspond respectively to the intangibility of the political world and the problem of appearances; to *fortuna* and women; and to peace or idleness. Political man struggles against all of these things through manufacturing necessity, establishing order, pursuing ideals of glory, and seeking larger scopes of control. He fights by attacking or constructing barriers against the seductive, the satisfying, the intangible and elusive and so also renders these forces more powerful as he grows more distant and alien from them. ("So much more at a distance than nearby the things that make a show are feared."[95]) These forces tempt and torment him, they foil and threaten him—just as women do.

Recall all that woman has come to symbolize. She is the "matter" that is man's own vulnerable and overwrought as well as potentially cowardly nature; the "matter" that is political situation or context; the "matter" that is a maleable people or polity. She is *fortuna*—times or situations man cannot fathom, always threatening to thwart or de-power him. To all of these kinds of "matter," Machiavellian man must strive to give form. Consider again the kinds of powers Machiavelli ascribes to women themselves. At times he suggests that women have power over men because men want something from them that is infrequently given. In this case, the power of women stems from their chastity in the face of insatiable male desire.[96] In other instances, Machiavelli portrays women as vengeful, calculating, shrewdly subversive of men's plans and activities.[97] This second kind of female power has an important relation to the first.[98] Women's intervention in the male world arises not from desire of him but for purposes of her own interests and power.[99] Thus, what man views as woman's power over him actually issues from his unrequited cravings. Man is controlled by her indifference to him or by her preoccupation with concerns that are mysterious to him because he does not share them. She appears to have power because both the motivations and the mode of her conduct are incomprehensible to him; when she rises against him, he neither understands where she came from nor what she is hitting him with.

In this battle, Machiavelli presents man with several options. He can struggle to fathom woman's nature and intentions and try to make his actions and desires intersect with hers. This is the *virtù* of insight, timing, perception, caution, and flexibility. Still, he must not pander to her, or he will have no *virtù* at all, he will be controlled by woman and thus be considered effeminate. Even if man manages to cooperate without pandering and maintains his focus upon his own desires, this mode of involvement with her has its costs: he must temper his own aims as they are submitted to or harmonized with hers. It also has its dangers: she is unreliable. However much he tries to harmonize his actions with hers, she may make a sudden turn, leaving him perplexed and powerless precisely because he heeded her so much, only to discover it was not enough.

He can also try to conquer her, to so fill the world with his power that she is forced to submit to him. This is the *virtù* of audaciousness and forcefulness in which his desire has largely been supplanted by angry enmity against the degrading experience of being in thrall to female power. Rapture becomes rape,[100] the weakness of desire gives way to the brutality of conquest, but man is not yet free. His forcefulness blinds him, he becomes more vulnerable as he strikes more sharply at a single target. Her many faces and dimensions appear to multiply as his focus and weapons have narrowed.

Finally, man may seek to acquire utter independence of woman, to become "self-sufficient" or, as it were, homosexual. This in no way means that he ceases to have any dealings with her nor that he ceases to fight other enemies, including himself. The *virtù* of independence, self-reliance, or self-sufficiency vitiates only one aspect of female power over man, and that is his *desire* for her offerings. He reduces her power by reducing his need for her. He seeks to form and control his world independently of her and to deal only with other hard, tangible enemies rather than with fluid or elusive ones. At the same time, he seeks to appropriate some of her techniques for himself—the use of illusion, deception, coyness, cunning and masked intentions. Thus, the self-sufficient/independent political actor is, in a sense, androgynous. He is manhood in drag, that is, clothed in his *perception* of female garb, attempting to use both male and female powers in the struggle with other men.

VI

Machiavelli's ideal—a lively, tempestuous polity spurred by the necessity of preserving itself against others and against time, making a few men glorious and all men free, striving for individual and collective immortality—has its darker side. Born of a "need" for power, it is nourished only by power, yet this power is without location in a purpose other than glory and political necessity. The polity keeps itself going through contrivance and war for it will collapse without spurs to greatness and explode without outlets for its surplus power. Thus, it must create enemies when it does not actually face them. The polity's value and *virtù* is indicated by its capacity to project itself beyond its boundaries, its strength is measured by its armaments, ardor, and order. It is threatened by tranquility and by time as well as by surprise attacks from others like itself. The flexibility essential to its survival is rendered almost impossible to achieve by the kind of order that is key to its existence at all and by the requisite obdurateness of the men who lead it.

The form or head of the polity is forever in tension with its matter or body, with its foundations or source of power, with what it has repressed, rejected, or reshaped to make itself strong. The head of the polity needs everything for its strength; yet very little that the head dominates actually needs the head—the matter is not actually formless, not actually in need of a ruling principle, not actually without function. The head is also perpetually threatened by its surroundings as well as by its body for these things move in directions, have needs or intentions quite different from those of the head.

The power of mental and physical force are man's greatest weapons in this kind of politics. The shortage of these powers, by comparison with other animals, was precisely what weakened and disadvantaged Machiavellian man in the wilderness. But in politics, his vulnerability is turned to aggression, his blindness is compensated by brutality, his precarious bearing in the world is cloaked by his *virtù*. Unfit to live in the jungle of the natural world, Machiavellian man creates a jungle of his own in civilization: Machiavellian politics.

Notes

1. *Discourses* I–1, pp. 193–95.
2. Ibid. pp. 193–94.
3. Ibid. p. 192.
4. Ibid. p. 194.
5. Ibid. p. 194.

6. *Discourses* I–3, p. 202.

7. *Discourses* III–12, p. 462.

8. *Discourses* I–7, pp. 210–11.

9. Ibid. p. 459.

10. *Discourses* II–12, p. 355.

11. Jerrold Seigel, "*Virtù* in and Since the Renaissance," p. 482.

12. *Discourses* I–4, p. 202.

13. *Golden Ass*, p. 763.

14. K. R. Minogue, "Theatricality and Politics: Machiavelli's Concept of Fantasia," *The Morality of Politics*, p. 153.

15. *Discourses* III–12, p. 460.

16. Ibid. p. 462.

17. Ibid. p. 462.

18. *Discourses* III–44, p. 523.

19. *Discourses* I–53, p. 303.

20. *History of Florence* I–19, p. 1057.

21. *Prince* 21, p. 84; *Discourses* I–6, p. 210.

22. Today these things go under the name of "national security" or "national interest."

23. Norman Jacobson, *Pride and Solace*, pp. 35–36.

24. Ibid. pp. 27–28.

25. Maurice Merleau-Ponty. "A Note on Machiavelli," *Signs*, trans. R. C. McCleary (Evanston, Ill.: Northwestern University Press, 1963) p. 212.

26. Jacobson, *Pride and Solace*, p. 35.

27. *Prince* 18, pp. 66–67.

28. K. R. Minogue, "Theatricality and Politics," p. 156.

29. Arendt, *The Human Condition*, p. 50.

30. Brown, *Love's Body*, p. 235.

31. See "Advice to Raffaelo Girolami" pp. 116–119. For four pages, Machiavelli details the acquisition of these two skills.

32. *Discourses* I–53, p. 303; *History of Florence* IV–27, p. 1219, 1220 and IV–31, p. 1227.

33. *History of Florence* IV–26, p. 1218 and IV–31, p. 1227.

34. "Remodeling Florentine Government," p. 110, 112; *Discourses* I–25, p. 253.

35. *Prince* 18, p. 82.

36. *Discourses* I–15, pp. 233–234 and I–14, pp. 231–33.

37. *Prince* 19, p. 68.

38. In the *History of Florence*, Machiavaelli gives accounts of entire wars carried out under auspices other than their actual ones, unbeknownst to everyone, on both sides, before, during and after the fighting. See V–17, pp. 1255–56 and V–18, p. 1257.

39. Minogue, *The Morality of Politics*, p. 152.

40. Robert Johnson, "Machiavelli and Gramsci," unpublished manuscript, p. 23.

41. N. O. Brown, *Love's Body*, p. 235.

42. *Discourses* II–11, p. 352.

43. *Prince* 18, p. 66.

44. Plato, *Gorgias* 482–527 (dialogue with Callicles) and *Republic* 336–51 (dialogue with Thrasymachus).

45. Thucydides, *Peloponnesian War* p. 331.

46. *History of Florence* III–13, pp. 1160–61.

47. *History of Florence* V–1, p. 1232; *Art of War* II, pp. 614, 619–20.

48. *Prince* 3, pp. 14, 16; *Discourses* II–19, p. 378.

49. *Art of War* I, p. 585; *Legations* II–53, pp. 136–137; *Discourses* I–21, p. 246; *Prince* 6, pp. 24–25 and 12–13, pp. 46–55.

50. *Prince* 21, pp. 83–84; "Words to Be Spoken on the Law for Appropriating Money, After Giving a Little Introduction and Excuse," p. 1440.

51. *Discourses* I–9, p. 219.

52. *Prince* 6, p. 25; 17, p. 64; and 24, pp. 88–89; *Discourses* III–11, p. 458.

53. *Prince* 3, p. 20.

54. *Prince* 7, p. 28.

55. *Prince* 9, p. 42.

56. According to Machiavelli, this is the case not only if one wants an empire like Rome, but even if one only desires a state which can maintain itself among adversaries.

57. *Prince* 6, p. 25.

58. *Discourses* II–19, pp. 217–19. Resonances can be heard here of Aristotle's depiction of women as "matter in need of form" and of women's contribution to the reproductive process as the "matter" or "material" for which the male supplies the "seed" or "principle." What mothers bring into being is thus ideologically appropriated from them and treated by man as his own doing just as the "whole" of the *polis* is regarded as supplying the meaning and integrity of its "parts." The parts are only the material for which political man supplies the form (Aristotelian version), or, the material (the people) lies limp and useless, in need of the man of *virtù* (Machiavellian version).

59. *Prince* 5, p. 23.

60. *Discourses* III–9, p. 453.

61. *Discourses* I–34, p. 268; I–59, p. 319; and II–15, pp. 360–362.

62. See the discussion of the etymologies of matter and mother on pp. 87–88.

63. *Prince* 5, p. 23.

64. Ibid. p. 31.

65. "Gratitude" is no minor theme in Machiavelli's political thought and it should now be clear why. Gratitude is linked to a construct of power in which the roots of power are meant to willingly give themselves over to another's purpose. See *Prince* 17, p. 62; *Discourses* I–28–30, pp. 255–261 and I–59, p. 318; "Tercets on Gratitude or Envy" pp. 740–744.

66. *Prince* 7, p. 31.

67. *Prince* 9, p. 39.

68. *Mandragola* III–9, p. 800.

69. *History of Florence* V–1, p. 1232.

70. *Discourses* I–2, pp. 197–99; see also III–1, p. 319.

71. *Discourses* II–24, pp. 392–94.

72. Much ink has been spilled on the subject of the sources of Machiavelli's conception of *fortuna*. (See, for example: Thomas Flanagan, "The Concept of *Fortuna* in Machiavelli," *The Political Calculus*, Vincenzo Ciofarri "The Function of Fortune in Dante, Boccacio and Machiavelli," *Italica* 24 (1947); Burleigh Wilkins, "Machiavelli on History and Fortune," *Bucknell Review* 8 (1959); J. G. A. Pocock, *The Machiavellian Moment: Florentine Political Thought and the Atlantic Republican Tradition* (Princeton: Princeton University Press, 1975); and H. R. Patch, "The Tradition of the Goddess *Fortuna* in Medieval Philosophy and Literature" *Smith College Studies in Modern Languages*, Vol. III, no. 4). That interest in this pagan goddess was current among poets, politicians, and literati of Machiavelli's milieu and was also prevalent among ancient and medieval minds is clear enough. Which of the various depictions of her most influenced Machiavelli's own rendition of the creature is less obvious, although it seems safe to choose Dante and Alberti over Aquinas and Aristotle. More significant is that Machiavelli was a sufficiently innovative and imaginative thinker to have constructed his own version of *fortuna*. This means that we would do best to look within his writings for an understanding of what he took *fortuna* to be and meant her to represent.

73. "Tercets on Fortune," pp. 745–46.

74. "Life of Castruccio Castracani of Lucca," p. 552.

75. *History of Florence* I–6, pp. 1041, 1042.

76. *History of Florence* III–23, p. 1177.

77. *Prince* "Dedication," p. 11.

78. *Letters*, p. 964.

79. *Prince* 25, p. 90.

80. "Tercets on Fortune," p. 747.

81. Ibid. p. 746.

82. Ibid. p. 747.

83. Ibid. p. 747.

84. Wood, "Machiavelli's Concept of *Virtù*," p. 171.

85. Machiavelli, in the *History of Florence* and elsewhere, makes frequent reference to times and places rife with internecine activity of too petty a sort to be called politics.

86. *History of Florence* V–1.

87. "It is impossible for a republic to succeed in standing still . . . because if she does not molest some other, she will be molested, and from being molested rises the wish and the necessity for expansion; and when she does not have an enemy outside, she finds him at home, as it seems necessarily happens to all great states." *Discourses* II–19, p. 379.

88. *History of Florence* V–1, p. 1233; see also I–39, p. 1079 and VI–1, pp. 1284–85.

89. *History of Florence* VIII–27, pp. 1420–21.

90. Here is the way Machiavelli speaks of the Florentine peace of 1471: "There appeared in the city those evils that are usually generated in the time of peace, for the young men, more unrestrained than usual, spent without measure on dress, banquets and similar luxuries; and being without occupa-

tion, they wasted on gambling and whores their time and their property. Their ambition was to appear magnificent in their clothing, to use speech that was pithy and clever; he who most deftly nipped the others was the smartest and the most highly regarded." *History of Florence* VII–28, p. 1372.

91. Wood, "Machiavelli's Concept of *Virtù*, p. 170.

92. Ibid. p. 170.

93. Ibid. p. 170.

94. See John Geerken, "Homer's Image of the Hero in Machiavelli: A Comparison of *Aretē* and *Virtù*," *Italian Quarterly* 14, no. 53 (1970), pp. 45–90.

95. *History of Florence* I–19, p. 1057.

96. See *Mandragola* (character of Lucretia), *Clizia* (character of Clizia) and "The Snake Charmers."

97. See *Clizia* (character of Sofronia) and "Balfagor: The Devil Who Married."

98. Machiavelli seldom speaks of women in politics without reference to their disruptive status as sexual objects. In addition to the plays, see *History of Florence* I–9, p. 1044; I–20, p. 1058; I–37,38, p. 1076–77; and II–3, pp. 1084–85.

99. Again, see *Clizia* (character of Sofronia who seeks to control her husband for purposes of her own power, not to obtain anything from him).

100. Ortega y Gasset insists that there *is* an etymological connection but that it runs the other way, i.e., that the first act was rape, then rapture. "The Sportive Origins of the State," *History as a System*, p. 31.

Modernity
Weber

7

Weber:
The Nature and Telos of Politics

M AX WEBER DREW A SHARP DISTINCTION between his "academic" writings and his political or "value-expressive" essays. Both, as well as the relation and blurring between them, are important to this study. In his "scientific" accounts of politics and society, Weber depicts a world that is a continuation of the intimate association between manhood and politics traced through the thinking of Aristotle and Machiavelli. The formations of political power, political institutions, and political purpose, which Weber claims not to evaluate but merely to codify and analyze, contain constructs shown to be bound up with manhood in the earlier thinkers' texts. Moreover, in his explicitly political writings, Weber develops and intensifies the specifically masculine political rationality and practices already identified. Finally, Weber's particular concern with "rationalization" and "meaninglessness" in the modern world signifies a crisis in the manhood-politics dialectic that has much bearing upon the politics of our own age.

Yet, with Weber, the nature of this study as an interpretative endeavor shifts in certain ways. In the writings of Aristotle and Machiavelli, it was possible to grasp one angle of the relationship between manhood and politics through their accounts of manliness, their (mostly perjorative) accounts of women and femininity, and their discussions of men's motivations for constructing and engaging in the political realm. Only the last of these is offered by Weber and that in quite abbreviated, inconclusive fashion. A more circuitous effort, therefore, will be required to relate manhood and politics in Weber's thought.

There are several dimensions to this effort. As already suggested, Weber represents a kind of culmination to this work—his writings embody the modern and crisis-ridden version of many themes elicited from the thought of Aristotle and Machiavelli. Thus, it is possible to examine Weberian political constructions with reference to the portrait of manhood with which the parallel formulations of earlier theorists were shown to be intertwined. For example, the *domination* intrinsic to the Aristotelian *polis-oikos* or public-private relation—justified by the superiority of male spirit and rationality in contrast to female enslavement by the body—is articulated by Weber in extremely stark terms. Similarly, the violent and coercive quality of Machiavellian political action—deriving from and reinforcing man's vulnerability, fear of entrapment, and lust for power as domination—is again presented by Weber as a simple *fact* of political life. Weber's formulations of political rationality, the characteristics of the political leader, the reified nature of political association, and an ideal of politics as autonomous from concerns of everyday or material needs also correspond to themes developed in earlier chapters.

If Weber's construction of politics embodies "inherited" elements of the manhood-politics relationship, it also contains some uniquely modern and uniquely Weberian contributions to this relationship. As a self-conscious inhabitant of a "disenchanted age" and less self-consciously, of a despotic and extremely patriarchal German nation-state, Weber denudes manly politics of ethical, religious, or other cosmological cloakings. This politics is laid remarkably bare—its ruthlessness as well as its hollowness is proffered without apology. Thus, for those inclined to think that the foundations of politics in manhood disintegrate with the rise of industrial capitalism, the welfare state or liberal egalitarianism, Weber loudly signifies the contrary.

There are other ways in which Weber can be drawn closer to the manhood-politics problematic than his works would at first seem to suggest. Although references to "female/feminine" and "male/masculine" are rare in his academic studies, these terms do appear in his letters and in records of his conversations.[1] Weber lived in an epoch and milieu strongly permeated by Freudian and neo-Freudian voices, and however critical he may have been of the Freudian "science," he was not impervious to it and occasionally reflected upon individuals, relationships, and social phenomena in such terms.[2] There are also moments when Weber's ambivalence about the virtues of masculinity is poignantly confessed. Consider the following excerpt from a letter to his fiancée:

> The world looks very different to me now than it did last autumn; for now I go forth to hard and great tasks of a purely human nature and for which it is worthwhile to exert one's strength, even if they appear to be less impressive than what the masculine profession, which goes on in

the midst of the market place of life, otherwise can offer us for goals . . . And since I have never, apart from the obligation "to make the most of one's talent" had more than *external* respect for the value of the masculine profession, I have a deep yearning that such daily, purely human tasks may be set before me.[3]

In a letter to his friend and student, Emmy Baumgartner, Weber offers an even more searching meditation on masculinity:

The life of a man in office shapes his understanding in a particular way. Human relations, when mediated through papers and documents, take on a peculiar kind of ghostly life—a picture as if one saw the outlined shadows of real living men performing a dance on a curtain. We know that real struggles are occurring on the other side of the curtain but only the colorless outlines fall upon it, often amazingly distorted. The masculine preoccupation with such shadows and, in general, with the interests of *external* life, makes it difficult for men to understand the reactions of those whose calling lies more on the inner side. For what comes from man as the mere expression of an external momentary mood is often felt by women more internally, with lasting pain.[4]

Lacking in definitive evaluation of "masculine" and "feminine" as these passages are, it is precisely the high degree of pathos and tension they evince that is of significance to this work. The extremes, crises, and contradictions contained both in Weber's life and his works are part of what make him such an important figure to analyze at this juncture in Western history. For Weber preeminently symbolizes and manifests crisis—in the words of Karl Jaspers, "Max Weber stood supremely for the meaning of failure in our time."[5] Weber both embodied and fought mainstream currents in politics, pedagogy, science, epistemology, in his values and in the way he lived his life. The very modes of power, organization, and knowledge he so powerfully criticized he also sought to bring to their fullest realization. This can be said of his methodological studies, his view of science and rationalization, and of power politics. He was a man in perpetual psychic crisis who fought back the dark by sheer willfullness. The same is true of his culture and his epoch: both were shattering from the weight of their own heritage as well as from crisis within and both struggled through might alone to pull forward. These crises, including Weber's own, I shall argue, are not independent of a crisis of manhood itself emerging in this period of modernity and Weber both speaks to and embodies this crisis. Rationality, born to deliver man from nature, now enslaves him as a machine. Politics, born to spiritually fulfill man, now reflects back to him his own hollowness. The irony, of course, is that Weber both fathered this knowledge and bowed before it; at best, he sought homeopathic cures for his own paralyzed manhood and for a manly politics. Each produced the toxins of its own disease: the whole of Weber's intellectual life represents a paradoxical recognition and refusal of this fact.

I

As with Aristotle, a consideration of Weber's formulation of politics is appropriately begun through his account of "prepolitical" associations. Unlike Aristotle, Weber locates the origins of political association, authority, and power in *two* distinct social formations. On one hand, he discerns the foundation of politics in the household, wherein collective life is organized according to production for human needs. On the other, Weber devotes much attention to "warrior leagues" or "men's houses," prepolitical social formations not specifically rooted in productive relations. In Weber's account, each of these social formations contributes to the origins of political consociation and contributes elements to what he takes to be universal characteristics of politics.

The household, Weber declares in *Economy and Society*," is the fundamental basis of loyalty and authority, which in turn is the basis of many other groups."[6] Political associations, especially nations, are included among these groups. In Weber's usage, the term "household" more closely corresponds to an *oikos* than to the contemporary family; the household is moored in production rather than in the biological bonds of the family:

> The size and inclusiveness of the household varies. But it is the most widespread economic group and involves continuous and intensive social action. . . . Its prerequisite is not a "household" in the present day sense of the word, but rather a certain degree of organized cultivation of the soil.[7]

According to Weber, marriage is neither the basis of the household nor a "mere combination of sexual union and socialization agency involving mother, father, and children."[8] Marriage as a social institution "comes into existence only as an antithesis to sexual relationships which are *not* regarded as marriage."[9] Nor does the household arise for the nurturance and protection of children: unlike state-of-nature theorists such as Hobbes and Locke, or even some of the nineteenth-century anthropologists, Weber is perfectly able to conceive of "maternal groupings" as preceding the paternal household, and of even more "primitive" biological-social groupings preceding these mother-child groups.[10]

From whence, then, comes the father-headed household that Weber denotes as the fundamental basis of loyalty and authority relations? A closer look at Weber's discussion of "maternal groupings" brings something quite intriguing to light, namely that there never existed "societies with maternal groupings only" and that

> the pure maternal gouping as a normal but obviously *secondary form* is often found precisely where men's everyday life is confined to the stable community of a "men's house," at first for militry purposes, later on for other reasons. Men's house [*Mannerhauser*] can be found in various countries as a specific commitment and resultant of militaristic development.[12]

Now if we leave Weber's discussion of the household for a moment in order to pursue the phenomenon of "men's houses," they are next and more fully discussed in the section of *Economy and Society* entitled "stages in the formation of political communities." The militaristic aspect of the *Mannerhaus* is still strongly emphasized here for Weber traces the genealogy of political community according to the origins and development of *organized violence,* initially nonlegitimate, later legitimate.[13] "Legitimacy," Weber argues, "originally had little bearing upon violence—in the sense that it was not bound by norms."[14] This is corroborated by the fact that primitive organized violence involved "situations where the most warlike members of a group on their own initiative consociate through personal fraternization to organize marauding raids."[15] Gradually, however, these primitive fraternities gain the legitimate monopoly of violence not only for the community's external adventures but within the community as well. Weber's detailed unfolding of this "evolutionary" process is significant:

> Violence acquires legitimacy initially only in those cases in which it is directed against members of the fraternity [the men's group] who have acted treasonably or who have harmed it by disobedience or cowardice. This state is transcended gradually, as this *ad hoc* consociation develops into a permanent structure. Through the cultivation of military prowess and war as a vocation, such a structure develops into a coercive apparatus able to lay effective and comprehensive claims to obedience. These claims will be directed against the inhabitants of conquered territories as well as against the militarily unfit members of the territorial community from which the warriors' fraternity had emerged.[16]

Here, starkly, lays Weber's first confession about the nature of politics: political organization is born from young male consociations developed to engage in "marauding raids," a myth of political origins which Norman O. Brown has called "politics as organized juvenile delinquency."[17] Although the members of the men's groups are primarily involved in armed rape and pillage, only these men are considered "free" and "equal" members of the territorial community.[18] All others, Weber reports, "those untrained in arms and those incapable of bearing arms, are regarded as 'women' and are explicitly designated as such in many primitive languages."[19] Moreover,

> in the sphere of political action, [the *Mannerhaus*] is almost the exact counterpart to the consociation of monks in the monastery in the religious sphere. Only those are members who have demonstrated prowess in the use of arms and have been taken into the warrior's brotherhood after a novitiate, while he who has not passed the test remains outside as a "woman," among the women and children, who are also joined by those no longer capable of bearing arms.[20]

While Weber thus establishes "men's houses" as the origins of organized violence and legitimate political domination, he has also declared the *household* to be the fundamental basis of elementary political relations. How may these two accounts be reconciled? Following his description of how warrior fraternities evolve into political organizations ruling a community in which all nonwarriors constitute "the ruled," Weber adds,

> only when the warrior group, consociated freely beyond and above the everyday round of life, is, so to speak, fitted into a territorial community, and when thereby, a political organization is formed, do both obtain a specific legitimation for the use of violence. . . . The larger community, among whose members are the warriors who had so far been organized as marauders or as a permanent warriors' league, may acquire the power to subject the freely consociated warriors' raids to its control.[21]

Now Weber appears to be suggesting that the formation of *political community* and *political organization* are distinguishable from the development of warrior groups into permanent structures of *political domination*. Weber does not clarify this shift in his argument, but by returning to his discussion of the role of the household in providing the foundations for political authority, the *meaning* of this confusion can be made clearer. Within this confusion too, lies the distinctly "masculine" roots of both political *authority* and political *action*.

According to Weber, authority and loyalty in the household stem from two of its essential features: the "solidarity" arising from communism of property and consumption and the revered "superiority" of the household's most able-bodied members.[22] As a purely economic phenomenon, Weber largely disregards household communism once he has mentioned it; it provides a basis for loyalty and authority but is not constitutive of them. Weber treats as quite significant, however, the authority he finds inherent in physical superiority. This authority is based on both superior strength and superior practical knowledge and experience.[23] It is thus, the authority of men as against women and children; of the able-bodied as against those of lesser capacity; of the adult as against the child; of the old as against the young. The "loyalty" is one of subjects toward the holders of authority and toward one another. As reverence for ancestors, it finds its way into religion; as a loyalty of the patrimonial official, retainer or vassal, it becomes a part of the relationships originally having a domestic character.[24]

As Weber here depicts the origins of political authority and loyalty, it would appear that he has departed altogether from the claim that politics is born from naked, organized violence. "Practical knowledge and experience" has been added to strength as a basis for the authority of men (fathers) over children and women. And since it is the household as an economic entity that is under discussion, one might assume that even the mention of superior strength refers not to physical coercion but to productive ability and capacity. However, in the discussion of "men's houses," Weber states explicitly that in the early stages of social and political formation, women were doing all of the agricultural work.[25] Thus, men's superior "practical knowledge and experience" in the household can only refer to their more "worldly" capacities, i.e., their knowledge and experience of marauding, pillaging, and defending their household against the same. This conclusion is corroborated by yet another discussion of the household in *Economy and Society*, ("Patriarchalism and Patrimonialism") wherein Weber seeks to debunk the notion that "natural filial piety" is the root of domestic authority. The truth of familial bonding, Weber says, lies in the fact that "the woman is dependent because of the normal superiority of the physical and intellectual energies of the male and the child because of his objective helplessness."[26]

At this point, a truly Weberian account of the origins of patriarchal authority has emerged: the mighty rule . . . not because they are most proficient or knowledgeable in the realm of "want satisfaction" or even because a need for rule exists. A man rules his household because he can physically and intellectually dominate and "protect" his wife and children. Male strength and familiarity with the male (violent) world outside the household or village are the basis for the household rule Weber calls the foundation of political authority. In short, household authority is moored in power rather than welfare, and this is what gives it its distinctly political character.

Despite the common theme of physical force in the domination exercised by the household patriarch and the warrior leagues, they contribute quite different elements to the foundation of politics. For Weber, the warrior leagues express the basis of political association and action. This is evident in their purely aggressive and extraordinary purposes, the exclusive status of their members as "free" and as "equals" with one another, their rites of initiation, their autonomy from those who sustain them materially, and not least of all, in their intensely self-conscious masculine identity. Other features signifying their historical role as founders of political association include their deliberate spatial separation from the territorial community off of which they live and their regular abduction and rape of the women of that territory.[27] Yet, even as they constitute the founding moment of politics, precisely because *all* the league's activities were distinct from the realm of everyday life, the warrior leagues were incapable of attaining a *continuous* and *grounded* mode of political association. While politics may be born of war, it, and human beings, cannot live by war alone. Political association must have some roots in everyday life if it is to exist on a sustained basis.[28] Thus Weber describes the process of "integrating" warrior fraternities and the territorial communities they dominated by force:

> The larger community, among whose members are the warriors who had so far been organized as marauders or as a permanent warriors' league, may acquire the power to subject the freely consociated warriors' raids to its control. It may achieve this success through either of two processes: the warriors' organization may disintegrate owing to a long period of pacification; or, a comprehensive political consociation may be imposed.[29]

Weber appears to be suggesting that when the warrior fraternity has been subdued or supplanted by the larger territorial community as a mode of political domination, the authority of fathers or household heads rises in relative importance. In other words, what Weber offers in two different accounts of the origins of political association and domination are actually two essential and relatively independent aspects of political founding, one more important initially, but the other equally vital if political life is to be sustained and developed.

This interpretation is corroborated by what Weber says elsewhere about the nature of "patriarchal patrimonialism" and the "welfare state." Loyalty and authority within patriarchal patrimonialism have a much stronger constitutive relationship with one another than is the case under earlier political formations. The domination of the warrior fraternity was only marginally "legitimate" and had as its clear basis violence (superior strength) rather than an aura of protectionism to engender loyalty consisting of more than mere obedience. In contrast, under patriarchal patrimonialism,

> the "good king," not the hero, was the ideal glorified by mass legend. Therefore patriarchal patrimonialism must legitimate itself as the guardian of the subjects' welfare in its own and in their eyes. The "welfare state" is the legend of patrimonialism, deriving not from the free

camaraderie of solemnly promised fealty but from the authoritarian relationship of father and children. The "father of the people" is the ideal of the patrimonial state.[30]

The "free camaraderie of solemnly promised fealty" is exactly the organizing principle of the men's houses. The "authoritarian relationship of father and children," on the other hand, derives from household relations. The latter is a more inclusive principle, as conducive to the organization and conduct of everyday life as it is to the occasions when that life must be protected from outside attack. Its basis of legitimacy, however, lies solely in the capacity for defense or protection by men against other men.

The household, Weber claims, was probably the earliest embodiment of the idea of "immortality." As older members of the household died out and new members were born or added through marriage, the joint economy of the household simply went on.[31] Such continuity, and the prospect for individual and collective immortality attendant upon it, were not available to the men's houses until and unless they were integrated into a community. Just as the polis was the necessary setting for the recognition of achievement by Greek political, athletic, and military heroes in Aristotle's account, the "territorial community," composed of "immortal households," was the necessary basis for continued memory of deeds by members of the warrior leagues.

The process of integrating warrior fraternities with patriarchal household authority raises a final and important point in this consideration of Weber's account of the origins of political action, authority, domination, and association. Weber's tendency to speak of politics as "domination" and of the state as the "legitimate monopoly of violence in society" often blurs the distinction between the *basis* of political authority and legitimacy on the one hand and the *exercise* of political domination on the other. But the distinction is there and it is a significant one. Both the basis of political authority and the exercise of political power are related to violence but they have distinct roots and characteristics. Political authority originates in household relations while political domination—power rooted in a monopoly of violence—has its origins in the marauding raids of the *Mannerhauser*. What Ortega y Gasset has termed the "sportive origins of the state" involved the sheer and decadent violence of men's groups who lived over and against the territorial basis of their existence.

In addition to constituting a founding moment of political association, men's leagues represent an archetype of manly political action insofar as (1) their activity bears no essential purpose other than that of their own achievement and glory, (2) their activities nonetheless impose a "political world of necessity" upon the territorial community they dominate and upon intergroup relations, and (3) from the perspective of those excluded from their ranks—the majority of the territorial population—their consociation is largely destructive and oppressive, *and* ultimately determinant of the structure of social life. By Weber's account, the men's leagues established the first principles of political consociation, exclusivity, equality, and freedom—all of these fundamentally and self-consciously linked with manhood. Put the other way around, the organized violence of groups wholly defined by and identified with manliness was the first form of political action and domination.

Yet these groups alone, precisely because they had no foundations in the communities they exploited, could never establish genuine political authority, with the legitimacy or belief system essential to such authority. Within the community, the origins of "legitimate domination" and the forms of political authority following from it could only issue from the father-household protectorate. This "protectorate" too had its essential basis in the capacity of the male household head to physically dominate his subjects and defend them from exogenous sources of violence or domination. This "defense" or "protection," of course, is purely necessitated by the omnipresence of male violence outside the household sphere. Thus, the "legitimacy" of the household patriarch is constituted by the assumed and accepted predatory nature of the male sex.

Both moments of political founding are sustained in Weber's depiction of modern politics and especially of the modern state. Both are also components of Weber's own political values. Indeed, with regard to the decades-old debate about whether Weber was essentially an imperialist-nationalist or a welfare-state liberal, this examination of what he understood as the dual foundations and purpose of political organization indicates that he was, in fact, both, and on an analytic level at least, this position was a coherent one. We turn now to a consideration of Weber's account of the specific dimensions and purposes of *modern* political formations.

II

Our aim . . . is so to create conditions, not that men may feel happier, but that under the necessity of the unavoidable struggle for existence the best in them—those physical and spiritual characteristics which we want to preserve for the nation—will remain protected.[32]

As the great theorist of "society" and social formations, indeed as the founder of bourgeois sociology, one would expect Weber to conceptualize politics in such a way as to lose all trace of autonomy from economy and social life. Instead, one learns from him that politics is "independent leadership in action"[33] and that the distinctly national purpose of the German state is in danger of becoming diluted or altogether subsumed by economic interests and a preoccupation with the "social question."[34] In his insistence upon the *autonomy* of politics, Weber resurrects an ancient tradition that is still less prominent today than it was in nationalistic and power-obsessed Prussianized Germany. Even in the context of his own milieu and epoch, however, Weber harbored more of a premodern conception of the nature of politics than most. At the same time, he formulated a specifically modern location for this understanding of politics: the imperial nation-state.

Hannah Arendt argued that "politics is never for the sake of life." In Aristotle's account, "mere life" is an instrument for the purposes of the "good life," political or contemplative life. For these theorists, genuine politics is independent of all activities related to the production and maintenance of life. In the study of Aristotle, we saw how this formulation of politics was linked to a fear of entrapment by nature and the body and also how it led to a conception and practice of manhood, freedom, and political action predicated upon repudiation and domination of individual bodies and the "body politic." In Machiavelli's thought too, political necessity as well as political achievement emerged as entirely distinct from human necessity. Similar themes can be found in Weber's work. They are more politically explicit yet much less overtly related to their origins in a formulation of manhood and politics specifically juxtaposed against woman, nature, the body and life itself. In Weber, we encounter the modern remnants of a tradition that has now forgotten its roots: a politics of purity and autonomy, a politics of "the extraordinary" which is antagonistic to and antagonized by "the everyday." Weber's devotion to an autonomous, noneconomic conception and practice of politics can be seen clearly in his evaluation of socialism, his formulation of national interest, and his discussion of the kind of man fit for political life.

Weber maintained a variety of objections to socialism and social democratic movements, some vehement and explicit, others discernible only in the shadows of his contrasting appreciation of capitalism and the figure of the entrepreneur. This is not the place to consider all dimensions of his views on public versus private ownership of the means of production.[35] Crucial is that "state ownership of production" is exactly the way Weber insisted upon formulating proposals for socialism, i.e., in purely economic terms. That there were other values and political claims at stake for many nineteenth-century socialists Weber certainly knew, both from controversies of his day and from his studies of Marxism. And that the transfer of production from private to state control was not the final end of even scientific socialism he must have also known, yet he insisted upon casting "the socialist program" in exactly these unlovely clothes.[36] Consequently, when Weber compared the merits of a private enterprise system ("anarchy of production") to socialism ("bureaucratic state-planned production"), he concluded easily in favor of the former. Capitalism offered greater economic productivity (hence greater national resources and power), greater political freedom and cultural vigor and above all, the possibility of keeping the state and political realm at least marginally independent of the economic realm.

> If private capitalism were abolished, the state bureaucracy would rule *alone.* Where now the bureaucracies of government and private industry can at least in principle counterbalance each other and hold the other in check, they would then be forged together into a single hierarchy.[37]

Prophetic as this evaluation of "state socialism" is, the question remains as to why the socialism Weber chose to analyze was its least defensible version. Weber's fear of increased bureaucratization through nationalization of industry was sincere and insightful, but why did he refuse to consider less authoritarian and more political accounts of socialism? Weber's understanding of politics was so thoroughly permeated by its power purposes that he simply could not fathom the heart of the socialist claim—that the ruled and the rulers shall be one, that the polity, economy, and society shall be united as a working community. He could not envision a stateless polity or a politics genuinely concerned with matters of collective well-being rather than with external exploits and internal domination. Or, to the extent that he could entertain these possibilities, he found them utterly unappealing. For Weber, the value of politics lay neither in addressing collective needs nor working out collective ideals. The state had a potential power and purpose far greater and more worthy than those of economic and social matters. For Weber, the modern *raison d'état* was the prestige and glory of the nation-sate itself.

In Weber's formulation of the "national interest," Aristotelian and Machiavellian concerns with the autonomy and purity of politics *vis à vis* "lower aspects" of human existence again chime loudly. In his Freiburg Inaugural Address of 1895, Weber argued for the subordination of immediate and sectarian economic interests to the long-term power-political ambitions of the German state. Nowhere does Weber display such acute awareness of the class basis of society and the class conflict to which it gives rise, yet he insists that politics must be lifted above such battles:

The nub of the social and political porblem is not the economic situation of the ruled, but rather the political qualifications of the *ruling* classes and those classes which are *rising* to power. The aim of our social and political work is not universal charity but the *social unification* of that nation which modern economic development has created in preparation for the difficult struggles of the future.[38]

In Weber's view, the battles for power between economic classes threatened to demote the power interests of the nation below material concerns. While he was striving to purge national politics of class interests, Weber took the opportunity to indict what he considered other pollutants of genuine political life:

The economic development of transitional periods threatens the natural political instincts with atrophy; it would be unfortunate if even economic science were to lead to the same result, by cultivating a feeble *eudaimonism* . . . behind the illusion of *independent socio-political' ideals.*[39]

And as "eudaimonism" and "social-political ideals" have no place in the guiding interests of the state, neither, Weber insisted, does "human ethics" belong among state concerns:

Other obstacles to the political education of the nation include that soft-headed attitude, so agreeable and even admirable from the human point of view, but nevertheless so unutterably philistine, which thinks it possible to replace political with "ethical" ideals[40]

Politics must wrest free of all of these claims and illusions, Weber declared, lest politics disappear altogether—if not in the grinding machine of bureaucratic officialdom, then in the stagnant broth of class squabbles, welfare concerns, and humanitarian ideals. At this point, yet another feature of Weber's distaste for socialism is made evident: the business of the state and of politics in general should not be the pedestrian business of running the economy. Moreover, the fact that production under capitalism is "anarchic" and competitive means that in scrapping for survival, the entrepreneurial class produces dynamism and prosperity for the nation. Not the gentility but the *agonism* of the bourgeoisie serves the power interests of the state even while the economy remains subordinate to the state.

It was with good reason that the *Communist Manifesto* emphasized the economically revolutionary character of the bourgeois capitalist entrepreneurs. No trade union, much less a state-socialist official, can perform this role for us in their place.[41]

In short, for Weber, the economy and polity are and must remain distinct from one another. The concerns of politics are other than those of life and livelihood and are imperiled should these matters occupy the attention of the state on any level other than which is relevant to the *power* of the state. Economic life has it political aspect, but that lies only in its capacity to empower the state. From the perspective of the state, the economy is an intrument, not an end. Mere life exists for the sake of the good life, power politics.

The third example of Weber's concern with the autonomous nature of political life can be found in his characterization of the ideal politican. Weber's famous plea for men who will live "for" rather than "off" of politics is accompanied by a twofold explanation. First, a man who truly lives "for" politics will make politics, and not simply pursuit of private interests, "his life, in an internal sense."[42] Secondly, a man who is of sufficient financial means to be indifferent to whatever remuneration he obtains from political office will think and act independently.[43]

Now Weber admits that fulfillment of the requirement that a politician be both "economically independent of the income politics can bring him" and "economically dispensable," i.e., the "recipient of completely unearned income," would necessarily result in political plutocracy—government by rentiers and wealthy lawyers.[44] And he further admits that despite their independence from a political income, even these men would inevitably live "off" politics in the sense that they would formulate policies tending to advance their class interests.[45] He admits as well that this would result in a certain degree of socially conservative policy: "a care for the economic 'security' of his existence is consciously or unconsciously a cardinal point in the whole life of a wealthy man."[46] Despite these problems, Weber looks to the wealthy strata as the source of true politicans because he wants those who have an instinct for power and who are reasonably unsusceptible to being bribed or fettered by the plethora of economic interest groups plaguing the halls of policymaking. He settles upon the upper echelon as a compromise: they care too much about money but are not dependent upon politics for it; in power instincts they are exceeded by the entrepreneurial class but the latter is not "economically dispensable;" they may make some policy with their own interests at heart but the prosperity of this class is usually in keeping with the general prosperity of the nation. In sum, this is the class most likely to circumvent both class interests and petty career interests in formulating policies of national interest. In contrast, Weber speaks this way of the political potential of the working class:

> The propertyless masses, engaged as they are in the harsh struggle for their daily existence, are much more predisposed to all *emotional* motives in politics, to impulsiveness and momentary impressions of a sensational character, as compared with the "cooler head" of the propertied man, who is freed from those cares.[47]

Weber's dread of politics being infested by the emotionalism and immediacy arising from the "harsh struggles of daily existence" is resonant of Aristotle's justification for excluding the majority of the population from political citizenship and suggests again an opposition between need and feeling on the one hand and freedom and rationality on the other. For the proper approach to politics, one must have both leisure and a sufficient distance from the contaminating activity of survival. Like Aristotle, Weber insists that the political man must have a sufficient stake (property) in the polity to establish a strong personal commitment but must not be so bound up with survival that his political concerns have too particularistic and immediate a character.[48] Yet in calling for a politically ruling stratum that is as free as possible of corrupting economic interests[49] and whose positive qualification consists of having a strong power instinct, Weber is striving for a political *aesthetic* of power, prestige, national glory, and heroic leadership. This aesthetic exists in contrast to a practice of politics that would have as its guiding purpose any sort of "common good"—ethical, social, cultural, or economic. For Weber, as for Arendt, Aristotle, and Machiavelli, politics occupies a rarified and precious space, where common concerns are unwelcome and common men are unsuitable. We pose to Weber, then, the same question posed to Aristotle after surveying all that was excluded from and threating to the polis: if it is not about life, collective well-being, justice or participation, what is politics about and why is it one of the highest and noblest endeavors to which a man can be "called"?

III

Politics, Weber states in his scientific writings, can be conceptually circumscribed only in terms of the *means* utilized for political association and domination. It is precisely "owing to the drastic nature of its means of control that the political association is particularly capable of arrogating to itself all the possible values towards which associational conduct might be oriented."[50] Weber continues:

> It is not possible to define a political organization, including the state, in terms of the ends to which its action is devoted. . . . There is no conceivable end which some political association has not at some time pursued . . . and . . . there is none which all have recognized. *Thus it is possible to define the "political" character of an association only in terms of the means peculiar to it, the use of force.* This means is, however, in the above sense specific, and it is indispensable to its character. It is even, under certain circumstances, elevated into an end in itself.[51]

What makes an association political is the use of force. Although Weber does not say that political ends are irrelevant, only that they cannot be codified, when he outlines the essential *conditions* for the existence of an autonomous political community, violence again has a definitive role.[52] And when he leaves altogether the terminology of means, ends, and conditions in order to strike at the *nature* of political association, there is no ambiguity whatsoever:

> The political community, even more than other institutionally organized communities, is so constituted that it imposes obligations on the individual members which many of them fulfill only because they are aware of the probability of physical coercion backing up such obligations. The political community, furthermore, is one of those communities whose action includes . . . coercion through jeopardy and destruction of life and freedom of movement applying to outsiders as well as to the members themselves. The individual is expected ultimately to face death in the group interest. This gives to the political community its particular pathos and raises its enduring emotional foundations.[53]

Born in domination through violence, the political association is also sustained this way and derives its essential nature from the threat of violence. A continuous line can be drawn from Weber's account of (1) the origins of political action and association in warrior leagues and patriarchal households through (2) the stipulations Weber establishes for the autonomous nature of politics and the men suited to it, to (3) the defining characteristics of a polity. "'Political community' applies to a community whose social action is aimed at subordination to orderly domination by the participants of a territory and the conduct of persons within it, through readiness to resort to physical force, including normally force of arms."[53]

The degree of autonomy Weber ascribes to politics and the violence characterizing it makes still more perplexing the question of what politics is ultimately for. What does political domination supply to its subject community other than power over it and the discipline of obedience within it? Weber says only this:

> Domination in the most general sense is one of the most important elements of social action. . . . In a great number of cases the emergence of rational association from amorphous social action has been due to domination and the way in which it has been exercised. Even where this is not the case, the structure of dominancy and its unfolding is decisive in determining the form of social action and its orientation toward a goal.[55]

In other words, political domination imbues purpose or aim, structure or rationality, to otherwise aimless, formless associations. Of course, what the colonizers view as "amorphous social action," the colonized may understand as their purposeful, traditional existence. Just as in Machiavelli's formulation, that which is "matter" to the prince who stamps it with his own "form" is formed existence to those who are stomped. There are also resonances of Greek political thinking here: in order to supply a higher purpose, a goal or *telos* to a people's pursuits, political domination is essential. The *polis*, Aristotle insisted, gives purpose and value to its "conditions," the lives and work of those excluded from political life.

If Weber does not convincingly relate the purposes of political domination to the needs or ends of the dominated, and more generally, does not answer the question of why political power is a good, we may still grasp why he found political domination of this sort so absolutely and everywhere inevitable. Although he never puts it in precisely these terms, Weber appears to locate the cause or engine of politics in a human "will to power." Politics is about struggle, he insists, not struggle over scarce material resources as economics is, but struggle for power in something very close to a Nietszchean sense.[56] "The struggle for personal power is the life blood of a politician.[57] As long as this will to power flourishes—and Weber surely cared for this as much as anything, that is would not be extinguished by bureaucratic rationalization—political life will be synonymous with political domination.

There is a second Nietzschean element in Weber's view of the inevitability of political domination and this pertains to his conception of "the mass."[58] We have already seen that Weber feared the "emotionalism" and immediacy of interest in the masses' political mentality.[59] "The political danger of mass democracy . . . lies first of all in the possibility that emotional elements will predominate in politics. The 'mass' as such (irrespective of the social strata which it comprises) thinks only in short-run terms.[60] Weber's terminology of "the mass" as opposed to prevailing socialist references to "the masses" is revealing. For Weber, the great body of society was just that, an undifferentiated collective with as little capacity for action, let alone great deeds, as any other large, undifferentiated organism.

> The *demos* itself, in the sense of a shapeless mass, never "governs" larger associations, but rather is governed. What changes [with democratization] is only the way in which the executive leaders are selected and the measure of influence which the *demos*, or better, which social circles from its midst are able to exert . . . by means of "public opinion.[61]

When Weber is not describing "the mass" as overwrought and cumbersome, he speaks of it as politically passive.[62] In both cases, one detects an essentially Machiavellian view of the body politic: the masses must not be ignored and they can be rallied around particular programs or leaders. They are potential "material" or instruments of state power or of an individual's aspirations to power. That is the extent of the "body politic's" relevance to politics.

Weber's devotion to an elite formation of political power is not limited to challenges against mass democracy. He scoffs as well at those who advocate diffused or shared political power.[63] "It is impossible for the internal or foreign policy of great states to be strongly and consistently carried out on a collegial basis. . . . Even the 'dictatorship of the proletariat' requires an individual dictator with the confidence of the masses.[64] For Weber, the essence of politics is power for purposes of organized domination. Such power can be consolidated and exercised only in the hands of a single leader whose "life blood" is the struggle for personal power.

But how do those who wield power acquire the legitimacy necessary to maintain power? Due to his reputation as the great theorist of legitimacy, little attention is usually given to the minimal relationship Weber claims actually exists between legitimacy and the power it supports. For Weber, legitimacy is a social and subjective phenomena—the only real bearing it has on the formation of power is its effect on what Weber terms the "empirical structure of domination.[65] As Roth and Wittich put the matter,

> Only after defining domination in terms of rule by a master and his apparatus does Weber add the ultimate grounds for its validity. He turns to legitimacy because of its inherent historical importance—the need of those who have power, wealth and honor to justify their good fortune.[66]

For Weber, legitimacy is about gaining loyalty, compliance, or obedience; it is about making a structure of domination appear "right," but it bears no relation to its actually being so. Legitimacy is instrumentally necessary to the powerful and is cherished at the level of values only by the powerless. Legitimacy figured so largely in Weber's sociological studies only because it had figured so largely in actual social history. It matters politically because, like the masses in general, it is something to which the powerful must always attend if they are to move as they would like.

Thus far, we have seen that Weber's formulation of politics is rooted in autonomy from economic and social life and in a complete preoccupation with power. This conception of politics distances it from any substantive concern with the just ordering or well-being of the political body. Anything that threatens to dilute or corrode the autonomy and power purposes of politics—whether it be socialism or simply social policy—Weber rails against. The preconditions for involvement with political life are a position near the top of the socioeconomic order and an overwhelming care for power. The essence and pathos of politics is violence, and of the political community, willingness to die for the state. The body politic is incapable of being properly political and is at best an instrument or means for the politician, a man whose ultimate concerns must be with his own power and the prestige of the state. Thus, the origins of politics in the autonomous organization and violent purposes of the *Mannerhauser* and in the organized domination of the household patriarch permeate modern political domination and association. Even rational-legal legitimacy is a modern gloss on inveterate pratices of naked domination.

Against this backdrop, one may well reconsider the meaning of Weber's insistence that the true politician, one who lives "for" rather than "off" politics, lives for "the consciousness that his life has *meaning* in the service of a "cause."[65] With Machiavelli, Weber presents politics as embodying the greatest potential for individual glory—this, despite the fact that in politics one cannot uphold Christian ethics or "the ethics of absolute ends." Well, then, what is this nonmaterial, nonnecessary, nonethical, nonsocial, yet uplifting and glorious cause? As with Aristotle and Machiavelli, does our inital encounter with Weber's thought not suggest that this rarified sphere to which only a few and very uncommon men are genuinely called ultimately has a hollow, contrived, or purely aesthetic nature? Are manhood and politics once again searching for a space occupied by no other so that they might assert their distinctiveness and importance above and beyond all "merely human" things? For answers to these queries, we turn now to Weber's analysis of the specifically modern realm of politics, the state.

IV

In one of his methodological essays, Weber argues:

> It is possible to defend quite meaningfully the view that the power of the state should be increased in order to eliminate obstacles, while maintaining that the state itself has no *intrinsic* value, that it is purely a technical instrument for the realization of other values from which it alone derives its value, and that it can retain this value only as long as it does not seek to transcend this merely auxilliary status.[66]

Weber makes these remarks in the context of seeking to distinguish between ascribing values to things and discerning "objective" value within them. Characteristically, he chooses as an example a subject that is most perplexing for his own work and politics. For while Weber does not mind emphasizing the status of the state as a "technical instrument," to actually refuse it any additional value is anathema to his own political concerns. If this were not obvious from his 1909 speech in which he expresses his belief in the power-position of the state as the "ultimate definitve value," it becomes quite evident from the textual situation of the confession cited above regarding the state's lack of intrinsic value. Just prior to this declaration, Weber has presented all the attributes of the state that would lead one to devote oneself to it as a secular diety:

> Of all the various associations, [the state] alone is accorded legitimate power over life, death and liberty. Its agencies use these powers against external enemies in wartime, and against internal resistance in both war and peace. In peacetime it is the greatest entrepreneur in economic life and the most powerful collector of tributes from the citizenry; and in time of war, it disposes of unlimited power over all available economic goods. Its modern rationalized form of organization has made achievements possible in many spheres which could not have been approximated by any other sort of social organization. It is almost inevitable that people should conclude that it represents the "ultimate" value—especially in the political sphere—and that all social actions should be evaluated in terms of their relations to its interests.[69]

The popular view that "all social actions should be evaluated in terms of their relation to the state's interests," of course, is exactly what Weber himself concluded and frequently urged upon others.[70] Yet if we take seriously Weber's admission that this ultimate value is assigned to a thing that has no intrinsic value, is only a means, and loses even its value as a technical instrument when it transcends its status as an instrument, we must look more closely at why Weber valued the state so highly.

We may approach this problem by considering Weber's formulation of the relationship between "nation" and "state." Separate entities for Weber, they also had separate, albeit interdependent, purposes. Although Weber found the concept of nation difficult to circumscribe, he settled upon "group prestige," "group honor," and the embodiment of "culture" as the essentials of a nation. "The significance of the "nation" is usually anchored in the superiority, or at least the irreplaceability, of the culture values that are to be preserved and developed only through the cultivation of the peculiarity of the group.[71] Thus, continues Weber, leaders of culture—the intellectuals—will necessarily invoke and propagate the "national idea" while those in political power promote the "idea of the state."[72]

What is the relation between nation and state? "Time and again we find that the concept "nation" directs us to political power."[73] Only because the Hungarians, Czechs, and Greeks strove for political power, i.e., sought to exist as nation-states, did they achieve cohesiveness as nations, Weber argues. Prior to this aspiration toward statehood, these entities were not nations but mere "language groups."[74] Thus the nation, although conceptually independent of the state, is completely bound to it genealogically. "The more power is emphasized, the closer seems to be the link between nation and state."[75] Recall that Weber views political domination as providing otherwise "amorphous social action" with a "goal." Consider now Weber's argument that until language groups, races, or tribes aspire to organized prestigious political power, they are not nations and they also lack any *raison d'être*.[76] The Africans, for example, who in Weber's words were "cultureless" (*kulturlos*), could be colonized legitimately while nation-states such as Poland deserved support for their strivings toward cultural and political autonomy.[77] The value as well as the "goal" of a people are established only through aspirations to organized domination in the form of a state.

What makes the state unique and autonomous is its total involvement with power and its occupation by power-seekers. The nation, from the perspective of the powerful, embodies everything else, i.e., those activities and persons at best indirectly concerned with power. Yet nation and state are mutually dependent: the state protects and advances the "prestige" of culture within the nation and the nation is the essential foundation for all the state's exploits.[78] Without national solidarity, the state cannot move. Again, it is possible to perceive quite clearly the instrumental relation the state bears toward the nation. Even if the protection and enhancement of the nation "justifies" or legitimizes state pursuits, this justification does not constitute the purposes of those wielding state power. As Weber says quite explicitly, the commitment of those in politics is to the idea of the state, not to the nation or the "culture" although they may have strong feelings of loyalty in these domains. The point is that as politicians, they are men concerned with the pursuit of power, for themselves and for the state. Just as Weber drew a firm line between politicians and intellectuals, he insisted upon a distinction between issues of *staatspolitsch* and national or *kulturpolitisch* issues. And he left no doubt as to which was primary:

> *Staatsraison:* With this slogan we want to raise the demand that in questions of German economic policy, even for example, the question of whether and to what extent, the state should intervene in economic life. . . . The last and decisive vote should go to the economic and political power interests of our nation and of their bearer, the German national state.[79]

For all his certainty that the power interests of the German state are of foremost concern in politics, Weber still has not clarified the ultimate point of state power. Why is the state worth valuing so highly? Weber never answers this question in substantive, noninstrumental terms. In *Economy and Society,* he notes that "the striving for prestige pertains to all . . . political structures[80] and in his political essays, the prestige and honor of the German state are heavily featured.[81] Weber also admits that the "prestige of power means in practice the glory of power over other communities, it means the *expansion* of power.[82] Thus, pursuit of the prestige of power is a major cause of war—"power-prestige always challenges and calls forth the competition of all other bearers of prestige."[83]

Once again we greet Aristotle's and Arendt's strutting young men in restless pursuit of honor, fame, and superiority. This time, however, it is nation-states rather than individual Greek heroes or cities who are seeking their share of glory and immortality through conflict and competition. The genuine value of state power is not established by Weber in terms of collective survival, prosperity, freedom or justice, but only in terms of prestige and glory. And the enormous cost of rendering this entity that has no intrinsic value as the ultimate value is one Weber himself squarely confronted. The specifically modern form of organized domination—rational-legal bureaucratic domination—Weber grasped as the deathnell of nearly all that is worth cherishing in human existence. Why he remained beholden to this institutionalized expression of manhood as domination when he perceived its danger and damage so keenly is what we shall explore in the next chapter.

Notes

1. See Arthur Mitzman, *The Iron Cage: An Historical Interpretation of Max Weber* (New York: Knopf, 1970); Marianne Weber, *Max Weber: A Biography*, trans. H. Zohn (New York: Wiley, 1975); and Martin Green, *The Von Richtofen Sisters* (New York: Basic Books, 1974).

2. Weber's general view of Freud may be glimpsed in Marianne Weber's *Biography*, pp. 372–80. His objections to its claims as a science and worldview are contained in a letter to Edgar Jaffe, *Selections in Translation*, ed. W. G. Runciman (Cambridge: Cambridge University Press, 1977), pp. 383–88.

3. Letter to Marianne Weber on the occasion of their engagement, cited in Mitzman, *The Iron Cage*, p. 93.

4. Letter to Emmy Baumgartner, cited in Mitzman, p. 59.

5. Karl Jaspers, *Three Essays: Leonardo, Descartes, Max Weber*, trans. Manheim (New York: Scribners, 1953), p. 194.

6. *Economy and Society*, eds. G. Roth and C. Wittich. (Berkeley: University of California Press, 1978), hereafter cited as *ES*. Volume II, III–1, p. 359.

7. Ibid. pp. 358, 359.

8. Ibid. p. 357.

9. Ibid.

10. Ibid.

11. Ibid.

12. Ibid.

13. *ES* (II) IX–2, 904–10.

14. Ibid. p. 905.

15. Ibid.

16. Ibid. p. 906.

17. *Love's Body*, p. 13; N.O. Brown takes his inspiration from Jose Ortega y Gasset's "The Sportive Origins of the State:" "It was not the worker, the intellectual, the priest . . . or the businessman who started the great political process but youth, preoccupied with women and resolved to fight—the lover, the warrior, the athlete." *History as a System*, p. 32. See pp. 26–32 for Ortega y Gasset's tale of the origins of men's leagues.

18. " 'Warriors, all equal' is fraternal organization." N.O. Brown, *Love's Body*, p. 12.

19. *ES* (II) IX–2, p. 906.

20. Ibid.

21. Ibid. p. 907.

22. *ES* (II) III–1, p. 359.

23. Ibid. p. 359.

24. Ibid. p. 359.

25. *ES* (II) IX–2, p. 906.

26. *ES* (II) XII–1, p. 1007.

27. Ibid. pp. 906–907.

28. The term Machiavelli used to identify this problem was "foundations." See chapter 6, p. 107.

29. *ES* (II) XI–2, p. 908.

30. *ES* (II) XIII–14, p. 1107.

31. *ES* (II) III–1, p. 359.

32. *Verhandlungen des 5. Evangelisch-sozialen Kongresses* (1894) pp. 80–81, cited in David Beetham, *Max Weber and the Theory of Modern Politics* (London: Allen and Unwin, 1974), p. 42.

33. "Politics as a Vocation," in *From Max Weber: Essays in Sociology*, eds. H. Gerth and C. Wright Mills (New York: Oxford University Press, 1946), hereafter cited as "Politics as a Vocation." p. 77

34. "Freiburg Inaugural Address," *Selections in Translation* ed. Runciman, p. 267.

35. Weber's technical or "scientific" refutation of socialism is contained in a fragment entitled "Socialism" (*Selections in Translation*, pp. 251–62. Most of his other analyses of socialism are untranslated, but a rather comprehensive discussion of them is offered by Beetham, *Max Weber and the Theory of Modern Politics*, pp. 82–89.

36. "In positive terms, what would socialism, as opposed to the present system amount to? In the widest sense of the word, what is usually referred to as a "collective economy." That is, first of all, an economy without profit, without the direction of production by private entrepreneurs on their own account and at their own risk. Instead, the economy would be in the hands of the officials of a public corporation. . . . Secondly, and in consequence, an end to the so-called anarchy of production, that is to competition between entrepeneurs." *Selections in Translation*, p. 253.

37. Cited in Beetham, *Max Weber and the Theory of Modern Politics*, p. 83.

38. "Freiburg Inaugural Address," p. 267.

39. Ibid.

40. Ibid.

41. Cited in Beetham, *Max Weber and the Theory of Modern Politics*, p. 83.

42. "Politics as a Vocation, p. 84.

43. Ibid. p. 106.

44. Ibid. pp. 85, 86.

45. Ibid. p. 86.

46. Ibid.

47. Cited in Beetham, *Max Weber and the Theory of Modern Politics*, p. 244.

48. In Weber's view, the quality of petty bourgeois life, too, was such that members of that class were unfit for national politics. Weber described the German petty bourgeois mentality in politics as "the absence of great national power instincts, the restriction of political goals to material ends or at least to the interests of their own generation, the lack of any sense of responsibility towards the future." Cited in Beetham, p. 145.

49. Elsewhere Weber refers to this strata as "persons who are economically independent of those above and below them." Appendix II, *ES*, p. 1447.

50. *ES* (II) IX–1, p. 902.

51. *ES* (I) I–17, p. 55, emphasis added. Weber repeats this formulation in "Politics as a Vocation," p. 77.

52. *ES* (II) IX–1, p. 902.

53. Ibid. p. 903.

54. Ibid. p. 901.

55. *ES* (II) X–1, p. 941.

56. Two interpreters who have cast explicit parallels between Nietzsche's "will to power" and Weber's formulation of a "power instinct" are Eugene Fleischman, "De Weber à Nietzsche" *Archives Europeenes de Sociologies*, vol. 5 (1964), pp. 190–238; and Raymond Aron, "Max Weber and Power Politics," *Max Weber and Sociology Today*, ed. O. Stammer (Oxford: Blackwell, 1971) pp. 83–100.

57. Cited in Beetham, *Max Weber and the Theory of Modern Politics* p. 76.

58. However little regard Weber held for the social and cultural, let alone political, potential of the masses, he did not share Nietzsche's view of them as "sheep," nor the Nietzschean conclusion that a great leader bore no responsibility toward them. The masses were contemptible perhaps, but this did not mean they were utterly without ethical and social claims upon the nation. See Wolfgang Mommsen, "Max Weber's Sociology and his Philosophy of World History," *Max Weber*, ed. D. Wrong (Englewood Cliffs, N.J.: Prentice-Hall, 1970), pp. 184–85.

59. When Weber spoke of "the masses," he was not referring exclusively to impoverished or propertyless groups. For him it was a cultural concept rather than one determined by class characteristics.

60. "Parliamentary Government and Democratization," p. 1459.

61. *ES* XI–8, p. 985.

62. "Parliamentary Government and Democratization," p. 1457.

63. Ibid. p. 1414.

64. *ES* (I) III–viii–15, p. 278.

65. *ES* (II) X–3, p. 953.

66. Roth and Wittich, "Introduction" *ES*, p. xc.

67. "Politics as a Vocation," p. 84.

68. The Meaning of Ethical Neutrality," *The Methodology of the Social Sciences*, trans. E. Shils and H. Finch (New York: Free Press, 1940), p. 47, Hereafter cited as *MSS*.

69. Ibid. p. 46.

70. "Freiburg Inaugural Address" and "Socialism," *Selections in Translation*.

71. *ES* (II) IX–5, p. 925.

72. Ibid. p. 926.

73. *ES* (II) V–4, pp. 397–98.

74. Ibid. p. 398. Consider the parallel in Athenian references to non-Greeks as "barbarians" *because* they did not have a polis form of political organization.

75. Ibid. p. 398.

76. "Only fifteen years ago, men knowing the Far East still denied that the Chinese qualified as a "nation;" they held them only to be a 'race.' Yet today . . . the same observers would judge very differently." *ES* (II) IX–5, p. 924.

77. Cited in Beetham, *Max Weber and the Theory of Modern Politics* p. 28.

78. "Cultural prestige and power-prestige are closely associated." *ES* (II) IX–5, p. 926.

79. Cited in Mitzman, *The Iron Cage*, p. 82.

80. *ES* (II) IX–3, p. 911.

81. *Selections in Translation*, p. 266, 268; Beetham, *Max Weber and the Theory of Modern Politics*, p. 39.

82. *ES* (II) IX–3, p. 911.

83. Ibid. pp. 910, 911.

8

Weber:
Political Rationality
and Political Institutions

O NE OF WEBER'S MOST INCISIVE DISCOVERIES about the modern state is that its enormous power is rooted in its structured alienation:

> Sociologically speaking, the state is an "enterprise" (*Betrieb*) just like a factory. This is exactly its historical peculiarity. Here as there the authority relations have the same roots . . . This all important fact: the "separation" of the worker from the material means of production, destruction, administration, academic research and finance in general is the common basis of the modern state in its political, cultural and military spheres, and of the private capitalist economy.[1]

An understanding of why Weber views the consolidation of institutional power as dependent upon alienation and of his ambivalent evaluation of this phenomenon requires an exploration of his formulation of instrumental rationality and "rationalization" in the modern world. Ultimately, I shall argue that by Weber's own account, the cultivation of instrumental rationality and its development into rationalization in the contemporary age is located in specifically "masculine" drives. Before doing so, I will indicate how what we have seen as an historically persistent ethos of manhood can be discovered at the root of Weber's construction of the relationship between rationality and rationalization. While instrumentally-rational action is itself "gender-neutral," Weber's analysis of modern political and economic institutions reveal instrumental rationality to have been harnessed to specific projects of manhood first discerned in Aristotle, Machiavelli, and aspects of Weber already discussed. These projects include a quest for freedom defined as liberation from constraint and for power defined as domination. When these things are driving the

152

use of instrumental rationality, rationalization on a massive scale is the consequence.

When instrumentally-rational action is bound to what has been identified as specifically masculine formulations of power and freedom, a dynamic of alienation arises that culminates in the domination of men by the very institutions designed to liberate and empower them. The alienation inheres in the peculiar means-ends relationship of instrumentally-rational action. The domination inheres in the institutionalization of the separation of means from ends and the subsequent subversion (rationalization) of ends. The specific institutions analyzed by Weber in this way are those of the capitalist economy and the bureaucratic state.

In short, while Weber saw rationalization and its attendant forms of domination and alienation as inevitable outcomes of the "disenchantment of the world" and the rise of instrumental rationality, I shall suggest that this "inevitable" development is actually rooted in constructions of power and freedom specific to Western manhood.

I

Weber distinguishes rational action from affectual and traditional action, and further divides rational action into two types: value-rational and instrumentally-rational.[2] Value-rational action is shaped by constant commitment to some value whereas instrumentally-rational action involves singleminded pursuit of a selected end such that all objects, issues, or values separating the actor from the end are mere tools or obstacles to the end. Instrumental action may serve value-rational action as a means but only in a limited way. However, instrumentally-rational techniques may be used to divine both ends and means.[3]

According to Weber, instrumental rationality produces the greatest efficiency of means to ends and thus also yields maximum *power* to achieve ends. Instrumentally-rational action is also "more free" than any other kind of action, since it is "based more extensively upon the actor's own "deliberations," which are upset neither by "external" constraints nor by irresistible "affect.'"[4] Instrumentally-rational action is also "free" in the sense of being liberated from custom, religion, tradition and morality. "With its clarity of self-consciousness and freedom from subjective scruples, instrumental rationality is the polar antithesis of every sort of unthinking acquiescence in customary ways as well as of devotion to norms consciously accepted as values."[5]

While Weber never sets out a full positive formulation of freedom, clearly he perceived the historical move toward embracing rationality (the rise of science, the death of God) as strongly linked to a quest for freedom. Karl Loewith casts the link between Weber's conception of rationality and freedom this way:

> To act as a free person . . . means to act purposefully . . . and to that extent to act logically or "consequently." The freedom of human action is evidenced concommitantly with rationality in the measuring and evaluation of the prospects and consequences inherent in the means available to a rational goal-oriented conduct. The more freely man considers and evaluates the necessary means to something (an end), the more he acts in terms of rational goal-oriented conduct, and therefore, acts all the more intelligibly.[6]

This is not to suggest that Weber's conception of freedom was limited to the pursuit of instrumentally-rational action. It is only to say that Weber posits a connection between this kind of rationality and freedom, and treated this feature of instrumental rationality as both the source of its appeal and its power to predominate in the modern world. Instrumental rationality provides the clearest path to any goal, entails use or domination of all objects in the path to the goal, and is the greatest liberator from nature, habit, religion, and tradition. The freedom of instrumentally-rational action is thus a freedom from external constraints for the power to achieve particular ends.

Even as Weber is merely defining rationality, he begins to introduce the notion of "rationalization." Rationalization of action, he says

> can proceed in a variety of directions; positively in that of a deliberate formulation of ultimate values; or negatively, at the expense not only of custom, but of emotional values; and finally, in favor of a morally sceptical type of rationality at the expense of any belief in absolute values.[7]

It is of course, the last possibility that Weber believes has come to prevail in the modern world and that threatens all activities and finally humankind itself with utter meaninglessness. Before this point is even reached, however, Weber suggests that instrumental rationality may cause ends to be overwhelmed or subverted by instrumental means. As moral scepticism increases, it simultaneously opens the way for the increased use of instrumentally-rational action and reduces the possibility of keeping such action in the subordinate position of means to value-rational goals.

> As that which was originally merely a means (to an otherwise valuable end) becomes an end or end-in-itself, actions intended as a means become independent rather than goal-oriented and precisely thereby lose their original "meaning" or end, i.e., their goal-ended rationality based on man and his needs.[8]

The reversal of the means-ends relationship and the disappearance of ends altogether are both aspects of the world-wide "rationalization" process leading Weber to find modern man trapped in an "iron cage." But the general prevalence of instrumental rationality and its effects upon ends is not by itself the source or cause of modern man's entrapment. To the *forms* of rationalization Weber depicts, specific content is also given. The two modern "systems" Weber identifies as both cause and effect of the rationalization of the modern world are capitalism and the bureaucratic state.

Capitalism as a mode of economic and social organization entails rationalization on two inter-related levels: first, in separating the producer from the means of production and second, in separating the productive means from the productive ends.[9] Capitalism is efficient— *the* most efficient mode of production in Weber's view—precisely because of these separations. The rational activity of maximizing profit required rationalizing the means to profit. This could be accomplished only by eliminating workers' control over the means of production. The factory, machinery or other means of production are organized rationally and the workers are then applied (as part of the means) in such a way that the machinery dominates them. The workers' labor too is thus rationalized since workers are reduced to a means (labor-power) and their labor is organized by the machinery upon which they work.[10]

As workers are separated from the means of production and themselves become means of production, so then do the ends and means of production come to be separated within society as two distinct classes of society. Capitalist rationalization on a *technical* level involved rationalizing the mode of production and separating the workers from their means of sustenance. Capitalist rationalization on a *social* level ensued from this rationalization of profit-seeking by turning the masses into means for profit-maximization. As means, the masses are forced to engage in purely instrumentally-rational action to survive because (1) they are deprived of all independent means to their own survival via "expropriation" and (2) the end for which they are the means is embodied in an altogether distinct class.

According to Weber, the original end for the entreprenuer was not wealth for its own sake but fulfillment of a calling in the service of God.[11] However, precisely because of the separation of means and ends entailed in capitalist rationalization of production, the ends of capitalism were themselves rationalized; the stipulations of profit-maximization ordered and constricted the capitalist realm of exchange with a set of inviolable, albeit implicit rules. Thus, the value of the entrepreneur's "calling" was supplanted by the requisites of survival in the world of free enterprise. No longer individuals but the system itself determined the ends and means of economic livelihood. As the original ends disappeared, the rationalized structure of production and exchange required involvement with capitalism by all, but now as servants rather than agents of the system. An organization of production designed to dominate *life conditions* thus becomes an organization that dominates *life itself*.

The capacity of capitalism to organize social life "automatically" led Weber, like Marx before him, to admire as well as deplore capitalism. But unlike Marx, for Weber the admiration won out and he sought to harness that system whose ends had been subsumed by its logic of means to a new end: the power of the national state. If capitalism could not be made to serve its own or individual ends, its dehumanizing, rationalized power could be made to serve that "ultimate value," state power. Thus Weber adds yet another layer of separated means and ends to those already entailed in capitalism: the nation as a whole, its involvement with and domination by the capitalist mode of production, becomes a means or instrument of state power. Before examining the implications of this for the problem of freedom and domination in the modern world, we need to see how the process of rationalization works in the other "system" Weber analyzes—bureaucratic state institutions.

The modern state entails the complete separation of state officials from the means of administration. In Weber's view, this is the essence of the concept of the state, its "historical peculiarity," and the basis of its extraordinary power.[12] Bureaucracy is the tool and concrete expression of this separation:

> The purely bureaucratic type of administrative organization . . . is, from a purely technical point of view, capable of attaining the highest degree of efficiency and is in this sense formally the most rational known means of exercising authority over human beings. It is superior to any other form in precision, in stability, in the stringency of its discipline, and in its reliability. It thus makes possible a particularly high degree of calculability of results.[13]

As with the separations entailed in the capitalist mode of production, separation of the bureaucrat from the means of administration (from actual state power) is the most rational, efficient, precise, stable, reliable, and hence most powerful form of organization. "Where administration has been completely bureaucratized, the resulting system of domination is practically indestructible."[14]

In addition to the common rationality structuring state and capitalist power, there is a similarity of *consequences* redounding from the means-ends separation in these two domains. The bureaucracy, separated off as a means, not only shapes the *character* of the state, but comes to predominate *as* state power. Not only the nation and the bureaucrats become enthralled to bureaucratic organization, but those whom the bureaucracy is meant to serve—the state leaders or politicians—lose power at the hands of bureaucratic organization. "In a modern state, the actual ruler is necessarily and unavoidably the bureaucracy."[15] Yet Weber also insists that "as an instrument of rationally organizing authority relations, bureaucracy was and is a power *instrument* of the first order for one who controls the bureaucratic apparatus."[16] Here we encounter an interesting difference between Weber's political writings, in which bureaucratic rule is disparaged, and his scientific writings, in which the bureaucracy is presented as a superior *instrument* of political power. In the former, Weber laments the "impotence" of the politician resulting from bureaucratic hegemony. In the latter, it is the "cage" of the bureaucrat that Weber describes in lurid detail:

> The bureaucrat cannot squirm out of the apparatus into which he has been harnessed. In contrast to the "notable" performing administrative tasks as an honorific duty or as a subsidiary occupation, the professional bureaucrat is chained to his activity in his entire economic and ideological existence. In the great majority of cases he is only a small cog in a ceaselessly moving mechanism which prescribes to him an essentially fixed route of march. The official is entrusted with specialized tasks, and normally the mechanism cannot be put in motion or arrested by him, but only from the very top. The individual bureaucrat is above all, forged to the common interest of all the functionaries in the perpetuation of the apparatus and the persistence of its rationally organized domination.[17]

Later in this chapter, the significance as opposed to the mere fact of this difference in Weber's political and scientific discussions of bureaucracy will be considered. At this point, it is important to note that one reason for the excesses of bureaucracy offered in both accounts pertains to bureaucratic specialization of knowledge. "Bureaucratic administration means fundamentally domination through knowledge."[18] Weber chronicles this form of domination through its "natural" power as simple expertise[19] to "official information" that the bureaucrat harbors for purposes of his own power and monopolizes as "official secrets."[20] Thus, the bureaucracy cultivates the power inherent in both its specialized training and its privileged access to information, and it does so for purposes of developing its own power.

More important than *how* the bureaucracy gains ascendency in the modern state is the fact that this process embodies the rationalization of political power. The ends of the state are usurped by its means, by its own instruments of domination. The extreme rationality of the bureaucratic mode of domination is precisely what makes it so powerful—its "precision, speed, unambiguity, continuity, discretion, unity, strict subordination, reduction of friction and of material and personal costs."[21] These are also the qualities that make bureaucracy "escape-proof" and that make conceivable the possibility that a "technically superior administration [could become] the ultimate and sole value in the ordering of men's affairs."[22] This possibility is the "shell of bondage" that comes to house not only bureaucrats themselves but all inhabitants of bureaucratic society.

We need to step back from Weber's discerning account of capitalism and the modern state in order to note what rests at the bottom of it. It is easy to be swept in by Weber's language of the dauntless march of rationalization without recalling the animating principle of this march. The impetus for both the development of capitalism and the bureaucratized state is, by Weber's own account, contained in the potential power and freedom held out by instrumentally-rational action. As Herbert Marcuse has pointed out, even technical rationality *could* be placed in the service of human liberation rather than domination.[23] It is the fact that Weber cannot conceive of this, that he can only link rationality to domination, which leads him to locate the oppressiveness of the modern state and capitalist economy in rationality itself, that is, in the inherent tendency of rationality to breed rationalization. This quest for a particular kind of power and freedom (embodied in the use of instrumental rationality) is not bound to the "struggle for existence" Weber denotes as the root of all economic and social activity.[24] Rather, this quest is autonomous from the struggle for life itself and both capitalism and the bureaucratic state have *intensified* the struggle for existence. Both superimpose a form of struggle in which individual, domestic, and international power and wealth are sought for their own sake in an endless battle to prevail over other individuals, groups, or nations. Finally, both capitalism and the bureaucratic state intensify the struggle out of which Weber insists they were born: the struggle for freedom.

The relation between instrumental rationality and freedom was considered briefly at the beginning of this chapter. We now need to understand the mechanisms by which this quest for freedom is subverted, by which it is converted into massive enslavement through the development of bureaucratic state and capitalist machines of domination. The potential freedom in both instrumentally-rational and value-rational action is linked with capacities for *control*. Even Weber's most moving expression of the freedom essential to the dignity of humans—the freedom to choose values—has these overtones:

The fruit of the tree of knowledge . . . consists in the insight that every single important activity, and ultimately life as a whole, if it is not to be permitted to run on as an event in nature but is instead to be consciously guided, is a series of ultimate decisions through which the soul—as in Plato—chooses its own fate, i.e., the meaning of its activity and existence.[25]

On a theoretical plane, this conception of freedom is only a step away from Weber's description of instrumentally rational action as liberation from "unthinking acceptance of ancient custom" and the "deliberate adaptation to situations in terms of self-interest."[26] Even closer to this philosophical conception of freedom is the "absolute clarity of self-consciousness" Weber ascribes to instrumental rationality.[27] While absolute freedom in selecting means differs from absolute freedom in selecting values, if one wants to maximize one's freedom in the sense of determining and controlling one's life, then the two shade together.

The quest for freedom in Weber's account is thus linked to a quest to dominate the conditions of one's life. In addition to obtaining control in a general fashion, this entails maximizing the prospects for *predictability* and *calculability* in any given situation and to this end, *routinization* of social, political, and economic life is essential. Weber described these three elements—predictability, calculability, and routinization—as key aims in separating individuals from the means of power and production in the state and in capitalism. These elements are all predicated upon the total rationalization of the means of power and production and in the resultant phenomenon of "organizational discipline."[28] The calculability issuing from organizational discipline lies in uniform obedience: "What is decisive for discipline is that the obedience of a plurality of men is rationally uniform."[29] This total rationalization of the means of power and production also entails rationalization of the ends of power and production. The behavior of state and capitalist power brokers is dictated by the rationalization of means such that their behavior, too, becomes rationally uniform.

Now the quest for freedom has come full circle. Beginning as a quest for control, the road to maximizing control ends in being controlled. Freedom diminishes as the power to obtain one's desires is expanded through systemization and routinization designed to achieve predictability and calculability.

An inanimate machine is mind objectified. Only this provides it with the power to force men into its service and to dominate their everyday working life as completely as is actually the case in the factory. Objectified intelligence is also that animated machine, the bureaucratic organization, with its specialization of trained skills, its division of jurisdiction, its rules and its hierarchical relations of authority. Together with the inanimate machine, it is busy fabricating the shell of bondage which men will perhaps be forced to inhabit some day, as powerless as the fellahs of ancient Egypt.[30]

Freedom, in the sense of choosing both ends and means, is wholly subverted by rationalization. In a fully rationalized society, one's choices are few and remarkably uniform.[31] The effect of the rationalized world upon the interiors of human beings is captured in Weber's famous lament about "specialists without spirit, sensualists without heart" as well as in some of his lesser-known writings:[32]

> It is . . . as though we knowingly and willingly were supposed to become men who need "order" and nothing but order, who become nervous and cowardly if this order shakes for a moment and helpless when they are torn from their exclusive adaptation to this order. That the world knows nothing more than such men of order . . . the central question is not how we further and accelerate it but what we have to set *against* this machinery, in order to preserve a remnant of humanity from this parcelling out of the soul, from this exclusive rule of bureaucratic life ideals.[33]

The death of the inner life of man is the final blow in the dissolution of freedom imposed by rationalization. For it is with the soul, "as in Plato," that freedom is made. Rationalization by its nature entails soullessness of action, obedience resulting from discipline, decisions issuing from calculation within system-constrained options.

II

It is important to recall at this point that Weber, like many before and after him, ascribed to *women* a stronger proclivity toward a deep inner life. By contrast, the calling of men is to the external dimensions of life, the world of appearance and the world of power.[34] This does not mean that Weber considered men devoid of an inner life but that he viewed it as a "feminine" dimension, a dimension without innate power yet from which all human meaning is derived. What Weber has described above, then, is a social and political order in which the "feminine" has been gradually suffocated by "masculine" techniques, and finally annihilated by the sheer weight of the masculine.

We have seen that what leads rationality unambiguously into rationalization is a quest for power as domination. The "birth of rationality" could, as even Weber acknowledged, "lead to the deliberate formulation of new values."[35] Instead, however, instrumental rationality gained ascendency over value rationality "at the expense not only of custom, but of emotional values and finally . . . at the expense of any belief in absolute values."[36] In order for this to occur, power-as-domination had to be the greatest goal for only this kind of power is obtained from the employment of pure instrumental rationality. Power, as a *value* of an external type, is alone compatible with instrumental rationality, which either subordinates the ends to the means or identifies them with each other. Instrumentally-rational action can only be used appropriately for an end that is itself instrumental and power is just such an end. If the end has some inner or ultimate value, instrumental means will contaminate or destroy this value. To put the matter the other way around, an inner-worldly value cannot make use of instrumental means and remain intact. One cannot be instrumentally rational in the pursuit of love, learning, religion, community, or art and reap the value of these things. When they are approached instrumentally, they are changed from ends-in-themselves into ends-for-something-else. Quite literally, their nature and value are transformed.

This is not to say that instrumentally-rational action cannot be made to serve "convictions;" indeed, that is just how such means are most often justified. Precisely because men serving "an ethic of absolute ends" are likely to use instrumental means to achieve them does Weber inveigh against the presence of such men in politics and call instead for those who would pursue "an ethic of responsibility."[37] The omnipresence of instrumental rationality makes the "ethic of absolute ends" not simply irrelevant to politics (as Machiavelli implied) but positively dangerous.[38] The point is that merely having convictions, such as that the power of the state is an "ultimate value," is not the same thing as having what Weber calls an inner life. These men of "order and nothing but order" could surely recite a list of their convictions as well a litany of the way in which their daily activities constitute fulfillment of these convictions.

It is the particular goals Weber ascribes to man—the goal of freedom in the sense of control and domination—that make instrumental rationality his most desirable tool. Power and control are maximized through instrumental rationality, especially in the domains of the economy and state. But precisely because instrumental rationality involves a potential discrepancy between ends and means, in this type of action the end itself is relatively diminished. With instrumentally-rational action, the means do not derive from the nature of the ends but from the purpose of obtaining the ends. The inner meaning or worth of the end is largely irrelevant to the type of means used to obtain it. In other forms of social action, e.g., value-rational action, the nature of the end determines the means; the nature of the end remains primary. Since another important feature of instrumentally-rational action is that the means-ends relationship tends to get inverted, the inner worth of the end is not only relatively diminished compared to other forms of action, but may disappear altogether.

A parallel may be drawn between this feature of instrumental rationality in relation to a goal and the effect of instrumental rationality upon those who are engaged with it. One can only be instrumentally rational, Weber tells us, if one is not caught up in traditional, affectual (emotional), or value-rational modes of action.[39] Conversely, if one is detained in one of these other modes of action, one will be "less free" *vis à vis* means, hence less efficient in pursuing the goal, hence less effective and less powerful.[40] Thus, to obtain power, one must rid one's mind of all but the range of options for obtaining it, with the exception of the tiny corner reserved for the "passion" or "habituation" driving the pursuit of the goal in the first place.[41] So much for cultivation of an inner life.

The emergence of instrumental rationality is thus the *technique* by which Weber's conception of "the feminine" is menaced while the culmination of the will to domination in rationalization is the *weight* under which the feminine finally collapses. The complete realization of rationalized economic and political life, with its qualities of disciplined obedience and conformity, creates men who are calculable and predictable, models of behavioralist analysis, fully conditioned into automatons. This last turn suggests that it is not the feminine alone that is imperiled under conditions of rationalization. Indeed, the will to freedom, control, domination, and power, which according to Weber embodies "the external world of masculinity," has engendered such total systems of domination in the form of capitalism and the bureaucratic state that manhood itself, at the moment at which it is fully realized, is wholly crushed. Completely dominated by its creation and its demands, manhood can be expressed nowhere except in the perverse forms of meaningless accumulation of wealth or pursuit of power for the intrinsically valueless state. Moreover, even man's contribution to these things only increases their domination over him. Both his worth as a being with an inner life who consciously determines meanings and values, and his quest for external power, freedom, and autonomy have been destroyed by the systems of domination arising from his manly ambitions.

All of these themes are brought together in Weber's devotion to the *Machstaat*, the instrument that has no intrinsic value but which he names the supreme political value, the institution that epitomizes the rationalization of ends symptomatic of masculinist instrumental rationality. For at one point Weber compares the great power states to smaller nations (e.g., Norway, Holland) in language which perfectly parallels his discussion of "masculine" and "feminine":

> It is naive to imagine that a people which is small in terms of numbers or power is any the less "valuable" or important in the forum of world

history. It simply has other tasks and thus other cultural possibilities.
. . . It is not only a question of the simple civic virtues and the possibility
of a more real democracy than is attainable in a great power state; it is
also that the more intimate personal values, eternal ones at that, can
only flourish in the soil of a community which makes no pretentions to
political power.[42]

Intimate personal values—presumably all that identifies human beings as such in Weber's eyes—can only flourish in political communities that do not aspire to power over others yet Weber urges absolute
allegiance, indeed devotion, to the power of a state in which these
values will be destroyed.

III

Weber's complicity in buttressing the systems and powers he
deplored is surely the greatest irony of his work and life. Wolfgang
Mommsen insists that "assertion of the value of the individual
personality in a world-historical setting that is basically antagonistic
to it was the keystone of Weber's thinking."[43] Mommsen's claim,
however, eschews the intensity of Weber's devotion both to science
and to the power of the state. In fact, in view of Weber's attachment to
a methodology, a politics, and a body of study that served to entrench
if not develop this "world historical setting" so destructive to the
value of the individual, one can only read his piteous cries against
that world as agonized self-flagellation:

> Given the basic fact of these irresistible advances of bureaucratization
> . . . how can one possibly save *any remnants* of "individualist" freedom
> in any sense . . . how can there be any guarantee that any powers will
> remain which can check and effectively control the tremendous influ-
> ence of this stratum? . . . How can modern society be preserved from
> "mechanical petrification?"[44]

These questions embody profound concerns for Weber and he addressed them tirelessly and passionately in his political writings and
activities.[45] However, nearly every other aspect of Weber's work and
commitments collided head-on with the values implicit in these
questions and contributed to their destruction. In his politics, Weber
elevated the power of the nation-state above all else and decried
attempts to valorize democracy, peace, and social or economic justice
in its place. Certainly he had excellent reasons for his antipathy to
socialism and his small regard for popular government in the era of
the modern nation-state. Both, he insisted, nourished the growing
beast of a completely rationalized society.[46] Pacifism he deplored for
other reasons, finding it irrelevant to politics at best, pernicious to
power concerns, and the preaching of it "corrupting of the youth."[47]

But Weber's commitments to political "realism" and to "an ethic of responsibility" do not by themselves justify his devotion to the power of the state, to the exercise of that power for purposes of supremacy in international politics, to the productivity of capitalism, and to the ruthless entrepreneurial spirit propelling capitalism. Weber, who knew so well what these institutions and practices were doing to society and individuals, who perceived so insightfully that these were means that had become ends, nevertheless defended and advocated them.[48]

It is with Weber's methodology, however, that the irony grows deepest. For through this methodology Weber rationalized the study of human existence, culture, association, and action. Both by seeking to separate his own values from his studies and by attempting to analyze human behavior through the application of rational, "ideal-type" categories, he performed a massive and grotesque exercise in rationalization. Science could never be an end in itself and had no end—its purpose was to codify, clarify, and demystify.[49] Science conceived in this way could only be a tool of rationalization, as well as an expression of it. "Scientific work is chained to the course of progress" and is based on "the knowledge or belief . . . that one can, in principle, master all things by calculation."[50] Moreover, the methodology Weber developed and espoused entailed rationalizing its very subject matter: "The construction of teleological schemata of rational action is possible only because the employment of the categories of "means" and "ends" requires the rationalization of empirical reality."[51] Heart and spirit, inner life and value, insofar as they defied means-ends classification, had to be eliminated from subjects of scientific investigation.

So also must the heart and spirit of the scientist himself take leave of the study. Repeatedly in the course of his writings does Weber whisper, "but here I cannot tread, for this would take us beyond the bounds of science."[52] Thus, the analytic capacities of the scientist too, are divided off from the rest of his being as a "means" to the end of science, an end without meaning and productive of greater meaninglessness in the disenchanted world. Of himself Weber demanded the very "parcelling out of the soul" he so disparaged in the rule of bureaucratic ideals. Nor was Weber content to make only his own work an exercise in rationalization. He demanded that others, too, leave their commitments, cares, beliefs and desires behind when they embarked upon the pursuit or dissemination of knowledge. Specialized knowledge, without a consciously chosen and agreed-upon value, is an essential ingredient of bureaucratic domination. Yet fellow teachers and researchers who sought to make their research serve their values Weber called unworthy.[53] And students who cried out for "useful," "political," or value-laden knowledge Weber called misguided.[54] Not satisfied merely to force himself and others to "know the devil in order to realize his power and limitations," Weber insisted upon incarnating and proselytizing for the demons of science, bureaucratic rationality, and rationalization.[55] While his "inner life" often tormented him to an incapacitating degree, Weber was determined, above all, to be a man.

IV

A paradox persists: however much Weber was complicit in rationalizing thought, life, and study, he opposed the specific rationalization of *politics* as strongly as he opposed anything. That the province of politics and its highest expression in leadership had been invaded by bureaucrats was for him the most regrettable manifestation of the reversal of the means-ends relationship inherent in rationalization. Bureaucracy, generated as the most powerful means of domination, had transgressed its value as means to become the source of domination. Still more disturbing to Weber, bureaucracy constricted the power and range of political leadership. Weber called for political "heros" to counter this process and to resuscitate the virtues, glory, and possibilities of political action. In this regard, Weber looked to a model of ancient manhood to fight contemporary, institutionalized consequences of manliness.

Before exploring the nature of Weber's heroic politician, we need to grasp fully what this figure is up against, i.e., the extent to which rationalization as bureaucratization casts death blows not only to the "feminine" and "masculine" as Weber conceived them but to that highest arena of manhood, politics itself. Recall first those aspects of bureaucracy that contribute to its tendency to exceed its domain as a *means* of administration. As the most perfect institutional embodiment of instrumental rationality, Weber declared bureaucracy to be the most precise and technically efficient form of organization known to humanity. The power of bureaucracy also lies in its highly specialized organization of knowledge—through such preserves, the bureaucratic subordinate can always dominate his "master."[56] A second aspect of the bureaucratization of politics Weber deplored pertains to the bureaucratic structures through which a modern politician rises to power, i.e., bureaucratization of political parties. As Weber notes in "Politics as a Vocation," it is the "party machine" that today selects, grooms and installs men of political power.[57] "By their very nature such parties develop a salaried officialdom" which, in turn, controls political patronage and other aspects of the structuring of political power.[58] Thus, both the rise to political power and the exercise of political power is everywhere conditioned and constrained by bureaucracy. Weber's objection to this is twofold: first, bureaucratic officials who by nature, training and mentality are not suited to politics are nevertheless engaged in it, and second, true politicians, "men with a strong power drive," are discouraged from entering politics because of bureaucratic constraints upon the exercise of power.

Weber's antipathy to the presence of the "official" in politics is strong but ambiguous. On the one hand, he describes the bureaucratic official as being capable of nothing other than duty and officiousness, subservience to a master, and obedience to a set of rules. On the other hand, he accuses petty bureaucrats of incessantly grabbing for power via the bureaucratic machinery. Still more confusing, these objections tend to get grafted onto one another in Weber's tirades against bureaucracy's usurpation of political life. The fundamental issue for him, however, is that while "nowadays specialized training is indispensable for the knowledge of the technical means necessary to the achievement of political goals . . . *policy-making is not a technical affair*, and hence not the business of the professional civil servant."[59] In an essay entitled "The Political Limitations of the Bureaucracy," Weber elaborates:

> The "directing mind," the "moving spirit"—that of the entrepreneur here and of the politician there—differs in substance from the civil service mentality of the officials. . . . If a man in a leading position is an "official," in the spirit of his performance, no matter how qualified—a man, that is, who works dutifully and honorably according to rules and instruction—then he is as useless at the helm of private enterprise as of a government . . . The difference is rooted only in part in the kind of performance expected. . . . The real difference . . . lies in the kind of *responsibility*, and this does indeed determine the different demands addressed to both kinds of position. "To be above parties"—in truth to remain outside the realm of the struggle for power—is the official's role, while this struggle for personal power, and the resulting personal responsibility, is the lifeblood of the politician as well as of the entrepreneur.[60]

"Our officialdom has been brilliant wherever it had to prove its sense of duty, its impartiality, and mastery of organizational problems in the face of official, clearly formulated tasks of a specialized nature," Weber declared in a discussion of post-Bismarck Germany. But "that bureaucracy failed completely whenever it was expected to deal with political problems."[61]

The second way in which bureaucratization threatens genuine politics lies in its constriction of the range and role of politicians. Not only does the knowledge hegemony of the bureaucracy force the political leader into a more dependent, less autonomous position *vis à vis* his staff and party, but the bureaucracy also dilutes the possibilities of a politician fulfilling the "power-instinct" making him aspire to leadership in the first place. In a discussion of the bureaucracy's effect in weakening the German parliament, Weber asks,

> why in the world should men with leadership qualities be attracted by a party which at best can change a few budget items in accordance with the voters' interests and provide a few more benefices to the protegés of its bigshots? What opportunities can it offer to political leaders?[62]

In an equally sardonic tone, Weber delivers the answer to his question:

> A man with a strong power drive, and the qualities that go with it would have to be a fool to venture into this miserable web of mutual resentment . . . as long as his talents and energies can apply themselves in fields such as the giant industrial enterprises, cartels, banks, and wholesale firms. . . . Stripped of all phraseology, our so-called monarchic government amounts to nothing but this process of *negative selection* which diverts all major talents to the service of capitalist interests.[63]

Just as bureaucratization chokes the realm of political action, so it prevents the rise and development of true politicians. Between control by bureaucratized political parties and the bureaucratization of the state itself, there is less and less room to rise to power, seek power, and exercise power by those who are truly drawn to the work. Yet, Weber insists, the cause must not be given up. "Politicians must be the countervailing force against bureaucratic domination."[64] A savior is needed; now we must see just what sort of creature this savior is.

V

Weber's call for politicians who are charismatic heroes "in a very sober sense of the word" is well-known and I shall not rehearse at length the argument contained in the last half of "Politics as a Vocation." What I do want to examine is the *nature* of this type of leader in terms of its relation to the general characteristics of politics set out in the previous chapter and the specific characteristics of politics in the disenchanted, rationalized age. Weber designs his political hero to counter the specific failings of modern political life and to lead the nation on to whatever greatness may be possible in the age of rationalization and disenchantment. But this hero is ultimately a monstrous figure: he wears the mantle of classical manhood and wields modern manhood's creation, the massively powerful nation-state. Moreover, this hero is meant to assert his power over and through, not against, the bureaucratic state and capitalist economy. He is not to dismantle the machinery of rationalized political and economic life that issued from the masculine quest for control and domination; rather, he is to mobilize that machinery for his own political ends.

We begin with Weber's demand that the true politician be a charismatic figure. The invocation of charisma raises the specifically antimaterial, "above necessity," aspect of Weber's formulation of true politics. In the charismatic leader, this antimaterialism has two aspects: (1) the leader himself must be detached from or "above" material issues and (2) the spirit and concerns constitutive of his charismatic status must be "extraordinary." With regard to the former, Weber says:

> Pure charisma is specifically foreign to economic considerations. . . . The elective ruler or the charismatic party leader requires the material means of power . . . and a brilliant display of his authority to bolster his prestige. What is despised . . . is tradition or rational everyday economizing, the attainment of a regular income by continuous activity devoted to this end.[65]

As it was in the Greek formulation, a material basis is required for political power, but it must be treated solely as a *means* to higher purposes in order not to contaminate the character of charisma. Politics, and especially political leadership, is not about life, survival, or sustenance.

With regard to the second element of the antimaterial nature of charisma, Weber is equally blunt: "Bureaucracy and patriarchalism . . . both are structures of everyday life rooted in the need to meet ongoing routine demands. All extraordinary needs . . . have always been satisfied on a charismatic basis."[66] When the leader's following or when external conditions require that charismatic leadership turn its attention to everyday life, charisma is "routinized" and thereby subverted.[67] Thus, charisma is not merely distinct from the politics of everyday life, its existence is explicitly antagonized by the demands of the ordinary.

> Charisma is a phenomenon typical of prophetic or expansive political movements in their early stages. But as soon as domination is well established, and above all as soon as control over large masses of people exists, it gives way to the forces of everyday routine.[68]

In these remarks about the relationship of the charismatic figure to social and economic life, we recognize Weber's stipulation that the true politician live "for" rather than "off" politics, be free of personal economic cares, pursue a politics "above class interests" and above the banal concerns of everyday life. He must, as Weber insists in "Politics as a Vocation," have "distance both to things and to men."[69] But the passage cited above raises a second feature of charismatic leadership and this is the fact that it is an exercise in domination. By Weber's account, charismatic leadership is an extremely powerful form of domination because it commands loyalty, devotion, and obedience not merely through injunction but through capturing the "souls" as well as the external compliance of the followers. For this reason, Weber terms charismatic leadership the "specifically creative revolutionary force of history."[70]

> Bureaucratic rationalization . . . revolutionizes with *technical means* . . . as does every economic reorganization "from without": It first changes the material and social orders, and through them the people. . . . By contrast, the power of charisma rests upon the belief in revelations and heroes. . . . It rests upon "heroism" of an ascetic, military, judicial, magical or whichever kind. Charismatic belief revolutionizes men "from within" and shapes material and social conditions according to its revolutionary will. . . . The decisive difference—and this is important for understanding the meaning of "rationalism"—is not inherent in the *creator* of ideas or of "works" or in his inner experience; rather, the difference is rooted in the manner in which the ruled and led experience and internalize these ideas. . . . Rationalization proceeds in such a fashion that the broad masses of the led merely accept or adapt themselves to the external, technical results which are of practical significance to their interests whereas the substance of the creator's ideas remain irrelevant to them . . . whereas charisma, if it has any specific effects at all, manifests its revolutionary power from within, from a central *metanoia* of the followers attitudes.[71]

Weber's call for charismatic leadership of mass democracy necessarily entails the "soullessness of the following, their intellectual proletarianization, one might say."[72] The soul and intellect of the people are "proletarianized" by the charismatic leader of a rational legal state because (1) the people are solely means to the leader's power, i.e., the purpose of his activity is unrelated to their wants and needs and he remains charismatic only insofar as he abstains from such concerns; (2) the people are completely dominated by a power upon which they are utterly dependent; and (3) the people are without even the power available under a pure rational-legal form of domination because they are wedded to charismatic power in a spiritual, nonrational manner and hence cannot "make use" of the domination either through value-rational or instrumentally-rational modes of action. The followers of a charismatic leader wholly surrender their minds, souls, and labor to the leader. In this regard, they are utterly and nonrationally in thrall to his power. The expression of individual personality—charisma—on the part of a great leader thus involves corresponding suppression of individuality and freedom on the part of the followers.

Insofar as charismatic leadership does not pertain to material or everyday life but only to the "extraordinary," the structure, organization and administration of the body politic may well be unchanged by the charismatic leader's attainment of political power. In a modern state, this means that the domination of individual lives through capitalism and the bureaucratic state will be *entirely unaffected* by the presence of a charismatic leader and to these modes of domination will be added a third, that of the charismatic leader himself. Charismatic leadership thus arises in the thoroughly rationalized state and society not to free its inhabitants, not even to lighten the burden of bureaucratic domination, but as final and complete enslavement of the body politic. The charismatic leader "proletarianizes" the people's souls and intellects while bureaucracy and capitalism control their bodies and external lives.

Only at the level of "prestige of culture" or national glory does Weber's call for plebiscitary leader-democracy offer anything to the life of the nation. Yet what it offers is not participation or freedom— not democracy in any meaningful sense—but only the collective knowledge that one is part of a great nation led by a great man. The democratic aspect of plebiscitary democracy is for Weber a *means* to the revitalization of political life. In fact, the value of plebiscitary leader-democracy appears to reside primarily in its potential to lengthen the life-span of charismatic leadership, precisely by keeping in place those "everyday" structures of domination that administer routine social and economic needs. ("Every charisma is on the road from a turbulently emotional life that knows no economic rationality to a slow death by suffocation under the weight of material interests; every hour of its existence brings it nearer this end."[73]) Where true leadership prevailed, bureaucratic domination would cease encroaching upon the explicitly political realm and would dominate social life alone. Politics, as the realm of the extraordinary, would be preserved from the fate of total rationalization, while the rest of human activity would continue under this suffocating form of total organization. As Wolfgang Mommsen notes, Weber's plebiscitary leader-democracy is really charismatic domination under the form of rational, formal, legal constitutionalism.[74] I would go further: it combines the two forms and the consequence is heavier, more thoroughgoing domination than would be entailed in either one alone.

In "Politics as a Vocation," Weber declares that the politician may serve "national, humanitarian, social, ethical, cultural, worldly or religious ends;" he may even want to serve the "external ends of everyday life."[75] Yet what Weber says about those who serve an ethic of absolute ends and his insistence upon the devotion of the politician to the power-interests of the nation diminish the expansive tone of this declaration. In several of his works, Weber identifies the true politician simply in terms of a capacity to expand state power.[76] He denounces the notion that the point of political leadership is ever to be a "servant of the people" and asserts baldly that a leader must develop his own power and the power of the nation-state.[77] "It is not a policy of comfort and ease that we are after but one of national greatness."[78] In countless ways, Weber reiterates his primary message about politics and politicians: "the struggle for personal power . . . is the life-blood of the politician."[79]

Yet, Weber insists, this personal power drive must be combined in some way with devotion to a "cause." This is not because a cause is ethically superior to pursuit of power for its own sake, but because unattached power-instincts turn in on themselves:

> The sin against the lofty spirit of the politician's vocation . . . begins where this striving for power ceases to be objective and becomes purely personal self-intoxication, instead of exclusively entering the service of "the cause." For there are only two kinds of deadly sins in the field of politics: lack of objectivity and—often but not always identical to it—irresponsibility.[80]

Thus, the politician must want power for himself but not only for himself, and the state being the appropriate thing for a man interested in political power to attach himself to, the individual's reasons for aspiring to political leadership now correspond perfectly to the social reasons for requiring it. A genuine politician pursues politics as a vocation because "either he enjoys the naked possession of power he exerts or he nourishes his inner balance and self-feeling by the consciousness that his life has meaning in the service of a 'cause.' "[81] This is the individual side. On the other hand, when Weber explains what is needed to lead a mass society to greatness, he calls for men who have a strong power drive, know how to play the modern instruments of power, and have the power interests of the nation at heart.[82] This is the social or "objective" side.

Yet as there is no responsibility on the part of the political leader to the general well-being, material needs, or even spiritual welfare of the citizenry, there is also none but his own convictions to guide him in the pursuit of power for himself and the state. Tirelessly Weber repeats, the distinguishing aspect of the genuine politician is his personal responsibility to his own values and for his own actions.

> The elected official will conduct himself entirely as the mandated representative of his master the electors, whereas the leader will see himself carrying sole responsibility for what he does. This means that the latter, so long as he can successfully lay claim to their confidence, will act throughout according to his own convictions and not, as the official, according to the expressed or supposed will of the electorate.[83]

Weber is concerned to liberate politics and politicians from all that constrains them in the modern state: "people" with class interests and particular needs, "parties" with their huge bureaucratic machines, and the state bureaucracy itself with its monopoly of specialized knowledges and its careerist officials. It is for purposes of overcoming all these constraints upon political leadership and action that Weber designs his charismatic political leader. Weber has given up on the many but he still holds out a bit of hope for the restoration of individual manhood—the pursuit of personal power—and of collective manhood—the pursuit of glory for the expansive nation-state. His hopefulness is hardly optimism, however, for he was certain that in most cases the bureaucractic state and especially the party machines would seek to *"castrate* the rise of charisma."[84]

VI

Weber's concerns for the redemption of political life and the development of true politicians are not without importance and integrity. One cannot scoff at Weber's effort to envisage a genuine politician in the age of rationalization, nor at his gloomy prediction that the forces of rationalization are more likely to win out. But his political hero would not solve the problems of modern political life, let alone social or economic life, which Weber identifies. Weber's ideal politician is a male warrior marshalling the forces of institutionalized manhood— the bureaucratic state. He embodies all the manly political values these chapters have uncovered: devotion to personal power, heroism, violence, domination and "the extraordinary," antipathy to everyday existence, and the instrumental rationality with which all of these things are infused. Despite Weber's insistence that a genuine politican must obey an "ethic of responsibility," instrumental rationality alone procures and wields the level of political power Weber is after, and instrumental rationality is utterly incompatible with an ethic of responsibility. There is probably no better evidence for this than the political "scandals" that have come to routinely plague the modern American presidency.

Weber's notion of leadership, indeed of politics itself, is predicated upon an instrumental relationship to the means of power, i.e., to the people and their provision of the material requisites of power. The people, the economy, the bureaucracy are all instruments or means to Weber's politician, whether he approaches them with a profound sense of responsibility for his actions or whether he justifies his actions according to some higher end they are meant to serve. Finally, the politician's devotion to the state is devotion to an instrument that has become an end; this is the most advanced symptom of instrumental rationality become rationalization.

Politics, which in Weber's account originates with the "marauding raids" of the men's houses, culminates in Weber's most optimistic view with a more "civilized" raid upon the nation by a single powerful man and his bureaucratic machine. Driven by a desire for power unharnessed to any human need, the masculine formulation of politics Weber depicts and advocates has no purpose save fulfillment of its own ideals of individual and national power and prestige. Born from the domination of life by warrior leagues and patriarchs, it threatens and suffocates life at every turn while presenting itself as the distinctly human, the highest calling, the greatest cause, the salvation from lower orders of rationalized existence. This is the conception and practice of politics and political life that centuries of involvement with manhood has bequeathed to us.

Notes

1. "Bureaucracy and Political Leadership," Appendix II-ii, *ES,* p. 1394.

2. *ES* (I) I–2, pp. 24–26.

3. "Action is instrumentally rational when the end, the means, and the secondary results are all taken into account and weighted. This involves rational consideration of alternative means to the end, of the relations of the end to the secondary consequences, and finally, of the relative importance of different ends. . . . Instead of deciding between alternative and conflicting ends in terms of a rational orientation to a system of values [the actor may] simply take them as given subjective wants and arrange them in a scale of consciously assessed relative urgency. He may then orient his action to this scale in such a way that they are satisfied as far as possible in order or urgency, as formulated in the principle of "marginal utility." From [this] point of view . . . value-rationality is always irrational." Ibid., p. 26.

4. "Knies and the Problem of Irrationality," *Roscher and Knies: The Logical Problems of Historical Economics,* trans. G. Oakes (New York: Free Press, 1975), hereafter cited as *Roscher and Knies,* p. 191.

5. *ES* (I) I–4, p. 30. Weber adds: "One of the most important aspects of the process of "rationalization" of action is the substitution for the unthinking acceptance of ancient custom, of deliberate adaptation to situations in terms of self-interest."

6. Karl Loewith, "Weber's Interpretation of the Bourgeois-Capitalist World in Terms of the Guiding Principle of Rationalization" in Wrong, *Max Weber,* p. 112.

7. *ES* (I) I–4, p. 30.

8. Loewith, "Weber's interpretation of the Bourgeois-Capitalist World," p. 114.

9. In discussing Weber's analysis of the relationship of capitalism to rationality and rationalization, I will be concerned only peripherally with his study of the origins of capitalism in *The Protestant Ethic and the Spirit of Capitalism* [trans. T. Parsons (London: Unwin University Books, 1930)]. This

most famous of Weber's works is relevant to the present study only in its concluding pages wherein Weber argues that the religious "calling" of the Protestant entrepreneur has been rationalized into a mode of behavior structured by the domination of capitalist organization itself. "For when asceticism was carried out of monastic cells into everyday life, and began to dominate worldly morality, it did its part in building the tremendous cosmos of the modern economic order. This order is now bound to the technical and economic conditions of machine production which today determines the lives of all the individuals who are born into this mechanism, not only those directly concerned with economic acquisition, with irresistible force. . . . Victorious capitalism, since it rests on mechanical foundations, needs [the support of religious asceticism] no longer." Pp. 181–82.

10. Weber discusses these features of the capitalist mode of production in a variety of places but does so most forthrightly in his harangues against socialism. See, e.g., "Socialism" in *Selections in Translation*, pp. 252–53.

11. *Protestant Ethic*, see especially pp. 155–70.

12. "Politics as a Vocation," p. 82; "Bureaucracy and Political Leadership," p. 1394.

13. *ES* (II) III—ii–5, p. 223.

14. Ibid.

15. "Bureacracy and Political Leadership," p. 1393.

16. *ES* (II) XI–9, p. 987.

17. Ibid. p. 988.

18. *ES* (II) III-ii–5, p. 255.

19. "The political "master" always finds himself *vis à vis* the trained official, in the position of dilettante facing the expert." *ES* (II) XI–11, p. 991. See also IX–11–C, pp. 993–96.

20. "The Right of Parliamentary Inquiry and the Recruitment of Political Leaders," Appendix II-iii, ES, pp. 1417–18.

21. *ES* (II) XI–6, p. 973; "Bureaucracy and the Naivete of the Literati," p. 1401.

22. "Bureaucracy and the Naiveté of the Literati," p. 1402.

23. Herbert Marcuse, "Industrialization and Capitalism" in Stammer, ed., *Max Weber and Sociology Today* (Oxford: Blackwell, 1971), p. 149.

24. "Objectivity in the Social Sciences," *MSS*, pp. 63–64.

25. "The Meaning of Ethical Neutrality," *MSS*, p. 18.

26. *ES* (I) I–4, p. 30.

27. Ibid. p. 30.

28. *ES* (II) XIV-iii, p. 1156. "Organization discipline . . . has a completely rational basis. With the help of suitable methods of measurement, the optimum profitability of the individual is *calculated* like that of any material means of production."

29. Ibid. p. 1149.

30. "Bureaucracy and the Naiveté of the Literati," p. 1404.

31. *ES* (I) I–4, p. 30.

32. *Protestant Ethic*, p. 182.

33. *Gesammelte Aufsatze zur Soziologie und Sozialpolitik*, cited in Mitzman, *The Iron Cage*, p. 178.

34. See chapter seven, pp. 128–29.

35. *ES* (I) I–4, p. 30.

36. Ibid.

37. "Politics as a Vocation," pp. 120–26; see pp. 171–72 of this chapter for discussion of the limitations to the "ethic of responsibility."

38. Ibid. pp. 121–22.

39. *ES* (I) I–4, p. 30.

40. *Roscher and Knies,* pp. 191–192.

41. See pp. 84–86 for the parallel formulation by Machiavelli of the kind of "mental *virtù*" required to address situations in which one's power is threatened by indecipherable sources.

42. "Max Weber's Sociology," pp. 186–87.

43. "The Political Limitations of the Bureaucracy," p. 1403.

44. As I have sought to suggest in this chapter and the previous one, more than occasionally Weber expressed these concerns in his "scientific" writings as well.

45. On socialism, see "Socialism" and "Prospects for Democracy in Tsarist Russia," *Selections in Translation,* ; and "Bureaucratization and the Naiveté of the Literati," pp. 1393–95, 1399–1403. On democracy and rationalization see *ES* (II) XI–6, p. 980; XI–8, pp. 984–85; IX–11, p. 991; and Appendix II-v, pp. 1442–59.

47. From a letter cited in Marianne Weber's *Biography,* p. 412.

48. It is not going too far, I think, to say that Weber was intoxicated by the conflict, war and sacrifice that were part and parcel of these institutions and thus was not even defending them as the "best of all possible evils.' See Marianne Weber's description of Weber's response to World War II, Ibid. pp. 617–78.

49. "Science as a Vocation," pp. 138, 139, 143, 144.

50. Ibid. pp. 137, 139.

51. *Roscher and Knies,* p. 191.

52. *Protestant Ethic,* p. 182; *ES* (II) IX–5, p. 926.

53. "Objectivity in Social Science," *MSS,* pp. 49–62 and "Freudianism," *Selections in Translation.*

54. "Science as a Vocation," pp. 148–52.

55. Ibid. p. 152.

56. "Right of Parliamentary Inquiry and the Recruitment of Political Leaders" *ES,* Appendix II-iii, p. 1418; and *ES* (II) XI-11–C, pp. 993–98.

57. "Politics as a Vocation," pp. 100–112; "Bureaucracy and Political Leadership," pp. 1395–99.

58. "Bureaucracy and Political Leadership," pp. 1396, 1398.

59. "Right of Parliamentary Inquiry," p. 1419.

60. "Bureaucracy and Political Leadership," pp. 1403, 1404.

61. "Right of Parliamentary Inquiry," p. 1417.

62. "Bureaucracy and Political Leadership," p. 1414.

63. Ibid. p. 1413.

64. "Right of Parliamentary Inquiry," p. 1417.

65. *ES* (II) III-iv, p. 244; see also XIV-i, p. 113.

66. *ES* (II) XIV-i, p. 1111; see also p. 1118: "In contrast to the revolutionary role of charisma, the traditional everyday needs in politics and religion are met by the patriarchal structure."

67. *ES* (II) III-v, pp. 252–254; see also XV–1–2, pp. 1158, 1162: "Routinized charisma," Weber explains, is the truth behind every legitimate ongoing order and bears little relation to the manifestation of *actual* charismatic elements.

68. *ES* (II) III-v, p. 252.

69. "Politics as a Vocation," p. 115.

70. *ES* (II) XIV-i, p. 1117.

71. Ibid. pp. 1116–17.

72. "Politics as a Vocation," p. 113.

73. *ES* (II) XIV-i–6, p. 1120.

74. "Max Weber's Sociology," p. 186.

75. "Politics as a Vocation," p. 117.

76. "Bureaucracy and Political Leadership," p. 1407.

77. Ibid. p. 1407.

78. *Verhandlungen des 8. Evangelisch-sozialen Kongresses* (1897), pp. 108–109, cited in Beetham, *Max Weber and the Theory of Modern Politics*, p. 126.

79. "Bureaucracy and Political Leadership," p. 1404, 1413, 1411, and 1414.

80. "Politics as a Vocation," p. 116.

81. Ibid. p. 84. See also pp. 114–15: "What inner enjoyments can this career offer? . . . The career of politics grants a feeling of power, the knowledge of influencing men, of participating in power over them, and above all, the feeling of holding in one's hands a nerve fiber of historically important events can elevate the professional politican above everyday routine even when he is placed in formally modest positions."

82. "Bureaucracy and Political Leadership," p. 1407.

83. Cited in Beetham, *Max Weber and the Theory of Modern Politics*, p. 231.

84. Marianne Weber, *Biography*, p. 638, emphasis added.

Toward a Post-Masculinist Politics

9

What is to Be Overcome: The Politics of Domination

WHILE HISTORICAL AND THEORETICAL SPECIFICITY are essential in tracing the relationship between manhood and politics, we may now fruitfully consider the common and contemporary themes found among the political theories explored in the previous chapters. We may ask what kind of politics we have inherited from a history in which manhood and politics were born symbiotically and have come of age together. In this chapter, a few of the most dramatic and persistent aspects of this complex history are distilled and drawn into reflections upon contemporary political life. In the next, the perspective offered by this history on the question of where we might go from here is explored in somewhat finer detail.

I

Politics . . . is never for the sake of life. . . . Whoever entered the political realm had first to be ready to risk his life, and too great a love for life obstructed freedom, was a sure sign of slavishness.[1]

In their own more subtle voices, Aristotle, Machiavelli, and Weber, each offered a variant of Arendt's bald claim. Concern with life was conceived by all of them not simply as foreign or irrelevant to politics, but as threatening or debasing to the political realm and manhood. This is why Aristotle excluded from *polis* citizenship all who were involved with human necessity. Slaves, women, and other workers taint politics with matters of "life." This is why Arendt calls for a literal, physical separation of the realm of the "good life" from the realm of "mere life." Weber, too, insisted upon politicians who were free from the cares of everyday life, who "have a distance from both things and men." He despaired at the infestation of politics by "emotionalism" or "petty concerns" and sought to reassert politics in a bureaucratized world by forging its autonomy from all other activities, by purifying it of the life-bound concerns of the social and the economic. These are the concerns Arendt believes have invaded the public realm, producing a politics she disparagingly names "collective housekeeping."[2]

> It requires courage even to leave the protective security of our four walls and enter the public realm, not because of particular dangers which may lie in wait for us but because we have arrived in a realm where the concern for life has lost its validity. Courage liberates men from their worry about life for the freedom of the world.[3]

The realization of manhood lies in transcendence of life, mere life, mortality, routines, rhythms, involvement with nature and necessity. Manhood is acquired through a relentless quest for immortality, through constructing ideals and institutions specifically contrasted to or with life. Man strives to transcend his body, his needs, his mortality, and locates his realization in a range of activity above these things, in a realm that banishes them. The sometimes loud, sometimes subtle reverberations of this effort are inscribed both in the projects he designs for himself and in the "life" he repudiates, oppresses or suppresses; these projects are distanced from the "baseness of life" while this "life" is reduced to nothing but baseness.

II

Let us go back to the body, the well-spring of life that has plagued man ever since he has known that he thinks. Western political man has regarded the body as a trap, a weapon, an instrument, a foundation, and a curse upon the mind, all more or less simultaneously. He carries these valuations of the body into his construction of politics and institutionalizes them there. Men's individual bodies, the realm of bodily maintenance, and the body politic—all are regarded as instruments or foundations at best, more often encumbrances, irritants, or threats to man and his political projects.

> If it should be true that the Greeks perished through their slavedom, then another fact is much more certain, that we shall perish through the lack of slavery.[4]

Political freedom is rooted in opposition to confinement by the body, by natural needs and desires, by the body politic. Freedom from bodily necessity was the prerequisite to the freedom of political life for the Greeks. Freedom to indenture other bodies is the essence of the realm of "free enterprise" Weber regarded as a "condition" but not a "part" of the political life of the modern state. Mortality and mortal needs are left at the threshold of the properly constituted political realm, an arena where immortality is pursued by individual men, by the *polis*, by the state.

The mind of man, the head of the polity, bears an instrumental, dominating relationship to the body. This is the key to the head's freedom and exaltedness. The body politic—the territorial population—exists for the sake of political life, for the higher purposes of the head. The only place for the body *in* politics is as a finely disciplined instrument of force, carrying out the will and aspirations of the head. The head's rationality is shaped by its relationship to its most immediate environment, its own body. What the head conceives of as Rationality is the specific kind of rationality emanating from its alienated, instrumental relationship with its body.

The greatest evil adheres to the greatest rationality. . . . There is political alienation because polity is relatively autonomous.[5]

The head cut loose from the body is dangerous. It declares itself the form-giver of all life and it declares war upon life. This is the heart of Western manhood. The head provides form, projects form, imposes form upon matter. The head that has repudiated its body regards all life as formless and construes itself as providing life with purpose or function. "Domination . . . provides amorphous social action with a goal."[6] The head declares itself the "whole" of which the body is a "part" or "condition." (What a remarkable inversion—only a metaphysically severed head is capable of such casuistry!) Man identifies himself as form-giver, constructs politics as that which gives form, calls politics the *telos* of man, and conceives an inherent right to impose form upon all that is living. Power to impose form, to control, master, and conquer larger and larger domains of life is the *raison d'être* and *raison d'état* of the politics of manhood.

Stamping matter with form for the purpose of domination requires singleness of purpose and unwavering attention to opportunity and strategy. As peoples and situations are transmuted into "matter" upon which a man strives to impose his form, their internal nature, structure or spirit may elude him. But, says Machiavelli, be bold and audacious, brutal and determined with what you do not comprehend. And so Western man has brutalized the planet nearly to extinction, obliterated peoples who pray to strange gods or live in tribes rather than nuclear families, and sought to refashion whole nations after the image of his own. Occasionally, the strategy of beating and raping the unknown into submission fails: twenty-eight years of brute force in Vietnam could not bring it back under colonial or imperialist control. Will the effort to impose the "form" of liberal capitalism upon nations emerging from *latifundia* despotism, where it simply does not fit, meet with similar results?

The essence of political community is willingness to risk death in the group interest. This gives political community its particular pathos.[7]

Willingness to risk death is the proof that life has been discarded as a fundamental value. To be willing to *die* for something is considered more glorious than to be willing to *live* for or through something. "Courage liberates men from their worry about life for the freedom of the world."[8] Political courage is construed as risking life, not struggling with or championing life, risking pride, risking desire. A real man lays his life on the line. For what is death risked? For honor, for glory, for a value greater than life, for freedom from enslavement by life, for immortality, or for the "ultimate value" of the state.

The essential characteristic of the state is violence.[9]

Politics originates in "senseless violence"—organized plunder, pillage, and rape—male bonding to appropriate and devastate bodies and the fruits of bodily labor. It pauses to construe itself as the *telos* of human existence, and proceeds to develop as institutions of domestic domination and foreign aggression. "The strong do what they can and the weak suffer what they must."[10] The Athenians opted for truth-telling before the metaphysicians arrived to doctor their words and deeds with teleologies and hierarchies. The weak do what they must: even in the household, Weber insists, "the woman is dependent because of the normal superiority of the physical and intellectual energies of the male and the child because of his objective helplessness."[11] So, he concludes, spare us "that soft-headed attitude, so agreeable and even admirable from the human point of view . . . which thinks it possible to replace political with 'ethical' ideals."[12] The first politicos were tribal warriors engaged in marauding raids; today Rambo and Ronald Reagan aim the laser beams of "Starship USA" while the CIA and National Security Council coordinate ultra-sophisticated marauding raids involving guns and money from around the globe. There have been protesting voices in between, even male ones, but all men are not Men.

III

When life is banished by the living, a new project is required. A higher, better purpose must be constructed, internalized, and justified by its bearers. What is this higher purpose? "The perfection of man," answered Aristotle. What is the perfection of man? "Fulfillment of his nature which has a purpose greater than life." Perhaps Machiavelli can help: why is politics the realm of greatest glory?

"Because there a man expresses his *virtù*, he achieves fame and pursues glory, he imposes form on matter, and is supremely challenged." But what, beyond his own fulfillment, does all this accomplish? "Possibly the unification of Italy or at least, the greatness of Florence." And what will Florence do or be with her greatness? "She will make her people proud and glorious, and able to dominate or plunder whomever they choose." Let us try Weber: why is politics such a noble calling? "Because there a man can feel the satisfaction of holding a nerve-fiber of history in his hands." But what does this satisfy in him? "An instinct for power." And those who follow him or who are dominated by him, those over whom he has power, what do they obtain? "The prestige of greatness."

Politics and manhood thrive in the realm of the "extraordinary," above the realm of ordinary life and cares, routine needs, human necessity. Necessity is an essential component of this kind of politics but it is a politically engendered necessity, a consequence of striving for power, projecting one's self or one's state beyond its bounds in a context where other men and states are doing the same.

For Machiavelli and the Greeks, the "extraordinary" nature of politics is embodied in the character of the political hero, symbolized by *virtù* and *aretē*. Weber, too, refers to the true politician as a hero but the extraordinary dimension of Weberian politics emerges even more sharply in the identity he establishes between the genuine politician and the charismatic leader. Charisma flourishes only on a plane "beyond the ordinary" and is quickly eroded by the demands of everyday, life-bound matters.

IV

"But," cries the sympathetic critic, "Weber's charismatic hero is anachronistic. We have no grand politics today but only the politics of interest, of bodily and social existence. Our politics is banal, trivial, corrupt. The modern liberal state constitutes itself as a means to our individual ends, it exists to protect and administer 'mere life' so that individuals may pursue freedom and happiness in the private or social realms. The welfare state is legitimized by its care for bodies and material life. Society, economics, and self-interest have been completely victorious in their overthrow of the political. Arendt insists upon this: 'There is perhaps no clearer testimony to the loss of the public realm than the almost complete loss of authentic concern with immortality.'[13] Real politics and real manhood are moribund: the politics of "life," of "collective housekeeping," is the paltry offering of the modern welfare state."

No, neither manhood nor politics, nor their relationship, are finished. The increasing entanglement of the liberal state with the capitalist economy does not add up to a politics of or for life. Yes, the bureaucratization of the state *has* hamstrung the manly quest for glory and immortality in an autonomous political realm. But from Weber we learn that manhood did this to itself. Moreover, within the rationalized machinery of modern political institutions, the manhood-politics relationship persists.[14] And ensnared, crisis-ridden manhood is even more dangerous than its "healthy" predecessor.

The formal political power of the liberal state is expressed in its assertion of the "national interest," a "cause" usually juxtaposed to the particular interests and general well-being of the citizenry. The notion of national interest permits the state to jettison its erstwhile concern with life to assert and pursue concerns higher than life. It is for "national security" or "national honor" that the state sacrifices its youth in foreign military interventions, engineers right-wing coups in the Third World, spends millions on subverting domestic and foreign voices of dissent, and builds its nuclear arsenals. It is for "national prosperity" that the state manages recessions to slow down a racing economy, pays farmers to bury rather than reap their crops, sanctions depletion and destruction of the environment, tolerates carcinogenic industrial operations, and slashes welfare programs while expanding defense expenditures. Little remains of the welfare state's protective posture toward "mere life" when such lives can be made into instruments of aggressive warfare, subjected to working conditions threatening to their mental and physical health, or subjected to an environment in which the prosperity of the state is held in higher esteem than its citizens' need to breathe air, drink water, and eat food that will not kill them. Ours may not be a polity that cultivates the pursuit of heroic deeds and honor but neither is it a polity that values life. To the extent that public figures still invoke the language of heroism, it is usually to rationalize and glorify the sacrifice of life for empty causes, whether it be marines in Lebanon or schoolteachers hitched to the project of conquering yet another "frontier"—the domain beyond planet Earth.

Those who seek to resuscitate "genuine politics" in the modern age nearly always do so by invoking the qualities of classical manhood and classical politics. Consider Weber's heroic politician, Arendt's courageous political actors, Nietzsche's *Übermensch*, Norman Mailer's "real men," some of the more notorious Black Panther Party leaders, Carey McWilliam's "citizen-warriors," the President's cultivation of machismo as he ducks bullets and sacks Carribean islands.[15] Manhood grown impotent reaches back for its youthful days of conquering virility. It would be pathetic or hilarious if it were not so dangerous.

V

Women struggling to gain *entrée* into humanity and into politics generally accept the definition of the species and of politics redounding from the cult of manhood. Jeanne Kirkpatrick, Golda Meir, Indira Ghandi, and Margaret Thatcher are almost parodies of modern-day *virtù*. The women of the Weather Underground, however brave and well-meaning, were sad imitations of the machismo revolutionary.[16] More disturbing still are the some of the philosophic founders of the contemporary women's movement. Here is Simone de Beauvoir's neo-anthropological account of the origin of women's subordination:

> The warrior put his life in jeopardy to elevate the prestige of the horde. . . . And in this he proved dramatically that life is not the supreme value for man, but on the contrary, that it should be made to serve ends more important than life itself. The worst curse that was laid upon woman was that she should be excluded from these warlike forays. For it is . . . in risking life that man is raised above the animal; that is why superiority has been accorded in humanity not to the sex that brings forth but to that which kills.[17]

In the *Second Sex*, de Beauvoir swallowed whole the drama of manhood and tried to get women a part in it. Men have always been synonymous with Human, she begins, while women have been Other, subhuman, nonhuman. In fact, she continues, women *do* have an inherent problem with being human—our cloying bodies will not turn us loose. "Instead of being a pure mind set like a flawless jewel at the center of everything, I took on flesh; it was a painful fall from grace."[18] Still, since women have minds as well, we can approach being human by attempting to transcend our bodies and seeking to shape the world rather than being passively shaped by it. "Fortuna may be mistress of one half of our actions but . . . even she leaves the other half . . . under our control."[19] 'Women,' urged de Beauvoir, 'become form-givers, develop projects, loathe your bodily enslavement, make others into the Other, tyrannize nature. Abortions and the pill are good technical assists, hostility toward all that is immanent and growing is essential, training in philosophy will clinch the matter.'

Marxist-feminism offered similarly rough beginnings. Thirty years after Engels urged women to seek their liberation through the smashing of the bourgeois order, August Bebel elaborated:[20]

> The moment when all the means of production become the property of society, when collective labor by the application of all technical and scientific advantages and aids in the process of production reaches the highest degree of fertility . . . *women shall be like man, a productive and useful member of society.*[21]

Lenin was the next great inspiration. He understood that women were an important source of revolutionary proletarians, indeed half the population and nearly one-third of the industrial labor force during the years preceeding the Russian Revolution.[22] Through the experience of organizing women, however, Lenin's top female cadre learned that there were far more complex, and indeed, theoretically and politically exciting features of "the woman question" than Marx or Engels had imagined. Clara Zetkin sought to take women's experience and concerns seriously on their own terms and Alexandra Kollontai sought to build a new political understanding out of this experience.[23] Zetkin was immediately pulled back into line with a lecture from Lenin that she later recounted in loving detail. Kollontai was officially denounced for her feminist and democratic politics; she eventually recanted and withdrew from active political life.[24]

Fifty years later, Shulamith Firestone sanctioned Bebel's vision but found his analysis of women's oppression thin. From her own theoretical explorations emerged Marxist-feminist revolutionary demand number one:

> The freeing of women from the tyranny of their biology by any and every means necessary.[25]

Firestone's belief that women can and should be liberated through test-tube babies is quintessentially Western and masculine: freedom is equated with and achieved through freedom from the body. Nature has enslaved us all, women are the last to be released because nature oppresses us most fiercely, but now, finally, we can have the same weapons, the same freedom. Women, too, can have *aretē, virtù*, the courage to risk life, freedom through the conquest of nature and necessity.[26] It is not a felicitous vision.

Preserving, extending, and politicizing the "maternal ethos" is not the answer either.[27] Mama is neither a saint nor a citizen but a woman who has been constructed for a particular and largely thankless purpose in a sphere generally characterized by powerlessness and inequality. This figure varies tremendously by culture and class (a matter which the literature in praise of her rarely recognizes) and may be more singularly identified by the common devaluation of her work than by her particular bearing in the world; she is everywhere oppressed, but she is not everywhere more protective, empathic, nurturant, pacifistic, and communal in orientation than her male counterpart. Moreover, the division between the genders, between all that they have been identified with and made responsible for, has crippled and constrained both sexes, both spheres of activity. The oppressed do not have a monopoly on truth, virtue, or correct sensibility.

VI

Is this a clarion call for the death of politics, of heroism, of striving and glory, of men? No, we must keep them all, relieve them of their pathologies and incorporate into them what they have excluded, repudiated, suppressed, and denied. Not maleness but institutionalized ideals of manhood are the problem. Not politics but the politics of estranged men is the horror. Not power but power against life and for hollow purposes is the enemy. Life and the human projects that extend beyond life must be reintegrated. The body and the head must be returned to one another. This is not a utopian, anonymous, passive, or naturalistic politics, an antipolitics or a politics in which life is never set at risk. It *is* a politics that parts ways with manhood as it has been traditionally constructed.

Notes

1. Arendt, *Human Condition*, pp. 36, 37.

2. Ibid.

3. Arendt, "What is Freedom?," in *Between Past and Future*, p. 156.

4. Nietzsche, "The Greek State," pp. 8–9.

5. Paul Ricoeur, *History and Truth*, trans. C. A. Kelbey (Evanston: Northwestern University Press, 1965) p. 249.

6. Weber, *ES* (II) IX–1, p. 902.

7. Weber, *ES* (II) X–1, p. 941.

8. Arendt, "What is Freedom?," p. 156.

9. Weber, *ES* (I) I–17, p. 55.

10. Thucydides, *The Peloponnesian War*, p. 331.

11. Weber, *ES* (II) XIII–1, p. 1007.

12. Weber, "Freiburg Inaugural Address," p. 267.

13. Arendt, *Human Condition*, p. 55.

14. See Kathy Ferguson, *The Feminist Case Against Bureaucracy* (Philadephia: Temple University Press, 1984).

15. All should be familiar except Carey McWilliams: "Weapons and Virtues," *Democracy*, vol. 2, no. 3 (July 1982). See especially pp. 103–105.

16. See Susan Stern, *With the Weathermen* (Garden City, N.Y.: Doubleday, 1975).

17. Simone de Beauvoir, *The Second Sex*, trans. H. M. Parshley (New York: Vintage, 1974), p. 72.

18. Simone de Beauvoir, *Memoirs of a Dutiful Daughter*, trans. J. Kirkup (New York: Harper and Row, 1974), p. 113.

19. Machiavelli, *Prince* 25, p. 90.

20. Frederick Engels, *The Origins of the Family, Private Property and the State*, ed. E.B. Leacock (New York: International Publishers, 1972).

21. August Bebel, *Woman Under Socialism*, cited in Lorenne Clark, "The Rights of Women: The Theory and Practice of the Ideology of Male Supremacy," p. 58.

22. V. I. Lenin, *Selected Writings: The Emancipation of Women*, ed. N. K. Krupskaya (New York: International Publishers, 1934), see esp. pp. 66–72. For the modern version of Lenin's position, see Charnie Guetell, *Marxism and Feminism* (Toronto: Hunter Rose, 1974). Labor force statistics are from Rose L. Glickman, *Russian Factory Women: Workplace and Society 1880–1914* (Berkeley: University of California, 1984), pp. 83, 86.

23. Clara Zetkin, "My Recollections of Lenin" in Lenin, *Emancipation of Women*, pp. 101–4. Alexandra Kollantai, *Selected Writings*, trans. and ed. Alix Holt (New York: Norton, 1977), see pp. 127–41; 216–49, 276–92.

24. Zetkin, pp. 103, 123; Kollantai's tale is told in Holt's commentary in the *Selected Writings*, pp. 121–22, 214–15, 298–99. See also Beatrice Farnsworth, "Bolshevism, the Woman Question and Alexandra Kollantai," *American Historical Review* vol. 81, no. 2 and Jacqueline Heinen, "Kollantai and the History of Women's Oppression," *New Left Review* 110.

25. Shulamith Firestone, *The Dialectic of Sex: The Case for Feminist Revolution*, revised edition (New York: Bantam, 1971), p. 206.

26. There are countless works, especially in the "corporate success" field, advocating this position. A small sample includes: Grace Lichtenstein, *Machisma: Women and Daring* (New York: Doubleday, 1981); Betty Harragan, *Games Mother Never Taught You: Corporate Gamesmanship for Women* (New York: Warner Books, 1977); and Marilyn Kennedy, *Office Politics: Seizing Power, Wielding Clout* (New York: Warner Books, 1980).

27. A variety of moderate and radical feminists put forth some version of this position. Jean Elshtain, drawing upon Sara Ruddick's "Maternal Thinking" [*Feminist Studies* 6 (Summer 1980)] offers the moderate version in *Public Man, Private Woman*, and "Antigones' Daughters." Mary Dietz offers a neo-Arendtian critique of Elshtain and Ruddick in "Citizenship with a Feminist Face: The Problem With Maternal Thinking" *Political Theory* 13 (1985). Valerie Hartouni makes an explicitly feminist critique of Elshtain's interpretation of *Antigone* in "Antigone's Dilemma: A Problem in Political Membership," *Hypatia*, vol. 1, no. 1 (Spring 1986). Radical feminists who present women and women's contribution to the world as inherently "life-affirming" include Mary Daly, [*Gyn/Ecology: The Metaethics of Radical Feminism* (Boston: Beacon, 1978)], Susan Griffin *Women and Nature* (New York: Harper and Row, 1978)], and the growing genre of spiritual feminism and eco-feminism. This issue is discussed at greater length in chapter ten, p. 189–91.

10

What Is To Be Done: Toward a Post-Masculinist Politics

"If the body stays a shackle, then the mind remains a chain
That'll link you to a destiny
whereby all good souls are slain."[1]

—Ferron

Radical visioning always carries certain perils and in thinking about a post-masculinist politics, there are any number of foolish casuistries into which one can stumble. In this regard, it may behoove us to muse briefly upon directions to be avoided in the project of conceiving alternatives to our inherited constructions of politics. We cannot avoid them all and still continue to speak, but, to borrow Norman Jacobson's phrase, we may at least guard against "some of our more absurd attempts at trying to pull ourselves up by our own metaphysical bootstraps."[2]

Because both female and male, private and public, have been developed in crude and limited fashion as a consequence of their antimonious construction, neither is a model for an alternative politics. Simple reversals—such as substituting "feminine values" for masculine ones in the public sphere—are both impossible and inappropriate avenues to liberated political thinking and practice. Yet this is the route intentionally or inadvertently taken by a quite diverse array of thinkers, from Jean Bethke Elshtain—a pro-family feminist, to Starhawk—a self-proclaimed witch and ecofeminist, to Mary Daly—a radical, spiritual feminist, to Kathy Ferguson—an anarchist-

189

socialist feminist.[3] Ironically, the problem is one that Ferguson herself identifies: "female values" have not been shaped for public purposes nor under conditions of freedom but rather have been developed under conditions of oppression and bent to the service of power in the private sphere.[4] Moreover they do not, any more than their masculine counterpart, bear our full humanity. Although we may find some of women's historically developed qualities more appealing than those of men, women cannot be called the more "fully human" gender in a history that dichtomizes women and men along almost every dimension of human being and activity. Within the partiality of the construction of both women and men, there has been no ungendered *human* experience, only the experience of women and men.

A second set of problems attendant upon the attempt to transform political life by supplanting masculinist values with those historically developed by women converges upon the fact that the heritage of "feminine values" is as little "essentially female" as its masculine counterpart. Certainly the cultural construction of gender has some ties to physiology but either humans are more and other than their physiological sex, or gender and culture are not worth talking about. Although some of those who celebrate "female values" and advocate their infusion into public life claim to be able to distill "essential" female values (such as caretaking, self-sacrifice, or identity developed through connection with others) from their sometimes disagreeable cultural expression (such as overprotectiveness, masochism, or fear of autonomy), it is not at all obvious how this can be done.[5] Either a subtle biologism, essentialism, or sneaky Hegelian dialectic is the operative dynamic in claims such as this: "feminist discourse . . . stands at the intersection of femininity and femaleness, opposing the strategies of the former while endorsing the values of the latter."[6] If human beings and values have essences that can be betrayed by their concrete expression, then God is not dead and neither is Plato. That we like some of the sensibilities women have developed pursuant to the role they have been assigned historically is a good reason to explore the political potential of these sensibilities but does not mean we can develop them into an idealized and mobile value *system* that abstracts from the context in which the sensibilities were formed and eschews their less lovely aspects. Similarly, while the traditional work of women as mothers and managers of emotional life provides rich material for rethinking political relations, this experience cannot simply replace political relations.

Finally, the whole idea of distinctly female or feminine values and especially revolutionary ones, is quite hard to sustain when differences of race, class, culture, and religion are attended to. While it is true that most women mother, we do not all do it in the same way, with the same consciousness, with the same value attached to it, under the same conditions, or within the same kinds of social relations. A young white academic mother in New York City and an Indian mother in Peru might well have more in common with their male counterparts than with each other in any number of respects but especially with regard to basic values and understandings of identity and community. To put this point slightly differently, while women are everywhere "the second sex," we do not in consequence necessarily develop a set of values that stand in opposition to the dominant, male ones; dominant discourses may always produce subjugated discourses but the latter are not necessarily oppositional or subversive.[7] Moreover, one of the most dangerous things we can do to ourselves is to believe, as have no small number of feminists, that women are what men say we are, e.g., naturally maternal or closer to nature, and proceed to develop an alternative politics out of the uninterrogated stereotype. Men may treat nature as a woman and a woman as nature, but this does not mean that women actually experience this ideologically assigned proximity to nature.

If "feminine" is not female, and female is neither "everything good" nor an historical or cultural constant, and women's historical experience in the household is not sufficiently worldly for it to be imported wholesale into a reformulated politics, then not only must we avoid the theoretical ruse of attempting to invert the old hierarchies, we must beware as well of trying to reconcile historical opposites. The oppositions themselves have led our imaginations and deeds astray: that female and male are identifiably different in any number of physiological and cultural respects does not mean that they are dichotomous. Man is no more the opposite of woman than the United States is the opposite of the Soviet Union, technology the opposite of nature, or the moon the opposite of the sun. Dichotomy is the simplest, most reductionistic and uninteresting way to render and organize difference. Social dualisms are not only oppressive (for one side is always valorized and both sides are always violated by the construction) but boring. Active/passive, dominant/submissive, aggressive/receptive, violent/peaceful—what living creature finds its own complexity or its relations with others accurately rendered by these terms? Instead of simple reversals or reconciliations, then, we need to search for the grounds of transformed human beings and polities on a plane apart from these wars between falsely constructed opposites.

As we approach this new ground, however, we immediately encounter another snare to be avoided in this kind of work. Political transformations are not accomplished through conceptual, linguistic, or ideological alterations. Rather, a new politics must be located *within* history and directed toward the concrete construction of a future. Thus, for purposes of alternative world-building we must hedge against inclinations to create, in abstract fashion, a new "political discourse" or a utopian feminist polity, although such endeavors may be of great value as vehicles or standpoints for criticism. We need to avoid formulating values, ethics, and aims that do not take their starting point in real, existent, historically shaped human beings and polities. If the critical work constitutive of the body of this book has any significance for political projects of our time, it lies in confronting who and where we are and rooting our understanding of possibilities for political transformation in that knowledge.

I

Among the features of our species distinctiveness is our capacity to think and do, deliberate and act, rather than merely survive. More than creatures who merely live, we *make* a world and imbue it with meanings. We are shaped by forces of external nature but bear as well the mind, impulses, and tools to create and transform the world we inhabit; in so doing, we create and transform ourselves. In the history of the West, these aspects of being human have been dealt with narrowly and problematically in several important ways. As was most starkly revealed by Aristotle, but evident as well from the other theorists considered in this study, the activity of maintaining and sustaining life has been ideologically and practically divided off from the activity of creating history and meaning, with most women made responsible for the former and mostly men taking credit for the latter. The consequences have not only been oppressive for a vast portion of the population but have entailed alienation from life itself for those who appointed themselves the form-givers and meaning-makers. The division also contains an enormous ideological obfuscation. On the one hand, as we know so well from Marx, the activity of maintaining and sustaining life is not uncreative or "purely natural" for human beings.[8] Even procreation has a distinctly historical form when humans perform it; particular modes, mores, structures, and meanings shape the way procreation is organized, practiced, and valued in any human culture. On the other hand, as we also learn from Marx, those who are "free" from the activity of maintaining and sustaining life for the activity of "world-making" are in fact not so; they are powerfully determined by the realm and activities from which they believe themselves to be independent.[9]

Still, there are differences between procreation and creation, and between replenishing or sustaining life and developing a world. The differences are not absolute and I shall argue that the parallels and connections between them can be grasped and incorporated into practice to a greater degree than we are accustomed to. Before making this argument, however, the differences need to be drawn out so that we can see the many dimensions of human existence to be given a home in a reformulated politics. Then we can conjecture about how they might be harbored within us as individuals and among us in society.

Human beings are capable of engaging in at least three kinds of activities: reproducing ourselves—without which we cannot exist at all; producing for ourselves—without which we cannot continue to exist; and those intellectual, artistic, and physical endeavors, both individual and collective, that do not directly produce for or reproduce our existence. The brilliance of Marx was to recognize the importance of the second kind of activity in human history, a recognition so far-reaching in its implications for social theory that it blinded him and those who follow him to the importance and the care and feeding of the other two. After Marx, much twentieth-century political theory has been devoted to arguing about the appropriate status of and relation between production and human activities that are not distinctly productive but are active or creative.[10] And it has been the project of recent feminist theory to assert the historically invisible significance of the other major web of activities Marx neglected— reproductive work.[11] While various theorists have argued for the supremacy of one activity over another in terms of what constitutes our "essential humanness" or the appropriate basis and center of social organization, few have tried to explore each of these activities from the perspective of the others or formulate a just social order in which all three are recognized, valued, and performed under conditions of freedom.[12] This has a great deal to do with failing to address, in a fundamental way, the problematic of freedom itself.

II

Our heritage in thinking about and practicing freedom is a profoundly troubled one. As I have argued throughout this work, from the very beginning of our civilization, even the most appealing formulations of freedom have been rooted in a freedom *from* the body and its demands, freedom *from* necessity in general. Marx fits this description no less than the rest, although he did realize that the conditions for genuine freedom were collective ownership and control of the means of production in the realm of necessity. But freedom for Marx comes only with the mastering of necessity according to these conditions and it is predicated upon the technological possibility of such mastery. His is a formulation of freedom that indisputably involves thoroughgoing control, indeed conquest, of nature and of human neediness. Moreover, as no small number of feminists have pointed out, Marx's understanding of freedom severely neglects reproductive work, which is problematic to master technically and no easy thing to collectively own and control.[13]

When freedom is posited beyond the body and beyond necessity, concern with life becomes an encumbrance to freedom. If freedom only begins when humans transcend a concern with life or, in Arendt's account, literally jettison this concern, then mortality and mortal needs must be left at the threshold of the political realm or wherever freedom is sought. Courage becomes a willingness to risk death, heroism has as its essence placing life at risk, noble pursuits are those which have a cause higher than or indifferent to life. Freedom cast as freedom from the body, need, and necessity is therefore inherently oppressive as well as ultimately impossible— living things simply cannot transcend or overcome themselves, the fact of their lives. This construction of freedom breeds a politics against life, dooms the activities and persons involved with necessity to organization under domination, and renders life an instrument rather than a cause of freedom. The utter bankruptcy of this approach to freedom was revealed by Weber: under modern systems of power, the quest for freedom as control of necessity has utterly subverted itself and man appears dominated by and trapped within the cogs of his own machinery of mastery.

Finally, freedom in opposition to necessity is a praxis of freedom that necessitates colonization of others and whose partiality converts women into some of its most severe victims. While men have been busy overcoming their bodies and necessity to find their freedom, something had to absorb, ideologically as well as practically, the dimension of human existence men were seeking to deny in themselves. Women were an obvious receptacle and indeed, it is by now commonplace that in most of the dominant discourses of Western Civilization, Woman is almost synonymous with Body.[14] Women's subordinate and violable status is thoroughly entwined with being identified with her body within social constructions dividing individuals and societies into bodies and minds and valorizing Mind. While man can be anything, woman *is* her physiology, historically most often reduced to her sexual and reproductive aspects.[15] Not incidentally, woman is also identified with Nature, and again not incidentally, her daily existence is bound up with concern for life—bearing and caring for it. In view of these associations, it should surprise no one that woman has been historically conceived as among the most inappropriate and subversive things one can introduce into politics: precisely because woman has been made to stand for body, sexuality, and life maintenance, she is dreaded in the political realm insofar as she is seen as contaminating politics with these banned goods. Indeed, woman in the political sphere, although decried by nearly every political thinker from Aristophanes and Aristotle through Nietzsche and Norman Mailer, is most succinctly described by the seventeenth-century English thinker John Knox, who simply declared the phenomenon "monstrous."[16]

Arendt insists that "man's freedom is always won in his never wholly successful attempts to liberate himself from necessity" and I am intimating the converse, that these attempts have not only subjugated women but have subverted man's quest for freedom.[17] In patriarchal history, freedom and domination have always been regarded as a complementary pair—"violence is the prepolitical act of liberating oneself from the necessity of life for the freedom of the world"[18]—and I am suggesting that they are at odds with one another in a sense more dramatic than that which Marx detected. We cannot dominate anything we are related to and find our freedom through that domination. A part of ourselves is always contained in the object of domination and is lost or estranged from us through the process of domination. The attempt to thoroughly subjugate the body by Mind results in the construction and experience of the body as a demanding demon—foreign, irascible, and infantile. Male domination of women limits the range and possibilities of men insofar as they alienate themselves from all the human activities and characteristics ascribed to women. Class domination—whether in Ancient Greece or under modern capitalism—estranges the dominant class from all that is entailed in the development and sustenance of life. Domination of the environment limits our freedom as creatures of the natural world; it entails a denial of ourselves as organic creatures and limits our capacity to provide for ourselves.

Genuine freedom—freedom marked by constant and diverse invention of our individual and collective existence—will only be had when we stop trying to repudiate or conquer who we are, what we must do for survival, what we confront in the way of necessity. Clearly this involves realization of the basic democratic socialist precepts of collective, decentralized ownership and control of production and the basic radical feminist precepts of collective responsibility for reproductive work. But it also entails a good deal more. We must learn to engage with the materials of our existence in a manner that draws forth its possibilities rather than imposes a form upon it. We must learn to engage regeneratively rather than instrumentally with nature, with ourselves as bodily creatures, and with others.[19] This does not, as some feminists would have it, entail a move to cast nature as the natural habitat of human beings nor to glorify nature or the body as a garden of harmonious delights. Unreconstructed nature is not the *métier* of producing, tool-using, meaning-making animals; moreover, nature offers up tidal waves, draughts, and gratuitous interspecies violence as well as delicately flowered meadows and the eternal changing of the seasons. The human body has its own version of this spectrum—it harbors the capacity for pain, violence, and disease as well as for pleasure and poetic movement. In this regard, the spiritual feminist injunction to simply surrender to nature and the body is revealed as a simplistic and unfelicitous one. Again, rather than simply inverting the hierarchy of value between nature and *technē* or freedom and necessity, we need to find our freedom in and through relationships to necessity, by constructing free conditions through which to engage with necessity rather than by striving to overcome nature and necessity. This is not to suggest that we must cease to care for or strive toward things other than the production and reproduction of life. But we can learn to arrange and address these cares such that we are not individually divided creatures and are not impelled to divide the species into those who sustain life and those who live "freely" by transcending life.

Rejecting the antagonistic dualism between freedom and necessity does not entail a "downward adjustment" of our expectations of freedom but rather, a theory and practice of freedom encompassing the whole range of human activity, the *human animal* rather than the human mind or the human male. We need to discern how to be free *as* ourselves rather than free *from* what we are, what bears and sustains us. Above all this involves recognizing that *the body is the locus, vehicle, and origin of our freedom rather than the encumbrance to it Western political theory has always claimed the body to be*. We know that other animals are free until they are physically captured or rendered physically dependent—why is it so difficult to see that in this instance, we, too, are animals?[20] Our bodies bear us, our bodies *are* us—how can freedom be a problem of Mind? Hegel, that greatest of all metaphysical acrobats, has us standing on our heads again, this time quite literally. The ancient and unchallenged rejection of the body, repudiation of the body as animal-like, culminates in the absurdity of conceiving the most physical of human experiences as a problem of mind and resolvable through mind. While human freedom is different and more complex than animal "freedom," in both cases the body is the *medium* of freedom or, to put the matter the other way around, the body is the necessary target of slavery. Even Arendt recognizes that freedom is contained in our capacity for action. What Arendt cannot admit is that the body is the locus or vehicle of action, hence of freedom. Her rejection of this conclusion explains why action remains for her a rarified, unrealizable ideal.[21]

This is not to say that minds cannot be colonized—they can and they are. In our culture and epoch, bureaucratic, patriarchal, liberal capitalist discourse does so on a daily basis. But discursive power is legitimating or coercive power, not liberating power. The colonization of minds initiates, sustains or legitimates power over bodies. A counter-discourse can only serve a critical function, it cannot actually free us. We cannot talk or think our way into freedom any more than we can talk or think our way through a brick wall. Discursive power can rob us of our freedom and can reveal our unfreedom but discourse alone cannot imbue us with or deliver freedom. Freedom is rooted in, predicated upon, and finally, *experienced*, through the body.

Concretely, freedom through the body requires that we embrace our "natural" or necessity-oriented aspect and turn our attention to ways in which it is currently organized *for* us rather than *by* us creatively, collectively, in short—freely. It also means that we need to look closely at desire, especially sexual desire, but other kinds of longings and urges as well. For if necessity is one part of what is despised and oppressed when the body is cast at odds with freedom, desire is another. Plato's identification of desire as a tyrant, Aristotle's association of virtue with continence, Machiavelli's connection of self-control with autonomy and *virtù*, Weber's designation of thoroughly rational action as the mode of action bearing the greatest freedom—all of these are testimony to the dangerous terms in which desire is viewed. Both necessity and desire have been historically regarded as injurious to freedom, crippling if not mastered, and the resultant organization of both has been fundamental to institutionalized sexism and misogyny. Woman, labelled "body," has been the chief bearer of both necessity and sexuality in Western civilization, with the consequence that she is demeaned, isolated and oppressed in her work, objectified and violated in her sexuality.[22]

What if we organized and experienced necessity and desire as loci of creative possibility rather than as slavish, deterministic drives requiring subjugation? Indeed, both can be fields of creative possibility; neither inherently determines or enslaves us. For example, when we peer closely at any given sexual desire, we discover that it is remarkably open to being shaped, engaged in different ways, channelled, teased, developed, rallied for myriad purposes, postponed. Yet we have been made stupid about this just as we have been made stupid about the creative possibilities attendant upon providing food for ourselves or bringing up the next generation. We accept the ideological division of our being into deterministic drives versus conscious willing, passion versus reason, instinct versus thought. Yet if humans really are *constructed* through and through, then both halves of these antinomies misfire—our passions are not fixed, only unknown and in important ways, untapped. Moreover, our passions are not separate from what we call thinking, only reified, retarded, and rigidified through being set out in opposition to thought.

From Freud (and it is ironic that it took Freud, the "head doctor," to announce this to us), we know that the head does *not* operate independently of desires and the body, that it responds in myriad ways to bodily desire, need and pain, including neurotically and brutally. From Freud, as well, we learn some of the limits to the head's erstwhile capacity for rational thought independent of bodily existence. Rationality in the form of Western reason is the ultimate attempt at mastery of the body; pure reason claims to be finally free of the body—a feat that is in the end only a miserable and immiserating joke. Who has not marveled at the phenomenon that the most wounded or enraged individuals are often the world's fiercest logicians or that a pristine rationality underwrites some of history's most gruesome episodes?

Where Freud leads us astray, of course, is in his essentialist, unhistorical designation of desire (a designation Foucault has done much to expose) and in his depiction of desire as relatively rigid, crude, limited in plasticity and possibililty.[23] Freud discerns that desire is shaped by human institutions, specifically the family, but it does not occur to him that "the family" itself is shaped through other quite specific historical forces and that it could be ours to transform or abandon. We, like Freud, tend to regard our desires as powerful givens, yet they appear as such precisely because they have been banished; we dread them, deny them, never dream of knowing and engaging them as we know and engage, for example, our thinking. We regard our thinking not as fixed but as fluid and changing over time; we do not consider our thoughts simply determined or determining even as they issue in part from an inaccessible place within us; we can prod them, develop them, stretch and transform them through encounter with others and the world. We experience thinking this way because it has not been banished so thoroughly as desire—it does not terrify us to the same degree so we are more familiar with the possibilities within it, indeed, with the *freedom* thinking bears for us. Whatever we banish or are ignorant of will rule us, which is probably why Socrates, who actively engaged and explored Eros, thought it might be wisdom, while Plato, who shunned Eros in his philosophy, named it a tyrant.[24]

Of course, desire, like thinking, bears not merely delights but some very rude, nasty, antisocial aspects. Even when its historically constructed, plastic, and malleable nature is accounted for, under the rubric of desire we would probably find individual urges for power, possession, indulgence, destruction, and all the other things political theorists and psychologists have been cataloging and decrying for millenia. In calling for the liberation of desire, I am not, as I think Nietzsche may have been, calling for the indiscriminate admission of all these elements into public life nor for simply letting the "Id" (Freud's unhistorical conceptual container for those uncivil elements) have its way in social life. Rather, I am suggesting only that a post-masculinist politics will give up a fierce, disembodied rationalism to explore the creative range and possibility of desire and, in public as well as private life, give desire a well-lit field of play instead of a shadowy one. Again, what lurks in the shadows haunts and tricks us. Our uninterrogated fears make us conservative, our uninterrogated wants make us hungry and mean, our uninterrogated longings make us fix upon objects and relations that do not satisfy us.

III

Thus far, the insistence that a feminist politics entails moving away from the construction of freedom rooted in domination of necessity and the body has been proffered in mostly abstract terms. At the risk of oversimplifying the contours of this project, I want to offer two concrete examples of the alternative approach to freedom and power sketched to this point. Neither example has political life as its explicit subject, but both illuminate features of an alternative politics.

In the production of food for our existence, there exists a continuum of possible approaches to the natural resources of the planet, with replenishment and renewal at one end and exploition leading to permanent damage at the other. Selecting crops and growing methods according to a careful accomodation between our need and the requisites of ecological balance and regeneration offer a rarely adopted example of the former. Cotton and tobacco production in the antebellum South, contemporary agribusiness in central California, and deforestation in vast regions of the southern hemisphere are frequently cited examples of the latter. Does this mean that external nature *dictates* the specific ways in which our needs for food and clothing are met? Not at all. We are creatures of *technē*, capable of boundless innovation in addressing necessity and interacting with nature. The only constraint upon our innovativeness lies in the characteristics of the *live* materials with which we are working, and even this is not much of a "constraint" since the possibilities are infinite. Our freedom lies in our *power* to create and open up possibility as we engage with necessity. Yet for new possibility to continuously be born and thus for our freedom in working creatively with these materials and our needs to be sustained, we must engage with these materials in a manner that rejuvenates them even as we cultivate and consume them. The less we engage with nature and with our own needs in this manner, the less we will experience freedom in meeting necessity. Raw exploitation of nature—stamping matter with form—limits its power and possibility. Very little can be cultivated from depleted soil; small food for life prospers in a polluted river or bay. In such circumstances, the requirement of depending upon distant lands or highly specialized technology quite literally constrains our freedom, our creativity and choices in meeting needs; once initiated, we become enslaved to the process and consequences of domination.

When we attempt to dominate external nature—exploiting it by seeking to master it or impose our desires upon it—we simultaneously limit the powers of nature and of ourselves in engaging with it. This limitation, explored in detail in the study of Machiavelli, emerges whenever something living—a person, a people, or a patch of external nature—is converted into "matter" in the form-matter paradigm. The "matter" is depowered, deprived of its capacity to regenerate and direct itself and the form-giver is constrained by the lessened possibilities of this depowered material. Power and freedom are thus diminished as conquest and control in the form of domination are extended. Machiavelli taught us this basic logic even if he could not make himself adhere to it.

For a different and perhaps stranger arena of exploration of these themes, we may turn to the sphere of intimacy and ask what it would mean to find freedom through necessity there. We do not usually think of intimate relations as a terrain of freedom although it has lately become fashionable to bring the notions of need and reciprocity to them. Precisely because we generally regard and approach intimacy as being outside the pale of freedom or even as antithetical to freedom do we prevent the possibility of engaging closely with others in liberating or empowering ways. By seeking to control the domain where our some of our deepest emotional needs are engaged, domination and depowerment ensue where the opposite could emerge.

There are countless ways domination can be insinuated into a relationship. Most obvious is the phenomenon of one person wielding literal, institutionally- or physically-backed power over another, thereby establishing relations of dependence and subordination. There are, however, much more subtle and interesting forms of domination in personal life. One of Weber's most important discoveries about the power and effectiveness of bureaucratic organization is that formalization, adherence to rules of conduct, and containment in narrow spheres of domain are the basis of domination and unfreedom in social relations. Since institutionalization—marriage—is today the most common approach to the realm of intimate relationships, it would appear that we are more terrified of freedom in the "personal sphere," where we choose this institutionalization, than anywhere else.[25] The high contemporary marriage rate in the face of the extraordinary divorce rate further highlights this terror. Given the rare prospects for recognition and security in the rest of our social order, this fear of freedom is hardly surprising but it is disturbing.

When we attempt to fulfill the need to be wanted, recognized, or cared for through controlling the entity meant to do so, i.e., through rules, regulations, and routines, the experience is a far cry from freedom. On one hand, as we bind another to us with contracts and obligations, our desire for love and recognition is mirrored back to us as ensnaring, confining, controlling in its power. On the other, institutionalizing the mode of fulfilling these desires reduces the possibility of developing or transforming them. Through controlling that which is intended to fulfill the need, we remain in thrall to necessity, to the process and parameters of control. We limit what the other is and might become through focusing singly upon what we are certain we must have and through institutionalizing its provision.

The attempt to address "emotional necessity" by controlling or institutionalizing that which is meant to provide for it is precisely what causes us to regard intimacy and freedom as antithetical, to situate power and need upon mutually exclusive planes, to treat autonomy and connection as opposites. Recall that the Greeks regarded the realm of necessity as inherently oppressive and slavish because it was organized oppressively, because they practiced slavery. The generic activity of work appeared degrading and threatening to freedom because in ancient Greece it was practiced under conditions of domination and relegated to a sphere that stood in opposition to the sphere designed for freedom. I am suggesting that we do the same thing not only with work but with intimacy. In both domains, we continue to think that freedom can only mean suppressing, escaping, or controlling the domain of need. If, in our ideas and practices, we establish oppositions between relationships and freedom, power and need, autonomy and connection, we can only experience choices about connecting with others as unhappy trade-offs: we face either the miserable freedom of loneliness, the numbness of drastic emotional repression, or the depowering dependence and control by necessity often contained in the "security of marriage." Each choice issues from the same cultural pathology; each embodies the conventional oppositions between freedom and necessity, autonomy and connection, power and dependence.

Imagine bringing the desire for love and recognition to relationship without striving to institutionalize or routinize the connection, without seeking control, without spinning sets of conventions upon which one can depend and is also ensnared. In this condition, we are extraordinarily vulnerable—indeed, much courage and willingness to risk is required for living and loving this way. But we are also extraordinarily free to develop myriad ways of meeting needs in the sense of encountering and transforming them rather than simply capitulating to them. In this condition we can experience power rather than dependence through connection because we freely act rather than conform or behave; we consciously make the relationship rather than letting it make and limit us. The very status of our "needs" is transformed in this kind of relationship because the needs develop and change as we engage with another autonomous being rather than being frozen in the institutionalized form of the relationship. We, the "material" of the relationship, produce a dynamic of development and change that is the fluid form of the relationship. Such a relationship is not without form but the form-matter distinction becomes meaningless. Imposition of a single form upon the relationship means an end to freedom within it, an end to the freedom to create and transform the relationship and ourselves.

In the kind of relations sketched above, there are two levels on which one can see freedom located in and through necessity. First, we experience freedom in addressing our own needs for recognition, protection, solace, love, comradeship or sex. These needs are not rigidly fixed or addressed through an institution but are freely developed and transformed in the encounter with specific others. Second, as we confront the power of another human being whom we do not possess or control, we greet an autonomous and fluid being. We confront the necessity of engaging deeply with something we cannot control or predict, something we could master or conquer only at the expense of our freedom. We experience freedom here through our capacity to draw forth possibility through action and innovation.

Undoubtedly, these sensibilities and practices sound difficult, dangerous, and fragile. Indeed, they are all of these things. More courage, more willingness to risk, is required of living this way than of ways more familiar to us. It is easier to live under controlled conditions than to take responsibility for shaping a life, just as it can be easier to live under power than to take power or be powerful. But comfort and ease are not the rewards freedom promises.

IV

What of pursuits other than the creation and sustenance of life and the meeting of need? What of those impulses to shape and transform our world, to leave something of an individual or collective indelible mark of our existence in a world that outlives us? How is this desire for "immortality" reconcilable with or integrated into an understanding of freedom rooted in nature and necessity? How can it be incorporated into the rest of our activities without replicating the historic tendency to give such impulses a higher, nobler, or more fully human status than the rest of human activities? Before exploring these questions, we need to recall what is so troubling about the way in which this dimension of human existence has been dealt with in the patriarchal past.

The Greeks offer the starkest picture of the historical problematic of immortality; according to Arendt, the Greek pursuit of immortality expressed a noble longing not to be mortal creatures but instead "to be immortal like the gods they created."[26] In previous chapters, we saw that this longing entailed disparagement of the value of life itself and of the activities and people involved with making and sustaining life. Immortalizing oneself depended upon the achievement of individual fame achieved through the defeat of another and realized through recognition of this accomplishment by one's peers. Greek heroes took exceptional risks with their own or others' lives (especially in war) or bested their rivals in competitive games. Recognition acquired in this fashion was fragile and precarious, utterly dependent upon both the witnessing of one's heroic action by others and the remembrance of the deed over time. This recognition is also mythologizing—the actor becomes the act in historical memory, the name stands for the great deed done once upon a time.

Now on the one hand, all this seems a very strange thing to live for and on the other, there are at least a few commendable aspects to the Greek obsession with heroism and immortality. The yearning to create or accomplish something of unique or lasting value and to be recognized for it is nothing to deride. Most people want to do more than merely live life and long instead to live it creatively, in active engagement with the world, even to determine something of the course of the world. What else can explain that "problem which has no name" with which Betty Friedan inaugurated the middle-class feminist movement two decades ago—the widespread experience among "housewives" that despite the relevance of their daily tasks to physical and emotional sustenance, their lives were empty, shadowy, void of meaning?[27] It is not merely "the unexamined life which is not worth living" but the uncreative life, the life wholly determined by the past and by external conditions, that cannot be experienced as a meaningful life. Perhaps Socrates meant to convey precisely this through his famous utterance—that an unexamined life is not seized and borne forth by its possessor.

Does the impulse to shape the course of our lives and of history necessarily constitute a "pursuit of immortality?" The nomenclature may be unimportant—human beings do seem to have fairly deep desires for *creativity, recognition,* and *continuity* in the course of a life, desires to be more than anonymous workers and more than "creatures of a day," fleeting heroines or heros. This does not mean we are born with a yearning to last forever, to overcome death or transcend mortal things. Yet these are the terms in which our needs for creativity and continuity have been expressed in patriarchal history, primarily because concerns with life itself have been construed as concerns that preclude creativity and continuity. When the reproduction and maintenance of life are organized oppressively and regarded as demeaning, transcendence of life appears as the only road to recognition, continuity and creativity. The particular form of the quest for these things is shaped by the construction of an oppressive mortal life.

So how do we go about addressing this need for continuity and creativity in a fashion that does not replicate the perilous extremes of the Greeks, the misguided national glory to which Weber turned, or the stamping of matter with form sought by the man of Machiavellian *virtù*? A glimpse of the possibilities may be obtained by investigation of a surprising arena, the work of reproduction. (Actually, reproduction has often been spoken of as a means of immortalizing oneself—even Plato and Aristotle spoke of it thus.[28]) By no means is reproductive work a model for all that we do in life, but it contains an intricate combination of elements that may enable us to explore alternative modes for experiencing creativity, continuity, and recognition.

Mary O'Brien has argued that Western politics is founded in male anxiety about the continuity experienced solely by women in bringing new life into this world.[29] The biologism underlying O'Brien's genealogy of politics is highly questionable, but there may be something to her conviction that the work of childrearing has historically offered women partial satisfaction of a desire for continuity. And, while a mother has little control over the natural processes which gestate new life, much of her engagement with the child can be creative. At its idealized best, nurturing a child to maturity entails developing, protecting, and guiding the potential of a small being in a way which learns from and honors what is there as well as contributing to it. By no means is one simply imposing form on matter. Similarly, in the "socialization" aspect of childrearing, socialization at its best involves the introduction of society to the child *and* the introduction of the child to society. Again, the form-matter paradigm is an altogether inappropriate model for this process. Socialization involves a molding as well as an introduction into history, into society, of something new and culminates in *letting go* of one's work—allowing the creation one had a part in to take on its own life in the world. Thus, the continuity a woman experiences in childrearing is literally embodied in another live being, but this embodiment does not bear the name nor the unilateral imprint of its "founder." A woman is not "immortalized" in her child—*inter alia*, the child, too, is mortal—but she is carried on.

(The irony in all of this, of course, is that in patriarchal history, it is the father who is said to acquire immortality through his children, a phenomenon that actually reveals much about the different ways women and men have met the need for continuity through the ages. The child bears the father's name and the mother's care. The father is immortalized through a single deed (copulation) while the mother gains the experience of continuity through a life work. He acquires recognition through ownership; she experiences continuity but not recognition for bringing the child to maturity.)[30]

I hasten to note that no matter what the cultural value and organization of reproductive work, by itself, childrearing probably cannot completely address the desire for creative work, recognition and engagement with the world. It is too close to nature, too much of it is finally given, and it is too rife with relations of inequality and protection for it to fulfill these desires. It neither fully taps creative capacities nor our impulse to exert power and distinguish ourselves. While it can lead to history-making, it is not in itself history-making. Childrearing is, after all, the most common work in the world and it also has more than a few inescapably monotonous, routine aspects to it. This is why the mighty feminist project of reorganizing and revaluing reproductive work is an essential but insufficient project for feminism. This is why being a mother, no matter how freely arranged or how deeply valued by others, is not enough for any of us.

But we can learn from childrearing as a mode of creative work in which an experience of continuity and creative transformation of the world are simultaneously featured. A mother contributes to the making of a child but ultimately must release the finished "product" to the world and to the grown child's own intentions. The contribution a mother makes to the world outlives her and carries a part of her forward into history, but her satisfaction must lie in seeing her work in the world without her name attached to it, without owning or possessing this creation. It is not her's but it is partly her. The work of raising a child involves drawing forth possibility, shaping and guiding but not stamping this being with external form.

Drawing these dimensions of the work of childrearing toward our endeavors in public life is not, I think, impossible. We can engage with the environment and our bodies as if they were organic and sentient rather than passive matter awaiting our imposition of form. We can learn to develop new modes of life out of historically given ones, rather than staging coups or seizing history by force, impetuousness, or rape. We can find continuity in long labors of love in which we are truly invested and represented rather than in once-only deeds that record a performance rather than a person. We can prove and distinguish ourselves through our cares rather than by risking our deepest attachments or in an essentially superfluous space where performances witnessed by peers provide the only certainty that we are "real." We can achieve recognition for work rather than owner-ship, for devotion and not only daring, for ingenuity or imagination and not only audacity.

These alternative touchstones for creative and worthwhile en-deavor are not meant to suggest that a post-masculinist politics must refuse a place to bold, impetuous, forceful or daring actions. Rather such a politics calls for a different kind of action, with different motives and measures of boldness and heroism. Nor do I mean to diminish the importance of courage in politics and other dimensions of life. As one of the most important and inspiring elements of human and political existence, courage, along with its siblings daring and perseverence, is indispensible to constructive transformation of personal and political life. We require courage to push back bounda-ries and push toward ideas, relations, and endeavors before which we may be utterly terrified. We require courage to *engage* with nature or with others when our inclination is to reach our aims autarkically or instrumentally. Courage is prerequisite to trust, to a deliberate and conscious relinquishing of individual control in both public and intimate settings. Courage is also at the heart of a willingness to test or assert one's human powers and a willingness to act while acknowl-edging the frailty of human existence and webs of relations.

The historical symbiosis of courage and manliness has affixed courage with a comparatively narrow meaning and content. In the tradition of manhood, courage has been the willingness to risk death for an abstract aim and the effort to defy mortality through placing the body in peril. In the terms of manliness, courage is overcoming bodily fears and overcoming concerns for life. In contrast, I am suggesting that we need courage to *sustain* life, to fight for freedom as bearers of life and hence of possibility. A courageous deed is one which sets identity and security at risk in order to bring forth new possibility. Altering boundaries, not simply smashing or denying them, requires political courage, but the sacrifice of life for the achievement of immortal glory alters no boundaries. In this regard, the traditional formulation of courage as risking life can be seen as very crude and simplistic compared to the kind of courage I am sketching. To intentionally place one's life in peril for an abstract ideal entails a simple defiance of the animal instinct for survival. Man "proves" that survival is unimportant by jeopardizing it. In fact, in that moment he proves how much of an animal he really is for the thing he calls noblest in himself is a simple (and unconvincing) denial of his animal instinct. Truly human courage surely must lie in distinctively human things—intellectual and emotional life, building collective existence, inventing new possibility, stretching horizons.

V

Finally, what about power—what could a post-masculinist formulation of political power entail? I will not try to answer this difficult question but only to mark some features of the terrain. Several feminist theorists have tried their hand at this problem: Jean Bethke Elshtain offers a thoughtful essay on the subject that nonetheless fails its aims—her reflections on women and power ultimately collapse into attacks on other feminists and a call to keep trying to think.[31] Nancy Hartsock, despite her devotion to materialism, ironically ends up analyzing power more as a problem of conceptualizations than practices, thereby advancing our understanding of the gendered "idea" of power but doing little to investigate how power actually operates.[32] She joins Kathy Ferguson and a number of others in offering the idea of "empowering" as a possible feminist approach to power, a useful notion for breaking the common equation of power with domination but not much more.[33] Adrienne Rich and Marilyn Frye have both written insightfully on the significance of the male power "to name" as well as the power of "access," again useful notions but hardly approximating full theories of political power.[34] And Catherine MacKinnon, probably the most intriguing and controversial feminist theorist of power to date, offers a dazzling account of some of the mechanisms of men's power over women but joins other feminists in decrying male power without exploring alternative modes and possibilities of power.[35]

There are several reasons for the limited feminist attempts and even more limited successes in this arena. Power is one of those things we cannot approach head-on or in isolation from other subjects if we are to speak about it intelligently. There are so many different kinds of power that the workings and value of power cannot be generalized. We need distinctions among modes of power as the Eskimos distinguish among different kinds of snow and neither our language nor most thinking about power currently makes such distinctions.[36] Power embodies the remarkable paradox of being one of the most determining and elusive elements of human existence. Power is ubiquitous and also largely invisible. It is not a thing but a relational element; like equality, power only exists *between* its agents and objects, it is not contained within them. Nonetheless, we often and reasonably speak of someone *having* power and of others being depowered or without power.

Power is the elusive and central dynamic of human relations—it springs up wherever human beings act, collaborate, unite or contest with each other and wherever there is organization or arrangements.

At the very least, humans generate and bear sexual power, economic power, political power, discursive power, intellectual power, and physical power. Importantly, women have been rendered relatively powerless in almost all these domains: we have either generated power that has been appropriated from us and used over and against us (sexual and economic), or we have been sequestered from access to power (political, economic and intellectual), or our voices have been silenced or discounted (discursive). This severence from almost every institutional mode of power is why what is distinctive about women's oppression is not injury, exploitation, or discrimination but *dependence*.

Another consequence of the historical exclusion of women from most modes of power is that, as several feminist theorists have pointed out, many women fear power and are often quite wary of the prospect of overtly deploying power.[37] Thus, until fairly recently, radical feminists have mostly rebelled against power and expressed visions of a world without power rather than seeking to take power or envisioning alternatives to the particular ways power is currently formulated, used, and deployed.[38] Of course, feminists are not alone in constructing a politics that seeks to eschew power; as Foucault has argued, we moderns generally regard power in purely negative terms, as wholly oppressive or repressive.[39] But few political movements of the magnitude and scope of feminism have been so profoundly wary of power and so loathe to engage, theoretically or practically, the problem of power. Marilyn French's magnum opus, *Beyond Power*, expresses in its very title this feminist hostility to power and tendency to envision a feminist future void of power.[40] One of "eco-feminism's" leading thinkers opposes power more subtly by drawing a distinction between "power-over" (bad, "male," to be overcome) and "power-from-within" (good, "female," transformative).[41] The mother-worship strain of feminism, variously called cultural or spiritual feminism, claims not to reject power yet offers the following as its ideal of feminist power:

> Nurturant, generative, transformative, generous in its protection of life; harmonious in its relationship to the natural world and in its assertion of the equality of the Self among the equality of Others. It is, above all, a beneficient power, the enabling side of an "active gentleness . . . with no mere will to mastery, only care for the many-lived unending forms" of life. Like the feminist form of love, this power begins in the mother-infant bond.[42]

These formulations not only idealize and sentimentalize motherhood but are extremely limited in scope; because the emphasis is solely upon caretaking, they are inadequate to the task of constructing alternative modes of political power. That Western polities have too little emphasized caretaking is clear enough and has indeed been among the arguments of the foregoing chapters. But there are many other elements of politics, e.g., deliberations and conflicts over everything from resource allocation to basic values, in which the caretaking mode of power is essentially irrelevant. The excitement and the frustrations of politics, of dealing with the power and needs collectivities generate and the multiple faces of the individual will to power, can never be reduced to the warm ambiance of a quiet nursery or even the demands of a noisy one.

The foregoing reflections suggest that patience is in order for the project of developing a distinctly feminist theory of political power. Women have had very little comprehensive experience with political power other than as its vehicles and victims. Before all else then, we need to get to know power as something other than an enemy, to recognize power as potency and not simply domination, as exciting and not only dangerous, as productive and not simply repressive or injurious. In this regard, we may draw upon a Machiavellian insight considered in earlier pages of this work. Recall that when a prince strives to dominate the body politic, he suffers limitations upon his power by rendering his constituents dependent, thus powerless, thus incapable of supplying much power to him. Conversely, when the heads of state seek to energize and empower the body politic, unleashing its creativity such as occurred in ancient Rome, the empowered body tends to burst the bounds of the form imposed upon it from above. To be powerful means to be capable of altering conditions of life and severe limits were placed upon the Roman plebians in this regard. The problem with Rome was that the creative energy of the people was contained within a form imposed from without for purposes outside them. Of course, challenging this form was partly what the "tumults of Rome" were about. But the plebian challenge never became a wholesale effort at transformation, and ultimately, the form of the Roman republic was stretched beyond the limits it was designed to serve and Rome collapsed.

Suggestive here is the link Machiavelli establishes between freedom, power, creativity, and struggle. Freedom is not something bequeathed to a people but is realized through action and through engagement with necessity. In Machiavelli's depiction, freedom is the experience of oneself as *a being of power*, capable of opening up possibility with, through, and against other beings of power. This conception of freedom has struggle and conflict at its heart but it is not a struggle to master or control necessity. Rather, it is a struggle to draw forth possibilities from necessity and to transform both ourselves and the necessary as we struggle with it. Our experience of ourselves as powerful beings is contained in this struggle and in conflict with others. Similarly, our experience of equality is obtained through meeting the power of others. Equality, like freedom, cannot be bequeathed to us from above nor enjoyed as "equal standing" on an abstract legal plane. We can only know equality when our powers meet those of other beings—beings who are not necessarily antagonistic to us but are autonomous and empowered. Machiavelli recognized that it is conflict and struggle that make us strong, powerful, and free. Conflict and struggle open up new opportunities and possibilities that allow us to discover our power as actors and our freedom as creators of new ways to meet necessity. But the lessons Machiavelli drew from the tumults of Rome need to be placed in the service of human life, genuine freedom, and equality rather than devotion to the state, imperialism, class, or gender domination.

VI

This sketch of the parameters of an alternative politics is far from complete. The project of developing new possibilities in specific theoretical and practical domains can only be taken up in a much more particularist mode than the present study inhabits. My concern has been to establish that Western political thinking and practice is bound up with traditional constructions of manhood and that a divorce is in order. The execution of this divorce, and the creative possibilities that attend upon it and come after, is practical work. We will theorize about it intelligently only when that work is underway.

In the beginning, says Aristophanes, there were four-legged, four-armed creatures, female-and-male in one, genuine hermaphrodites.[43] These were strong, energetic and happy people, utterly self-sufficient and peaceable on earth. But they had just a little too much zest-turned-*hybris* and one day tried to scale the heights of heaven and set upon the gods. Zeus determined to come up with a way of weakening these creatures without destroying them since they did, after all, have many virtues and just this one vice. So, he split them in half, bound up their open wounds, and set them loose on earth again. These new creatures, female and male, were miserable at first, and spent their days running about searching for their lost halves, flinging their arms around each others' necks, and begging to be rolled into one again. To appease them, Zeus made some adjustments in their new bodies so that they might experience brief oneness with each other now and then, but he did not return to them the wholeness and strength they had once known.

Over many millenia, these half-creatures grew accustomed to their condition. And, even as Aristophanes tells the story, he exalts the masculine virtues over the feminine, praising the greater virtue of men and the bonding between men as the highest form of love. Men who seek "wholeness" with other men exhibit "daring, fortitude and masculinity," they are "the most hopeful of our nation's youth, for their's is the most virile constitution."[44]

Aristophanes did not live to see to what proportions this virile constitution could grow nor how complete and institutionalized this male bonding could become. Today, these bonded men are once again trying to scale the heights of heaven and set upon the gods. Their aspirations for power know no limits and the stakes of the game are now ultimate. But we cannot call upon Zeus this time—who threatened to divide the already halved creatures again if he had any more trouble with them—for he, like Aristophanes, has long since passed away. Nor can we resurrect myths of wholeness, hermaphroditism, or androgyny as visions, for they have gone, rightly, the way of the gods. Humans are complex, tension-ridden, discordant creatures and gender will never be a mere or minor biological "fact" for us—nor is there any reason to wish that it could be. We can, however, bear our complexities and construct both gender and politics in ways far more compatible with justice, with life in the largest sense of the word, and above all, with the rich possibilities contained in being human together.

Notes

1. Ferron, "It Won't Take Long" in her *Shadows on a Dime*, Nemesis Publishing, 1984.

2. Norman Jacobson, *Pride and Solace*, p. xv.

3. See chapter nine, note 27 and Starhawk, *Dreaming the Dark* (Boston: Beacon, 1982); Kathy Ferguson, *The Feminist Case Against Bureaucracy* (Philadelphia: Temple University, 1984; Mary Daly, *Gyn/Ecology: The Metaethics of Radical Feminism* (Boston: Beacon, 1978), and *Pure Lust* (Boston: Beacon, 1984).

4. This statement is in accord with Kathy Ferguson's argument in *The Feminist Case Against Bureaucracy*, pp. 166–73: "women's traditional experience, by itself, is both distorted and partial. It is distorted in that the commitment to caretaking is bent to the service of power." The partiality of women's experience pertains to caretaking in the context of a small number of intimate and unequal relationships, in short, to women's limited experience in the public world. Ferguson would not, however, appear to agree with my next claim, that feminine values bear as little relation to our "full humanity" as masculine ones do.

5. Feminists who have assumed that something like "essential" female values can be distilled from their contemporary limited context include

Ferguson, although she is certainly not guilty of a crude essentialism. Even more certain that there is such a thing as "female values" arising from woman's trans-historical experience of mothering are Jean Elshtain, "Antigone's Daughters," and Sara Ruddick, "Maternal Thinking," and "Preservative Love and Military Destruction: Some Reflections on Mothering and Peace" in Joyce Trebilcot, ed. *Mothering: Essays in Feminist Theory* (Totowa, NJ: Rowman and Allenheld, 1984). In the same volume, see also Eleanor H. Kuykendall, "Toward an Ethic of Nurturance: Luce Irigaray on Mothering and Power."

6. *Feminist Case Against Bureaucracy*, p. 174.

7. See Michel Foucault, "Two Lectures" in *Power/Knowledge*. To the extent that Foucault sometimes appear to treat subjugated discourses as if they are always oppositional or subversive, he is a Hegelian after all, seeing a particular power's antithesis as the natural and inevitable response to the presence of power.

8. "The German Ideology" in *The Marx-Engels Reader*, p. 150–57.

9. Ibid., pp. 159–63.

10. Consider the concerns of Existentialism, some members of the early Frankfurt School, Jose Ortega y Gasset, Walter Benjamin, and Maurice Merleau-Ponty, as well as the more obvious case of Hannah Arendt and her followers.

11. See for example, Clark and Lange, eds. *The Sexism of Social and Political Theory*, and Mary O'Brien, *The Politics of Reproduction*. See also the citations in chapter one, note 12.

12. Arendt, for example, sides with Aristotle in insisting that our "full humanity" is expressed only in political action. At the other end of the spectrum Lorenne Clark argues that "reproduction is . . . the central fact around which all theory about social organization ought to rotate." In "Rights of Women: The Theory and Practice of Male Supremacy", p. 54.

13. See Clark, "Rights of Women", and Wendy Brown, "Reproductive Freedom and the 'Right to Privacy.' "

14. See Elizabeth Spelman, "Woman as Body: Ancient and Contemporary Views," *Feminist Studies* 8 (Spring 1982).

15. This construction of woman within the tradition of political theory is developed and analyzed at length in my "Where is the Sex in Political Theory?," *Women and Politics*, vol. 7, no. 1, January 1987.

16. Cited in Nannerl Keohane, "Female Citizenship: 'The Monstrous Regiment of Women,' " unpublished paper for Annual Meeting of the Conference for the Study of Political Thought, April 6–8, 1979, p. 29.

17. Arendt, *The Human Condition*, p. 119.

18. Ibid. p. 31.

19. Regeneration is the term Donna Haraway uses to speak of healing and restoration without collapsing into the romantic language of reciprocity, rebirth, etc. See "A Manifesto for Cyborgs: Science, Technology, and Socialist Feminism in the 1980s," *Socialist Review* no. 80, p. 101.

20. Other than Marx, the only major political theorist who grasped this was Rousseau. In the origins tale he tells in the "Discourse on Inequality," he subtly and elegantly relates animal and human freedom through the body. Ultimately, however, Roussseau compromises this insight in the name of freedom as control, i.e., "moral freedom" in *The Social Contract*.

21. See Arendt, "What is Freedom?" especially pp. 152–53.

22. For a more thorough exploration of these connections, see my "Where Is the Sex in Political Theory?"

23. See Michel Foucault, *History of Sexuality*, vol. I, trans. R. Hurley (New York: Vintage, 1980).

24. I am contrasting Plato's claim in *Republic* 573b with the words ascribed to Socrates in *Symposium* 210–12. I have justified my controversial distinction between the authors of the two positions and more fully elaborated the relationship between eros and knowledge in Socratic thought in " 'Supposing Truth Were a Woman?': Plato's Subversion of Masculine Discourse."

25. In "The Family: Love It or Leave It," Ellen Willis develops this point with wit and poignancy. *Beginning to See the Light: Pieces of a Decade* (New York: Knopf, 1981), pp. 156–57.

26. Arendt, *Human Condition*, p. 18.

27. Betty Friedan, *The Feminine Mystique* (New York: Norton, 1963).

28. See, for example, Aristotle, *Politics* I.ii.1. and Plato, *Symposium* 207a–d.

29. Mary O'Brien, "The Politics of Impotence" in *Contemporary Issues in Political Philosophy*, eds. Shea and King-Farlowe (New York: Science History Publications, 1976).

30. I think the fact that women experience continuity through childrearing explains in part why women reconciled themselves to their oppressed lot for so many millenia. The deskilling and circumscription of motherhood in the last century also partly accounts for the recent revolt against this oppression. As schools, summer camps, television, psychotherapy, shopping malls, city streets, fast food, and the commercial world as a whole encroached upon and usurped the mother's role in developing to maturity a new being on this earth, her experience of continuity through child-raising was severely diminished. No longer is the child essentially the mother's creation but, instead, a product of all the social institutions that appropriated, interfered with, or contravened her role in the child's development. Of the many who chart pieces of this development, three of the most interesting for feminist theorists are Sheila Rowbatham, *Woman's Consciousness, Man's World* (Middlesex, England: Penguin, 1973); Linda Nicholson, *Gender and History: The Limits of Social Theory in the Age of the Family* (New York: Columbia University Press, 1986); and Ely Zaretsky, *Capitalism, the Family and Personal Life* (New York: Harper Colophon, 1976).

31. Jean Bethke Elshtain, "Power Trips and Other Journeys," paper presented to the Annual Meeting of the American Political Science Association, 1979.

32. Nancy Hartsock, *Money, Sex and Power: Toward a Feminist Historical Materialism* (New York: Longman, 1983).

33. Kathy Ferguson, "Feminism and Political Science," unpublished mss.

34. Adrienne Rich, "Compulsory Heterosexuality and The Lesbian Continuum," *Women, Sex and Sexuality*, eds. C. Stimpson and E. Person (Chicago: University of Chicago Press, 1980) and Marilyn Frye, "A Note on Separatism and Power" in *The Politics of Reality*, (Trumansburg, NY: Crossing Press, 1983).

35. Catherine MacKinnon, "Feminism, Marxism, Method and the State: An Agenda for Theory," *Signs*, vol. 7, no. 3 (Spring 1982).

36. Even Michel Foucault, easily the most interesting and nuanced con-

temporary theorist of power, often speaks of power in generic, undifferentiated fashion. See "Two Lectures" and "Truth and Power" in *Power/Knowledge*, ed. C. Gordon (New York: Pantheon, 1980).

37. Several feminist theorists have recently speculated about women's fears of power. See Marilyn Frye, "A Note on Separatism and Power," p. 107 and Helene Moglen, "Power and Empowerment," *Women's Studies International Forum*, vol. 6, no. 2, pp. 131–34.

38. Contemporary examples of this rather simplistic feminist opposition to power are Marilyn French, *Beyond Power: Women, Men and Morals* (New York: Summit Books, 1985) and many of the essays in R. Linden, *et al.*, eds. *Against Sadomasochism: A Radical Feminist Analysis* (Palo Alto: Frog in the Well, 1982).

39. *History of Sexuality*.

40. Marilyn French, *Beyond Power*.

41. Starhawk, *Dreaming the Dark*, pp. 4–18.

42. Haunani-Kay Trask, *Eros and Power: The Promise of Feminist Theory* (Philadelphia: University of Pennsylvania, 1986), p. 147.

43. Plato, *Symposium* 189–93.

44. *Symposium* 192.

Bibliography

Adkins, A. W. *Merit and Responsibility: A Study in Greek Values.* Oxford: Clarendon Press, 1960.

Agonito, R. *History of Ideas on Women.* New York: Putnam, 1972.

Allen, D. C. "Renaissance Remedies for Fortune." *Studies in Philosophy* 38. 1941.

Anglo, Sydney. *Machiavelli: A Dissection.* London: Gollancz, 1969.

Annas, Julia. "Mill and the Subjection of Women." *Philosophy* 52 (1977).

Apuleius, Lucius. *The Golden Ass,* trans. W. Adlington, ed. F. J. H. Darton. New York: Hogarth Press, 1924.

Arendt, Hannah. *The Human Condition.* Chicago: Chicago University Press, 1958.

———. *Between Past and Future.* New York: Viking, 1961.

———. *On Revolution.* New York: Viking, 1963.

———. *Crises of the Republic.* New York: Harcourt Brace, 1969.

———. *On Violence.* New York: Harcourt Brace, 1969.

Aristotle. *De Anima,* trans. R. D. Hicks. Cambridge: Cambridge University Press, 1907.

———. *Generation of Animals,* trans. A. L. Peck. Loeb Classical Edition. London: Heinemann, 1942.

———. *Politics,* trans. E. Barker. Oxford: Oxford University Press, 1946.

———. *Nicomachean Ethics,* trans. J. A. K. Thomson. Middlesex, England: Penguin, 1955.

Arthur, Marilyn. "Early Greece: The Origins of the Western Attitude Towards Women." *Arethusa,* Vol. 6, No. 1 (1973).

Barrett, Michele. *Women's Oppression Today: Problems in Marxist Feminist Analysis.* London: New Left Books, 1980.

Baron, Hans. *The Crisis of the Early Italian Renaissance: Civic Humanism in an Age of Classicism and Tyranny.* Princeton: Princeton University Press, 1966.

Beetham, David. *Max Weber and the Theory of Modern Politics.* London: Allen and Unwin, 1974.

Bendix, Reinhard. *Max Weber: An Intellectual Portrait.* Garden City, N.Y.: Doubleday, 1962.

Bonadeo, Alfredo. *Corruption, Conflict and Power in the Works and Times of Niccolo Machiavelli.* Berkeley: University of California Press, 1973.

Bondanella, Peter. *Machiavelli and the Art of Renaissance History.* Detroit: Wayne State University Press, 1973.

Bowra, C. M. *The Greek Experience.* New York: Mentor Books, 1957.

Brown, Norman O. *Life Against Death.* Middletown, Conn.: Wesleyan University Press, 1959.

———. *Love's Body.* New York: Random House, 1966.

Brown, Peter. *The World of Late Antiquity.* New York: Harcourt Brace, 1971.

Brown, Wendy. "Reproductive Freedom and the 'Right to Privacy': A Paradox for Feminists," in Irene Diamond, ed. *Families, Politics, and Public Policy: A Feminist Dialogue on Women and the State.* New York: Longman, 1983.

———. " 'Supposing Truth Were a Woman?': Plato's Subversion of Masculine Discourse," in *Political Theory* (forthcoming).

———. "Where Is the Sex in Political Theory?" *Women and Politics,* Vol. 7, No. 1 (1987).

Bruun, H. H. *Science, Values and Politics in Max Weber's Methodology.* Copenhagen: Munksgaard, 1972.

Burckhardt, Jakob. *The Civilization of the Renaissance in Italy,* trans. S. G. C. Middlemore. Vienna: Paidon Press, 1890.

Butterfield, Herbert. *The Statecraft of Machiavelli.* New York: Collier-MacMillan, 1960.

Camus, Albert. *The Myth of Sisyphus,* trans. J. O'Brien. Edinburgh: Penguin, 1975.

Cassirer, Ernst. *The Myth of the State.* New Haven, Conn.: Yale University Press, 1946.

Chabod, Federico. *Machiavelli and the Renaissance,* trans. David Moore. New York: Harper and Row, 1965.

Cioffari, Vincenzo. "The Function of Fortune in Dante, Boccaccio, and Machiavelli." *Italica* 24 (1947).

Clark, Lorenne M. G. and Lynda Lange, eds. *The Sexism of Social and Political Theory: Women and Reproduction from Plato to Nietzsche.* Toronto: University of Toronto Press, 1979.

Clark, Stephen R. L. *Aristotle's Man.* Oxford: Clarendon Press, 1975.

Cochrane, Eric W. "The End of the Renaissance in Florence." *Bibliotheque d'humanisme et renaissance* 27 (1965).

Collingwood, Robin G. *The Idea of Nature,* ed. T. M. Knox. Oxford: Clarendon Press, 1965.

Croce, Benedetto. *Politics and Morals,* trans. S. Castiglione. New York: Philosophical Library, 1945.

Dalla Costa, Mariaosa and James, Selma. *The Power of Women and the Subversion of Community.* Bristol: Falling Wall Press, 1973.

de Beauvoir, Simone. *The Second Sex,* trans. H. M. Parshley. New York: Random House, 1953.

———. *Memoirs of a Dutiful Daughter,* trans. J. Kirkup. New York: Harper and Row, 1974.

Debus, A. G. *Man and Nature in the Renaissance.* Cambridge: Cambridge University Press, 1978.

Dickason, Anne. "Anatomy and Destiny: The Role of Biology in Plato's Views of Women," in *Women and Philosophy,* eds. C. Gould and M. Wartofsky. New York: Putnam, 1976.

Dietz, Mary. "Citizenship With a Feminist Face: The Problem With Maternal Thinking." *Political Theory* 13 (1985).

Dodds, E. R. *The Greeks and the Irrational.* Berkeley: University of California Press, 1951.

Dover, K. J. "Classical Greek Attitudes to Sexual Behavior." *Arethusa* Vol. 6, No. 1 (1973).

———. *Greek Homosexuality.* Cambridge: Harvard University Press, 1974.

———. *Greek Popular Morality.* Oxford: Oxford University Press, 1974.

Eisenstein, Zillah. *Capitalist Patriarchy and the Case for Socialist Feminism.* New York: Monthly Review, 1979.

Elshtain, Jean Bethke. "Antigone's Daughters" *Democracy,* Vol. 2, No. 2 (1982).

———. *Public Man, Private Woman.* Princeton, N.J.: Princeton University Press, 1981.

———. "Power Trips and Other Journeys" Unpublished paper presented to Annual Meeting of 1979 American Political Science Association.

Elliot, T. S. "Niccolo Machiavelli," *For Lancelot Andrewes: Essays on Style and Order.* London: Faber and Faber, 1928.

Engels, Frederick. *The Origins of the Family, Private Property and the State,* ed. E. B. Leacock. New York: International Publishers, 1972.

Ehrenberg, Victor. *The Greek State.* Oxford: Blackwell, 1960.

Euben, J. Peter. "Political Equality and the Greek Polis," in *Liberalism and the Modern Polity,* ed. M. McGrath. New York: Marcel Dekker, 1978.

Farnsworth, Beatrice. "Bolshevism, the Woman Question and Alexandra Kollontai." *American Historical Review,* Vol. 81, No. 2.

Ferguson, Kathy. *The Feminist Case Against Bureaucracy.* Philadelphia: Temple University Press, 1984.

———. "Feminism and Political Science." Unpublished mss.

Figes, Eva. *Patriarchal Attitudes.* Greenwich, Conn.: Fawcett, 1970.

Firestone, Shulamith. *The Dialectic of Sex.* New York: Bantam, 1976.

Finley, M. I. *The World of Odysseus.* New York: Viking, 1965.

Fleisher, Martin, ed. *Machiavelli and the Nature of Political Thought.* New York: Atheneum, 1972.

Fleishmann, Eugene. "De Weber à Nietzsche." *Archives Europeenes de Sociologie* Vol. 5. 1964.

Forest, W. G. G. *The Emergence of Greek Democracy.* New York: McGraw-Hill, 1966.

Foucault, Michel. *History of Sexuality,* Volume I, trans. R. Hurley. New York: Vintage, 1980.

———. *Power/Knowledge,* ed. C. Gordon. New York: Pantheon, 1977.

French, Marilyn. *Beyond Power: Women, Men and Morals.* New York: Summitt, 1985.

Friedan, Betty. *The Feminine Mystique*. New York: Norton, 1963.

Freud, Sigmund. *The Standard Edition of the Complete Psychological Works*, trans. and eds. J. Strachey and A. Freud. London: Hogarth, 1964.

Frye, Marilyn. *The Politics of Reality: Essays in Feminist Theory*. Trumansburg, N.Y.: Crossing Press, 1983.

Fustel de Coulanges, N. D. *The Ancient City*, trans. W. Small. Garden City, N.Y.: Doubleday, 1956.

Giddens, Anthony. *Politics and Sociology in the Thought of Max Weber*. London: Macmillan, 1972.

Gilbert, Alan. *Machiavelli's Prince and its Forerunners*. Durham, N.C.: Duke University Press, 1968.

Gilbert, Felix. "The Humanist Concept of the Prince and the *Prince* of Machiavelli." *Journal of Modern History* IX (1939).

―――. "Machiavelli's Idea of *Virtù*." *Renaissance News* IV (1951).

―――. "The Concept of Nationalism in Machiavelli's *Prince*." *Studies in the Renaissance* I 1954.

―――. *Machiavelli and Guicciardini*. Princeton: Princeton University Press, 1965.

Gilmore, Myron P., ed. *Studies on Machiavelli*. Florence: G. C. Sansoni, 1972.

Glickman, Rose L. *Russian Factory Women: Workplace and Society 1880–1914*. Berkeley: University of California Press, 1984.

Gould, J. P. "Law, Custom and Myth: Aspects of the Social Position of Women in Classical Athens." *The Journal of Hellenic Studies* Vol. C. 1980.

Gouldner, A. W. *Enter Plato*. New York: Basic Books, 1965.

Green, Martin. *The von Richtohofen Sisters: The Triumphant and the Tragic Modes of Love*. London: Weidenfeld and Nicolson, 1974.

Grene, David. *Greek Political Theory: The Image of Man in Thucydides and Plato*. Chicago: Chicago Univerisity Press, 1962.

Griffin, Susan. *Woman and Nature: The Roaring Inside Her*. New York: Harper and Row, 1978.

Guetell, Charnie. *Marxism and Feminism*. Toronto: Hunter Rose, 1974.

Gurken, J. H. "Homer's Image of the Hero in Machiavelli: A Comparison of *Aretē* and *Virtû*." *Italian Quarterly* 14, No. 53 (1970).

Hale, John R. *Machiavelli and Renaissance History*. New York: Macmillan, 1960.

Hannaford, I. "Machiavelli's Concept of *Virtù* in the *Prince* and the *Discourses* Reconsidered." *Political Studies* 20 (1972).

Haraway, Donna. "A Manifesto for Cyborgs: Science, Technology and Socialist Feminism in the 1980s." *Socialist Review* 80 (1985).

Harragan, Betty. *Games Mother Never Taught You: Corporate Gamesmanship for Women*. New York: Warner Books, 1977.

Hartouni, Valerie. "Antigone's Dilemma: A Problem in Political Membership." *Hypatia* Vol. 1, No. 1.

Hartsock, Nancy. *Money, Sex and Power: Toward a Feminist Historical Materialism*. Boston: Northeastern University Press, 1985.

Hegel, G. W. F. *Philosophy of Right*, trans. T. M. Knox. Oxford: Clarendon Press, 1952.

Heinen, Jacqueline. "Kollantai and the History of Women's Oppression," *New Left Review* 110.

Hexter, J. H. *The Vision of Politics on the Eve of the Reformation: More, Machiavelli and Seyssel.* New York: Basic, 1973.

Hippocrates. *Hippocratic Writings*, ed. G. E. R. Lloyd. Harmondsworth, England: Penguin, 1978.

Hill, Melvyn, ed. *Hannah Arendt: Recovery of the Public World.* New York: St. Martin's, 1979.

Hinton, R. W. K. "Husbands, Fathers and Conquerors." *Political Studies* Vol. 15, No. 3. (1967) and Vol. 16, No. 1 (1968).

Jacobson, Norman. *Pride and Solace.* Berkeley: University of California Press, 1977.

Jaeger, Werner. *Aristotle.* New York: Oxford University Press, 1962.

———. *Paideia: The Ideals of Greek Culture*, trans. G. Highet, 2nd edition. New York: Oxford University Press, 1965.

Jaspers, Karl. *Three Essays: Leonardo, Descartes, Max Weber.* New York: Scribners, 1953.

Johnson, Robert. "Machiavelli and Gramsci." Unpublished mss.

Kelly-Godal, Joan. "Did Women Have a Renaissance?" *Becoming Visible: Women in European History*, R. Bridenthal and C. Koonz, eds. Boston: Houghton Mifflin, 1977.

———. "Notes on Women in the Renaissance and Rennaisance Historiography," *Conceptual Frameworks in Women's History.* Bronxville, N.Y.: Sarah Lawrence Press, 1976.

Kennedy, Marilyn. *Office Politics: Seizing Power, Wielding Clout.* New York: Warner Books, 1980.

Keohane, Nannerl O. "Female Citizenship: 'The Monstrous Regiment of Women.' " Paper presented to the Annual Meeting of the Conference for the Study of Political Thought, New York, April 1979.

Kitto, H. D. F. *The Greeks.* Edinburgh, England: Penguin, 1957.

Kollantai, Alexandra. *Selected Writings*, trans. A. Holt. New York: Norton, 1977.

Kristeller, P. O. *Renaissance Thought: The Classic, Scholastic and Humanistic Strains.* New York: Harper, 1955.

Lacey, W. K. *The Family in Classical Greece.* London: Thames and Hudson, 1968.

Lachmann, L. M. *The Legacy of Max Weber.* London: Heinemann, 1970.

Lange, Lynda. "Reproduction in Democratic Theory," *Contemporary Issues in Political Philosophy*, eds. Shea and King-Farlowe. New York: Science History, 1976.

Lefkowitz, Mary. *Heroines and Hysterics.* New York: St. Martin's Press, 1981.

LeFort, Claude. *Le travail de l'oeuvre Machiavel.* Paris: Gallimard, 1972.

Lenin, V. I. *Selected Writings: The Emancipation of Women*, N. K. Krupskaya, ed. New York: International Publishers, 1934.

Lichtenstein, Grace. *Machisma: Women and Daring.* New York: Doubleday, 1981.

Linden, R. et al. eds. *Against SadoMasochism: A Radical Feminist Analysis.* Palo Alto: Frog in the Well, 1982.

Lucas, R. A. "A Specification of the Weber Thesis and Its Critics." *History and Theory* X (1971).

Machiavelli, Niccolo. *The Chief Works and Others*, trans. A. Gilbert. Durham, N.C.: Duke University Press, 1965.

MacKinnon, Catherine. "Marxism, Feminism, Method and the State," Parts I and II. *Signs* Vol. 7, No. 3 (1983) and Vol. 8, No. 4 (1984).

MacPherson, C. B. *The Political Theory of Possessive Individualism*. Oxford: Oxford University Press, 1962.

Mahowald, Mary. *Philosophy of Women: Classical to Current Concepts*. Indianapolis: Hacket, 1978.

Mansfield, Harvey. *Machiavelli's New Modes and Orders: A Study of the Discourses on Livy*. Ithaca: Cornell University Press, 1979.

Marcil-Lacoste, Louise. "The Consistency of Hume's Position Concerning Women." *Dialogue* 15 (1976).

Marcuse, Herbert. *Eros and Civilization*. Boston: Beacon, 1955.

————. "Marxism and Feminism." *Women's Studies* II, No. 5 (1974).

Marx, Karl. *Marx-Engels Reader*, 2nd Edition, ed. R. C. Tucker. New York: Norton, 1978.

Maulde, LaClaviere M. A. R. *The Women of the Renaissance: A Study of Feminism*, trans. G. H. Ely. New York: Putnam, 1901.

Mayer, J. P. *Max Weber and German Politics: A Study in Political Sociology*. London: Faber and Faber, 1943.

Mazzeo, Joseph. "The Poetry of Power." *Review of National Literatures* Vol. 1, No. 1 (1976).

McWilliams, Carey. "Weapons and Virtues." *democracy* Vol. 2, No. 3 (1982).

Meinecke, Friedrich. *Machiavellism: The Doctrine of Raison d'État and its Place in Modern History*, trans. D. Scott. London: Routledge, 1957.

Merchant, Carolyn. *The Death of Nature: Women, Ecology and the Scientific Revolution*. New York: Harper and Row, 1980.

Merleau-Ponty, Maurice. *Signs*, trans. R. McCleary. Evanston, Ill.: Northwestern University Press, 1964.

Millett, Kate. *Sexual Politics*. Garden City, N.Y.: Doubleday, 1970.

Mitchell, Juliet. *Psychoanalysis and Feminism*. New York: Pantheon, 1974.

Mitzman, Arthur. *The Iron Cage*. New York: Knopf, 1970.

Moglen, Helene. "Power and Empowerment." *Women's Studies International Forum* Vol. 6, No. 2.

Mommsen, W. J. "Max Weber's Political Sociology and His Philosophy of World History." *International Social Science Journal* 7 (1965).

————. *The Age of Bureaucracy: Perspectives on the Political Sociology of Max Weber*. Oxford: Blackwell, 1974.

Nicholson, Linda. *Gender and History: The Limits of Social Theory in the Age of the Family*. New York: Columbia University Press, 1986.

Nietzsche, Friedrich. *Early Greek Philosophy and Other Essays* (Volume II, *Complete Works*) ed. O. Levy. Edinburgh: Darien Press, 1914.

O'Brien, Mary. "The Politics of Impotence," in *Contemporary Issues in Political Philosophy*, eds. Shea and King-Farlowe. New York: Science History, 1976.

————. *The Politics of Reproduction*. Boston: Routledge and Kegan Paul, 1981.

Okin, Susan. *Women in Western Political Thought*. Princeton: Princeton University Press, 1979.

Olschki, Leonardo. *Machiavelli, The Scientist*. Berkeley: University of California Press, 1945.

Osborne, Martha Lee. "Plato's Unchanging View of Women: A Denial that Anatomy Spells Destiny." *Philosophical Forum* 6 (1975).

Ortega y Gasset, José. *History as a System and Other Essays Toward a Philosophy of History*, trans. H. Weyl. New York: Norton, 1962.

Pateman, Carole. "Women and Consent." *Political Theory* Vol. 8, No. 2 (1980).

Pateman, Carole and Brennan, Teresa. "Mere Auxilliaries to the Commonwealth: Women and the Origins of Liberalism." *Political Studies* Vol. 27, No. 2 (1979).

Parekh, B. and Berki, R. N., eds. *The Morality of Politics*. New York: Crane, Russuk, 1972.

Parel, Anthony, ed. *The Political Calculus: Essays on Machiavelli's Philosophy*. Toronto: Toronto University Press, 1972.

Patch, H. R. *The Goddess Fortuna in Medieval Literature*. Cambridge: Harvard University Press, 1972.

Pitkin, Hanna. "Justice: On Relating Public and Private." *Political Theory* Vol. 9, No. 3 (1981).

———. *Fortune Is a Woman*. Berkeley: University of California Press, 1984.

Plamenatz, J. P. *Man and Society*. New York: McGraw-Hill, 1963.

Plato. *Collected Dialogues*, eds. E. Hamilton and H. Cairns. Princeton: Princeton University Press, 1961.

———. *Republic*, trans. A. Bloom. New York: Basic Books, 1968.

Pocock, J. G. A. *The Machiavellian Moment: Florentine Political Thought and the Atlantic Republican Tradition*. Princeton: Princeton University Press, 1975.

Pomeroy, Sarah. *Goddesses, Whores, Wives, and Slaves: Women in Classical Antiquity*. New York: Schocken, 1975.

Price, Russell. "The Senses of *Virtù* in Machiavelli." *European Studies Review* 3 (1973).

Rich, Adrienne. "Compulsory Heterosexuality and the Lesbian Continuum." *Women, Sex and Sexuality*, eds. C. Stimpson and E. Person. Chicago: Chicago University Press, 1980.

Ricoeur, Paul. *History and Truth*, trans. C. A. Kelbley. Evanston, Ill.: Northwestern University Press, 1965.

Rodolfi, Roberto. *Life of Niccolo Machiavelli*, trans. C. Grayson. London: Routledge, 1963.

Rousseau, Jean-Jacques. *The First and Second Discourse*, trans. R. and J. Masters. New York: St. Martin's, 1964.

———. *Emile*, trans. A. Bloom. New York: Basic, 1979.

Rowbatham, Sheila. *Woman's Consciousness, Man's World*. Harmondsworth, England: Penguin, 1973.

———. *Beyond the Fragments: Feminism and the Making of Socialism*. Boston: Alyson, 1979.

Ruddick, Sara. "Maternal Thinking." *Feminist Studies* 6 (1980).

———. "Preservative Love and Military Destruction: Some Reflections on Mothering and Peace," in *Mothering: Essays in Feminist Theory*. J. Trebilcot, ed. Totowa, N.J.: Rowman and Allenheld, 1984.

Runciman, W. G. *A Critique of Max Weber's Philosophy of Social Science.* Cambridge: Cambridge University Press, 1972.

Sachs, Hannelore. *The Renaissance Woman,* trans. M. Harzfeld. New York: McGraw-Hill, 1971.

Sargent, Lydia, ed. *Women and Revolution: A Discussion of the Unhappy Marriage of Marxism and Feminism.* Boston: South End Press, 1981.

Sartre, Jean-Paul. *Being and Nothingness,* trans. H. E. Barnes. New York: Simon and Schuster, 1956.

Saxonhouse, Arlene. "The Philosopher and the Female in the Political Thought of Plato." *Political Theory,* Vol. 4, No. 2 (1976).

————. *Women in the History of Political Thought: Ancient Greece to Machiavelli.* New York: Praeger, 1985.

Schein, Seth L. *The Mortal Hero.* Berkeley: University of California Press, 1984.

Schochet, Gordon J. *Patriarchalism in Political Thought.* New York: Basic, 1975.

Schweitzer, Arthur. "Theory and Political Charisma." *Comparative Studies in Society and History* XVI (1974).

Seigel, Jerrold. "*Virtù* in and Since the Renaissance." *Dictionary of the History of Ideas,* ed. P. P. Wiener, Vol. 4. New York: Scribners, 1973–74.

Shils, Edward A. "Charisma, Order and Status." *American Sociological Review* 30 (1965).

Skinner, Quentin. *Machiavelli.* Oxford: Oxford University Press, 1981.

Slater, Phillip. *The Glory of Hera: Greek Mythology and the Greek Family.* Boston: Beacon Press, 1968.

Spelman, Elizabeth. "Woman as Body: Ancient and Contemporary Views." *Feminist Studies* 8 (1982).

Stammer, Otto, ed. *Max Weber and Sociology Today.* Oxford: Blackwell, 1971.

Starhawk. *Dreaming the Dark.* Boston: Beacon, 1982.

Stern, Susan. *With the Weathermen.* Garden City, N.Y.: Doubleday, 1975.

Tarlton, Charles D. "The Symbolism of Redemption and the Exorcism of Fortune in Machiavelli's *Prince.*" *Review of Politics* 30 (1968).

Thucydides. *The Peloponnesian War,* trans. J. H. Finley. New York: Modern Library, 1951.

Trask, Haunani-Kay. *Eros and Power: The Promise of Feminist Theory.* Philadelphia: University of Pennsylvania, 1986.

Trebilcot, Joyce, ed. *Mothering: Essays in Feminist Theory.* Totowa, N.J.: Rowman and Allenheld, 1983.

Turner, Bryan S. *For Weber: Essays on the Sociology of Fate.* London: Routledge and Kegan Paul, 1981.

Villari, Pasquale. *The Life and Times of Machiavelli,* trans. L. Villari. New York: Scribners, 1898.

Weber, Marianne. *Max Weber: A Biography,* trans. H. Zohn. New York: Wiley, 1975.

Weber, Max. *The Protestant Ethic and the Spirit of Capitalism,* trans. T. Parsons. London: Unwin University Books, 1930.

————. *From Max Weber: Essays in Sociology,* trans. and ed. H. H. Gerth and C. W. Mills. New York: Oxford University Press, 1946.

————. *The Methodology of the Social Sciences,* trans. E. Shils and H. Finch. New York: Free Press, 1949.

————. *Max Weber on Universities: The Power of the State and the Dignity of the Academic Calling in Imperial Germany,* trans. and ed. E. Shils. Chicago: Chicago University Press, 1974.

————. *Roscher and Knies: The Logical Problems of Historical Economics,* trans. G. Oakes. New York: Free Press, 1975.

————. *Economy and Society,* ed. G. Roth and C. Wittich. Berkeley: University of California, 1978.

————. *Selections in Translation,* ed. W. G. Runciman. Cambridge: Cambridge University Press, 1978.

Wender, Dorothea. "Plato: Misogynist, Paedophile and Feminist." *Arethusa* Vol. 6, No. 1 (1973).

Wexler, Victor. "Made for Man's Delight: Rousseau as Anti-Feminist." *American Historical Review* 81 (1976).

Whitfield, J. H. "The Anatomy of *Virtù.*" *Modern Language Review* XXXVIII (1943).

————. *Machiavelli.* Oxford: Blackwell, 1947.

————. *Discourses on Machiavelli.* Cambridge: Heffer, 1969.

Wilkins, Burleigh T. "Machiavelli on History and Fortune." *Bucknell Review* 8 (1959).

Willis, Ellen. *Beginning to See the Light: Pieces of a Decade.* New York: Knopf, 1981.

Wolin, Sheldon S. *Politics and Vision.* Boston: Little, Brown, 1960.

————. "Max Weber: Legitimation, Method and the Politics of Theory." *Political Theory* Vol 9, No. 3 (1981).

Wollstonecraft, Mary. *Vindication of the Rights of Women,* ed M. Kramnick. Harmondsworth, England: Penguin, 1975.

Wood, Ellen M. and Neal. *Class Ideology and Ancient Political Theory: Socrates, Plato and Aristotle in Social Context.* Oxford: Blackwell, 1978.

Wood, Neal. "Machiavelli's Concept of *Virtù* Reconsidered." *Political Studies* 15 (1967).

Wrong, Dennis. "Max Weber: The Scholar as Hero." *Columbia Forum* Vol. 5, No. 3 (1962).

————, ed. *Max Weber.* Englewood Cliffs, N.J.: Prentice Hall, 1970.

Zaretsky, Eli. *Capitalism, The Family and Personal Life.* New York: Harper and Row, 1976.

Zimmern, A. E. *The Greek Commonwealth: Politics and Economics in Fifth Century Athens.* Oxford: Clarendon, 1922.

Index

225